DATE DUE

DEMCO 38-296

Dancing
Modernism/Performing
Politics

Dancing
Modernism/Performing
Politics

MARK FRANKO

*Indiana
University
Press*
BLOOMINGTON AND INDIANAPOLIS

Permission from the Evelyn Singer Literary Agency is acknowledged to reprint excerpts from
published material by Michael Gold.

Library of Congress Cataloging-in-Publication Data

Franko, Mark.
Dancing modernism/performing politics / Mark Franko.
          p.   cm.
Includes bibliographical references (p.) and index.
ISBN 0-253-32432-7. — ISBN 0-253-20947-1 (pbk.)
1. Modern dance—Political aspects. 2. Modern dance—History.
I. Title.
GV1783.F72   1995
792.8—dc20   94–31788

1 2 3 4 5 00 99 98 97 96 95

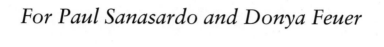

For Paul Sanasardo and Donya Feuer

Contents

The Politics of Expression / ix

ONE The Invention of Modern Dance / 1

TWO Bodies of Radical Will / 25

THREE Emotivist Movement
and Histories of Modernism:
The Case of Martha Graham / 38

FOUR Expressivism and Chance Procedure:
The Future of an Emotion / 75

FIVE Where He Danced / 93

Appendix: Left-Wing Dance Theory:
Articles on Dance from New Theatre,
New Masses, and Daily Worker / 109

Notes / 145

Bibliography / 178

Index / 189

The Politics of Expression

These essays contribute to a revisionary account of historical modern dance. Until recently, dance historians have been reluctant to reevaluate the modernist spirit of historical modern dance.[1] Paradoxically, the modern-dance master narrative is so inherently, that is, so "blindly" modernist that critical distancing from its tenets appears at first unconscionable, a betrayal of the art itself.

> First come the expressivist individuals, typified by Isadora Duncan. Then come the makers of expressivist systems, typified by Wigman and Graham. . . . Then, in reaction, comes Merce Cunningham . . . rejecting style and expression as generating a set of preferred movement and ways of combining movement, and substituting for it a method of making movement into dance.[2]

In this and various similar genealogical synopses, one easily imagines Isadora Duncan expressing herself, Martha Graham formalizing emotional expression into a set of movement procedures, Merce Cunningham organizing bodily movement into new configurations without expressive intent. The most salient trait of the modernist narrative is its progress from expression as spontaneity to expression as semiological system to the marginalizing of expressive intent. The Duncan-Graham-Cunningham cycloid, in particular, proceeds through a narrowing range of options that refine away each immediate precursor's stakes. Modernist accounts of modern dance history thus perform the telos of aesthetic modernism itself: a continuous reduction to essentials culminating in irreducible "qualities."

Recent reevaluations of aesthetic modernism, notably in new art history, expose the modernist narrative's omission of politics, mass culture, and sexual difference.[3] Although clearly present, these areas have been systematically refused critical treatment. For example, many of the dancer/choreographers studied here are women, which begs the question of how modern dance found itself allied with modernism at all. I answer that various positions on sexual politics were undertaken *within* (thanks to but also in spite of) modernism, that is, within ideological constraints countered by expressive strategies. The first three chapters, in particular, describe political options reenvisioned as feminist practices of modern dance. This orientation does not denigrate modernism *per se*, but it does render it a more flexible and ambivalent critical category even as it proposes a different sort of dance history.

In place of master narratives, I propose methodologies for opening the canon to theories of spectatorship. I juxtapose canonical figures—Isadora Duncan, Martha Graham, and Merce Cunningham—with their until recently lesser-known contemporaries—Valentine de Saint-Point, left-wing "revolutionary" dancers of the thirties, and Douglas Dunn, respectively. I am drawn particularly to contrasts through which noncanonical work suggests radical alternatives and deconstructive readings. Moreover, alternatives obscured by the canon reveal conditions under which canonical work itself was originally shaped. In the course of such comparative studies the relation of modern dance to sexual, class, and modernist cultural politics emerges, initially through expression theory analysis. My starting point is the affect trinity: stimulus—feeling impact—expression.[4] In the first chapter, I argue that Isadora Duncan's two dominant genres—the lyrical and the Dionysian—correspond to a pre-expressive and a post-expressive level. Expression theory analysis reveals that when she avoided the culmination of affective process in her performance, Duncan was not expressive, strictly speaking. I argue on this basis that the pre- and post-expressive levels were important for Duncan's staging of feminine subjectivity, that is, ultimately, for her dance as a sexual politics.

As discussed by M. H. Abrahms, expression is a phenomenon of "'overflow' [that] signifies the internal made external," an inherently Romantic concept. Abrahms cites Friedrich Schlegel for the meaning of the term expression: "The word expression (*Ausdruck*) is very strikingly chosen for this: the inner is pressed out as though by a force alien to us."[5] This concept of expression as the outwarding of inwardness, as Abrahms goes on to show, is inseparable from affect as stimulus and the experience of emotion. I invoke this straightforwardly physical sense of expression and the possibilities of troping upon it to uncover a political dimension in performance.

The Romantic notion of expression forcibly conflicts with aesthetic modernism's absolute: the reduction of art to the essence of its own formal means. Early twentieth-century primitivist choreography initiated claims to universal authenticity through purging subjectivism (emotion) and privileging the moving body's "presence" (expression). Thus, aesthetic modernism instituted a split between emotion and expression. This split was productive of theatrical impersonality. Consider Jacques Rivière's analysis of Vaslav Nijinsky's *Rite of Spring* (1913), the first modernist ballet and a famous example of the primitivism that marked early modernism.[6] Rivière identifies Nijinsky's *Rite* as an exemplar of absolute dance: "our only impressions were to come from the body's own movements and from the clearly visible and distinctly outlined figure drawn by the dancer with his arms and legs."[7] Rivière's analysis establishes a dichotomy between emotion and expression, which is the performative realization of modernism's split between subjectivism and subjectivity:

> On this undefined road on which the dancer sets out, the emotions find a too easy outlet and spend themselves in vain. Instead of the emotion being the object that the movement tries to describe and make visible, it becomes a mere pretext for erupting into movement. . . . By breaking up movement and bringing it back to the simple gesture, Nijinsky caused *expression* to return to the dance. All the angles, all the breaks in his choreography, are aimed only at preventing the escape of emotion.[8]

Rivière describes *Rite* as a perfect realization of desubjectified emotion, calling the result "expression." His analysis contains the key motifs of dance modernism: a defamiliarization of bodily emotion through the primitive, mechanical, or futuristic sources of movement innovation and the return of expression, once emotion is expunged, as a depersonalized ("universal") embodiment of subjectivity. Choreography is thought to organize movement as an absolute "self-speaking" material. Movement itself becomes a modernist object.

Historically, movement as a modernist object is tied to 1920s experiments with labor efficiency. In *Mechanization Takes Command,* Siegfried Giedion demonstrates that scientific management and contemporary art joined concerns in movement studies. "Motion acquires a form of its own and a life of its own," particularly in Frank B. Gilbreth's light curves and wire models.[9] The attempt to represent human motion in its "pure path" and visualized time frame is directly related to concerns for the autonomy of modern dance. If personal affect could be eliminated from dance, bodily movement would obtain an autonomous significance: It would appear aesthetically absolute in its physical self-delineation. Although apparently in conflict with the fact that modern dance was created and performed in many instances by strong-willed and charismatic individuals, modernist impersonality could nevertheless draw on personal charisma to project its vision of universal subjectivity. On the other hand, the politics of an overtly emotional and personal body belong principally to the antimodernist, left-wing branch of American modern dance that did not survive beyond the 1930s but whose influence continues to be felt confusedly, and without adequate historical perspective.[10] The underacknowledged left avant-garde of American modern dance is discussed in chapter 2. Supplementing this chapter is an appendix of left-wing dance theory. These virtually unknown texts reveal how central dance was to social activism and, for the historian, how aesthetic precision can emerge from politically situated critical writing. I reproduce these texts—they are not dance reviews, but actual theoretical reflections on dance as social action—to propose that a realist/modernist debate, of which, to my knowledge, no counterpart in contemporaneous American theater existed, did take place in the field of American modern dance during the 1930s.[11]

Rather than imagine aesthetic change as progress (modernization), I argue that new stylistic practices result from internal critiques of expression theory. The "internality" of these critiques displaces modernist scenarios of rejection and purist reformation because new positions regarding emotion were being manipulated but not reduced beyond recognition. They were altered as if from within, critically restylized. The notion of internal critique pertains to what Remo Guidieri and Francesco Pellizzi have called "the definition of an old identity in a 'modern' context. The recourse to innovation sets in motion a new becoming at the same time that it permits the preservation of that which, by its very permanence, continues to particularize and to define culture."[12] The issue of change is no longer uniquely one of progress, but partially one of return. That is, aesthetic innovation is no longer considered the product of "abstract confrontation," which is the way Lukacs described the supplanting of one school by another in aesthetic modernism.[13]

Rather, manipulations of expression theory leading to new aesthetic choices are reconceptualized here for their covert political value.

Internal critiques resituate aesthetic innovation as a poetics of politics.[14] For example, internal critique in the thirties can signal the response of a sexual politics under pressure from class politics. I will argue that Martha Graham's lack of personal emotion in her early concert appearances can be linked to a critical perception that Duncan's emotionalism was a "feminine" weakness.[15] I interpret Graham's intensely impassive visage at this time as a feminist response to a disparaging image of Duncan. I argue further that Graham's impassivity exposed her to pressure from a largely left-wing audience wanting to perceive the solidarity of modern dance with the working class through a more evident realism. What made Graham's early work modernist was her rejection of subjectivism at a time when much of her audience wanted to bring bodies and emotions together in an immediate synthesis. Graham's situation during the thirties thus became a complex site of tension between sexual and class politics.[16]

In the different social climate of the mid-fifties, Merce Cunningham's aesthetics of indifference appeared to carry modernist reduction to a new stage. Yet I suggest that his neutrality be reconsidered for its reassertion of inwardness as inviolable privacy. This has been identified by one commentator as a covert gay position.[17] Thus, the social conditions that Isadora Duncan struggled against—the containment of women in the private sphere—became the telos of a male-generated performance abjuring emotional display and commitment to appearances. Viewed from this politico-expressive rather than apolitically aestheticist perspective, dance history spirals back on itself rather than progressing inexorably forward.[18]

To posit a formative role for spectatorship—as I will do repeatedly in what follows—contradicts presuppositions about the body's purity and autonomy of presence, the tenets of modernist dance history. My view is that concert dance is glued to expectations, delusions, and agendas projected by spectators. Only under such collaborative and even conflicted conditions are public spaces of movement constituted. I call for a dance history that will discuss the construction of such spaces called performances. Movement's "object" is movement's purpose—its agency, if you prefer—but also its materiality as culture, its crystallization as experienced event.

Although proceeding chronologically through canonical figures and an admittedly narrow range of examples, the unity of the chapters is less teleological than methodological. No alternative master narrative of dance history will be created. Instead, the notion of "the dancing image" as a reflective relation of dance to culture is made increasingly complex. The chapters unsettle easy symmetries between performance and "the times," purportedly realized by dance as if through a relation of form to content. Social histories of dance influenced by the modernist paradigm conceptualize performance in such a passive yet illustrative rapport with culture. The cultural politics of dance tend thus to be swept aside by taste criteria. Formalist analysis of the dancing image has too often been appended to context as what Siegfried Kracauer called an ornament of "false concreteness."[19] I argue for a more intensive historicization of aesthetics, equated here with a previously ignored political dimension of "expressive" action.

The complexity I wish to introduce further implies that modern dance was a politically resistant and, in this regard, an asymmetrical or nonillustrative practice. But an equally important need for complexity hinges on asking how much of dance practice materializes as visible, or should be understood in visual terms alone. "There remains a vague concept of the image," writes Norman Bryson of art history and criticism, "as an area of resistance to meaning, in the name of a certain mythical idea of life."[20] Similarly, dance history has been marooned in tautological contextualizations whereby the visibility of dance assures minimal interpretation (realized as description) and maximal inevitability (confirming the genesis of, or promoting, success). Although these essays recognize and celebrate the visual impact of dancing, they call, too, for new ways of considering how bodies mold social space and are molded by it. My use of expression theory avoids, in this respect, reifying outmoded ideas of "inside" and "outside" as insuperable walls between the individual and culture. The flexibility of expression theory's manipulation in modern dance blurs such rigid boundaries. And interpretive ambiguities raised by such blurring introduce, in turn, a politics of expression in dance.[21]

To counter what could be called the visual fallacy of dance history, I apply Michel de Certeau's "practice of deviation," that is, historiographic procedures in which "qualitative (structural) differences" are measured with respect to "current formal constructs."[22] The qualitative differences this book sets to work are those of expression theory manipulated in response to particular historical pressures. The current formal constructs are drawn primarily from performance studies and art historical reevaluation of aesthetic modernism. Yet, although elaborated from neighboring disciplines in the humanities, theory does not herald the relinquishing of performance as a uniquely kinetic event. Theory identifies critical tools to address the politics of expressivity.

The final chapter, "Where He Danced," does not directly treat the modernist paradigm just discussed. Still, through a comparison of aerial artist/female impersonator Barbette in 1926 with Butoh dancer Kazuo Ohno in 1989, similar issues of dance, radicalism, and sexual politics are invoked. Both performances—one in modernism and one after modernism—suggest radical alternatives to the conventionally virile male role in Western modern dance. As a postmodern artist, Ohno himself comments on dance and expressivity from outside the Western enclosure. He enacts a striking version of the end of a continuum that began with Duncan: the celebration, but also the undoing, of dance as the feminine within high concert culture.

Although I draw on my own history of spectatorship where possible, I also assume the crucial methodological importance of what choreographers themselves have written. I read their personal statements of poetics, aesthetic theories, pronouncements, and manifestos performatively as idea-stagings and movement projections, but also as strategies for social intervention or tactical withdrawals from institutional constraint. In addition to deconstruction of the canon and historicized theories of spectatorship, the correlation of two "texts"—one written, the other performed—provides the third methodological axis of this book.

This project was completed thanks to faculty research funds granted by the University of California, Santa Cruz, and a residency at the Humanities Research Institute of the University of California, Irvine, with the research group "Choreographing History: The Construction of Dance's Past" (1993). I wish to thank the institute's director, Mark Rose, and his staff as well as Susan Foster, the group's convener, for their support. Sharing this work with others in the process of its formulation has been writing's best phase, and particular acknowledgments accompany essays published earlier in *Discourse*, *Res*, and *PMLA*. For the collection of these essays in one volume, however, I gratefully acknowledge the critical input of Evan Alderson, Norman Bryson, Selma-Jeanne Cohen, Susan Foster, Susan Manning, Randy Martin, Juliet Neidish, Edna Ocko, Francesco Pellizzi, Peggy Phelan, Nancy Ruyter, and Linda Tomko, as well as of my students in the Theater Arts Board of Studies at the University of California, Santa Cruz, and in the Department of Performance Studies, Tisch School of the Arts, New York University. Becky Brimacombe's editing has also been enormously helpful, and the research assistance of Jennifer Touchton and Christian Herold is greatly appreciated.

For permission to reproduce their work, thanks are extended to: Jane Dudley ("The Mass Dance" in *New Theatre*, December 1934), Douglas Dunn ("Talking Dancing" in James Klosty, *Merce Cunningham*), Evelyn Singer Literary Agency for permission to reprint Michael Gold's "The Loves of Isadora" (*New Masses*, March 1929), "Dance of Death" (in "Change the World," *Daily Worker*, June 14, 1934), "Remembering Isadora Duncan" (*New Masses*, September 1937), Al Hirschfeld (drawing of Martha Graham for *New Masses*, October 19, 1938), and Edna Ocko ("The Revolutionary Dance Movement" in *New Masses*, June 1934). I also thank the New York Public Library for the Performing Arts, Astor, Lenox, and Tilden Foundations, for permission to quote from the teaching notebooks of Louis Horst (the "Horst Manuscripts").

Dancing
Modernism/Performing
Politics

ONE

The Invention of Modern Dance

*1900: "For hours I would stand quite still, my two hands folded be-
tween my breasts, covering the solar plexus. . . . I was seeking and
finally discovered the central spring of all movement."*
                                                    —*Isadora Duncan*[1]

This passage from Isadora Duncan's autobiography recounts the emergence
of natural movement following a patient vigil at the site of her body's "central
spring." Whether we are to believe it or not, Duncan's personal discovery of
movement can be read as a foundational narrative of modern dance, its myth
of origin. Hands folded over solar plexus, the dancer detects movement's first
stirring as a conversion from soul to body. Despite the metaphysics of expression theory, in which what is invisible comes to visibility, Duncan makes
movement's origin wholly, although not purely, physical, in that she traces it
to the solar plexus, "the temporal home of the soul."[2] Thus, her discovery of
movement also implied that movements worth discovering retained something of their natural origins. A spiritualized nature inhabited dancing just as
the soul abided for a while in the solar plexus. In Paul Valéry's words, Duncan
redefined dance as "a kind of *inner life*, allowing that psychological term a
new meaning in which physiology is dominant."[3]

"New meaning in which physiology is dominant" marks the incursion of
the fetish into the realm of the idol, the incursion of the body's materiality
into the transcendence called expressivity. For William Pietz, "The truth of
the fetish resides in its status as a material embodiment; its truth is not that of
the idol, for the idol's truth lies in its relation of iconic resemblance to some
immaterial model or entity."[4] The idol, in other terms, retains the functions of
what Hazard Adams calls "religious allegory." Allegory is invariably "religious" in that it insists on the absence of the "stood for" in representation.[5] I
want to argue that the expressive idea informing Duncan's concept of the
activity of *dancing* was iconostatic (religious allegory) inasmuch as her body
was a means to an elsewhere rather than an autonomously independent material. "Do you not feel an inner self awakening deep within you—that it is by
its strength that your head is lifted, that your arms are raised . . ."[6] Expressivity,
then, is inseparable from an idealist perspective in which the body acts as a
"medium" giving the spectator access to an extra-corporeal self of which the
body's movement furnishes traces. Duncan portrays "inner self" as the physi-

cally absent or, let us say, nonspectacular and thus private presence of which dancing is the manifested echo. Consequently, expression induces "loss of body" which, like ecstasy, promotes a vacancy.[7] Louis Untermeyer called Duncan's dancing "an ecstasy that was as bodiless as the music with which it melted—austere, consecrated, compelling."[8] The expressive model proposes that her hidden self possessed the strength by virtue of which her body moved.

Yet the singular encounter of Duncan's solar plexus with her soul contradicts self-expressive iconostasis. Duncan fetishized her solar plexus as part-object of her "motor" or nature-soul. In direct contact with the "source," itself wedded to the source, the solar plexus may have been *inner* but was not *absent*. Rather, it put her audience in direct and unmediated contact with meaning "in person," with the person of meaning in the flesh.

Duncan's personal poetic statements weave between these two poles. In her writing, she becomes personally identified with a carnal source of inspiration, yet that present source retains its miraculous, elusive, evanescent connections to an elsewhere. Whereas the self-expressive theme in her writing highlights the activity of *dancing* and its effect on the public, the fetishistic theme calls attention to her discovery of movement as material in the making of *dances*. That is, the soul's invisible presence is a performance effect whereas the body's materiality is the impetus for designing that performance. The solar plexus as source of creativity introduces not only the how but the what, whereas discussions of inwardness interpret movement qualities alone. Dancing and choreographing dances constitute distinct yet interwoven pursuits allowing us to differentiate between expressive meaning translating a significant elsewhere as absence, and the body as a material signifier denying the loss of palpable presence.

INNER/OUTER POLARITIES

Founding mother in popular imagination of an "organic society,"[9] Duncan wished to contest the Victorian experience of female culture. Her efforts to reform the constricted movements of women's bodies in daily life and in theatrical self-display had meaning both *externally* for social life and *internally* for dance history. Externally, Duncan refuted, as did New Woman novelists of the 1890s, "the general separation of public and private spheres (and the relegation of women to the latter)."[10] Her career as a self-producing female soloist effectively challenged the separation of public and private spheres that immured women in the confines of domesticity. That is, by choosing dance as "woman's place," she inevitably raised the issue of woman as subject, of feminine subjectivity.[11] Duncan's subjectivity was unstably positioned on a threshold between privacy and publicity because her dance was an act of public display unveiling hidden nature as prior to or intrinsically outside society, from elsewhere by definition. Although opposed to the separation of these spheres, Duncan also relied on their segregation to dramatize her opposition. In this sense, she took performance where she found it as a public act for a

Figure 1. Portrait of Isadora Duncan. (Courtesy of Isadora Duncan Collection, San Francisco Performing Arts Library and Museum)

private self. Thus the image of a lone figure on an empty stage dancing to music. Although the consecrated historical interpretation understands Duncan's force as her personal charisma, how did her politics translate into aesthetic terms? How can performance theory reconstruct her work as social practice *internal* to dance history?

Duncan's writing narrates the discovery of *dancing* but rarely, if ever, the incremental and pragmatic construction of *dances*. Since the 1970s, however, reconstructions of Duncan's work have established that her dances have an objective historical status of their own: They qualify as dances in their own right, regardless of Duncan's now-absent body.[12] The paradox is, on one hand, that dance history has monumentalized Duncan's personal presence—her charisma, the Duncan myth—which depends on her own irremediable absence. She was unique, historically unrepeatable. On the other hand, her choreography itself, which had become undervalued (or perhaps one might say overpowered by her expressive theory and personal success), recovers Duncan's presence as would the relic of a material signifier with no strings to transcendence attached.[13] This is not to claim choreography can reanimate the dead, but rather that it "contains" a trace of performance inherent in the discovery of movement and the composition of dances, a trace unaccounted for by the solipsism of self-expression or the simulacra of impersonation. Reconstruction recovers the material of dances as the part-object of a deceased body, a relic.[14]

Duncan specialist Julia Levien recently stated that the dances as seen in 1990 were not "reconstructed" because that term implies loss, and the dances "were never lost."[15] All dance, however, is constituted by loss in the form of its own immediate disappearance which then engenders a desire for its reappearance, ultimately for its reconstruction. Reconstruction and choreography—two facets of the science of making dances happen—are distinguishable from dancing as the irretrievable mystery of what happened in those dances. The aim of recent reconstructions has *not* been to reconstruct Duncan's personality. They reveal instead multiple versions of Duncan just as Duncan herself may originally have evidenced multiple selves: mother, maenad, pre-Raphaelite girl, spirit of Music, political radical, priestess, darling of salon society, new pagan. . . . Reconstructions tell us there can be no totalized vision of ISADORA DUNCAN.

The decentered self of Duncan's reconstructed dances corresponds to a reappropriation of her choreographic poetic by reconstruction, that is, from a position *internal* to dance history but external to the legend of her personality. To extricate oneself from the Duncan legend, a public domain in which her privacy has been deposited, is also to displace intensely personal spectatorial accounts reinforcing Duncan's most essentialist discourse: "When she expresses her submission to the inevitable," wrote painter Eugene Carrière, "we, too, resign ourselves with her."[16] This sort of empathy records Duncan's mythical agency to the detriment of her dialectical struggle. Just as reconstructions are not in any original sense performances, but re-member vocabulary and composition (choreography) without simulating a particular and unique subjectivity, so they reveal a de-centered rather than consolidated self. My interest here is neither in a kinetic nor in a choreographic description, both of which might be afforded by examining reconstructions. Instead, I wish to theorize a political positioning of the body not as a representation but as a practice. I assume that practice is in some way encoded in Duncan's writing and particularly in her treatment of expression theory. My reading of Duncan's expression theory reveals the fetish emerging from the expressive model, practice emerging from representations.

> *Date unknown: "I did not invent my dance, it existed before me; but it was slumbering and I awoke it."* —*Isadora Duncan*[17]

Let us apprehend Duncan's performance, then, by attending directly to her dance theory. In a juncture between her statements of a personal poetic and the effects of reconstructed choreography emerges an intertextual field relating the "inside" of dance performance to the "outside" of social history. The starting point is fairly obvious: Duncan reproached the classical ballerina with a false consciousness of the mechanical origin of movement:

> The ballet school taught the pupil that this spring was found in the centre of the back at the base of the spine. From this axis, says the ballet master, arms, legs and trunk must move freely, giving the result of an articulated puppet.[18]

Ballet was not only wrong about the body, it was unsyntactical, noncumulative: "[in ballet] each action is an end, and no movement, pose or rhythm is successive or can be made to evolve succeeding action."[19]

It is seldom noted that Duncan's reform was syntactical as well as lexical. Syntax is a fundamentally choreographic problem of how one movement can be justified as following another. But the choreographic ramifications of Duncan's discovery of "natural" movement are problematic. She writes: "I also then dreamed of finding a first movement from which would be born a series of movements without my volition, but as the unconscious reaction of the primary movement."[20] Duncan sought not only natural movement, but syntactically natural movement sequences developed from the unconscious.

Moscow Art Theater director Constantin Stanislavski also conjoined nature with the unconscious in his method of emotional retrieval: "Many important sides of our complex natures are neither known to us nor subject to our conscious direction," he wrote. "Only nature has access to them."[21] Stanislavski explains how sense memory is a pathway to emotion memory. The life of the senses opens the way to the memory of old impressions, rendering emotions available to recall.[22] Both Duncan and Stanislavski subscribe to a conception of art as a "culture of feeling" broadly opposed to the "philosophy of mechanism."[23] Despite the Stanislavski "method," emotions elude the conscious control of actors and directors. "Nature" and the "unconscious" are terms preserving the domain of privacy as a source of art. Method acting, then, is a scientific technique for developing access to the private in public. As a technique, however, it was considered natural rather than artificial because it presupposed the integrity of privacy.

In dance, however, the syntactical problem is more complex than is the presentation of emotion in drama. It amounts to asking how entire choreographic sequences can be rendered wholly natural, how transitions between individually natural movements can be as uncalculated as the movements they link, and how the closure or resolution implied in dance composition can appear inevitable.[24] Duncan's choreographic "dream" asks these questions and ventures this response: In order for the content of dance to be inherent in its structure, expressive movement should play a double and, in fact, divided role.

The "new kinaesthetic" of modernism has been analyzed by Hillel Schwartz as not only expressive, but also "operative" and "transformative." Across a broad spectrum of physical practices between 1840 and 1930, Schwartz locates a common tendency of physical practices to operate on and/or transform their expressive agency.[25] In other words, expressive movement confirms the continuity of its own production, its own ability to reproduce itself, by a feedback of gesture into character, "as if by 'going through the motions' one might (wordlessly) discover and redefine oneself."[26] The movement from inner to outer on which Duncan's dance seems to depend is regenerating provided it accommodates reciprocal movement from outer to inner. Similarly, Duncan's dream has movement unfold into space from the solar plexus only to reincorporate itself as catalyst of the next in a series of movements. Autonomous reincorporation of the "first movement" enables "unconscious reaction." The centrifugal turning outside-in of dance, the reappropriation of its own gestural outside by its essentialist and internalist presence, could be viewed as compromising for the inner/outer polarity itself. What was thought to be purely "self-expressive" movement is generated from the "outside" of the self's closure. I explore in what follows how this process necessarily entails displacements of intentionality or temporary losses of subject-position at odds with organic wholeness, and how such desubjectification suggested a transgressive reading of the inner/outer binary. That binary is a fundamental condition of thinking about embodiment. We are in space and space is outside of us. Yet the binary is subject to manipulation. Each twist given to its phenomenology establishes a new site of ideology.

1929: "Isadora Duncan was a genius. She denied the rights of private property in the dance."   *—Michael Gold*[27]

My question could be rephrased thus: Was Duncan really that "expressive" woman dancing the dance of "herself"? Ample evidence, of course, exists for Duncan's belief in the self-expressive basis of her art. ("My Art is just an effort to express the truth of my Being in gesture and movement.")[28] Yet such an image—the status of Duncan herself as image—conflates Duncan's performance with the unproblematic vision of her charisma: "She shall dance the freedom of woman."[29] Duncan performed women's rights; Duncan's dance was a transparent medium through which her personality sent a message of social reform. This emblematic approach provides attractive motifs for social histories organized around the dancing "image" *and* for dance history's institutional need to maintain Duncan as a pure origin of modern dance. This last point requires a short digression.

Several years after Duncan's death in 1927, a modern dance establishment began to take shape in New York. Duncan's links to Soviet Russia and the revolutionary sentiments her writing and interviews displayed endeared her to the New York literary left, influential in late-twenties and early-thirties cultural life. "Stupid, pernicious, ignorant, intolerant America disgusts me," Duncan confided to the *San Francisco Examiner*, "and I am going back to Russia, the most enlightened nation of the world today."[30] Duncan used the terms "dreary" and "routinized" to characterize America, much as she used the terms "mechanical" and "puppet-like" in her indictment of European classicism.[31] The technological aesthetic in opposition to which Duncan founded modern dance was most clearly epitomized in America's unorganic society in which capital enslaved labor, mechanism subdued energy. Duncan's rhetoric, by which I mean her tendency to evaluate social situations with aesthetic criteria, draws near to the sort of interaction between dance and politics that I am attempting to imagine in her performance as a practice.

Despite Duncan's professed radicalism, the patronage network she cultivated in America and abroad as well as her perceived aestheticism established her appeal to the right. In the second issue of the *Dance Observer*, one reads an emotionally more neutral, if just as historically appropriative, assessment:

> If the art of the dance is imbued with a renewed vitality and significance, it is because the year 1878 gave birth to an American dance genius who was destined to rescue the art from the sterile infantilism which had possessed it in bondage, unbroken since the fifteenth century. That she was essentially an American phenomenon is indicated by the fact her principles of movement and feeling for change and growth are the identical characteristics of our own dancers of today.[32]

Duncan's date of birth is henceforth brandished to reaffirm the origins of an institutional discourse on modern dance. Her reputation as originator safeguards the integrity of American modern dance as a discursive field and, more generally, of twentieth-century dance history within aesthetic modernism. In this sense, too, Duncan is fetishized if one admits William Pietz's historical contextualization of fetish theory as "the theory of value articulated from that comparative standpoint located . . . at the point of encounter between the values and value consciousness of societies with different modes of production."[33] Duncan's natural dance—the specter haunting America—contains a vision of socialism as organic, ultimately as a feminine community without capital. I will return to this point with reference to Duncan's fascination with the Greek chorus.

If Duncan's choreography in reconstruction escapes the unbearable tautology of "natural dance," and I believe that, from a postmodern perspective, it can, it is not in small part due to the detachability of her personality from the reconstructed dance and the corresponding idea that detachment was integral to the original performing of those dances. How can such detachment be expressed without countering our image of the "original" Duncan as self-expressive social reformer, as mobilizer of her "self" in the name of others? What consequences follow for dance history if the founding mother of modern dance is recast as a modernist who, in T. S. Eliot's terms, seeks "a continual self-sacrifice, a continual extinction of personality."[34]

EN-GENDERING DANCE

Date unknown: "Each movement retains the strength to engender another."   *—Isadora Duncan*[35]

The dream of a choreography beyond volition perpetuating itself with the inevitability of birth contractions can also be explained in the analytical terms of expression theory. According to this theory, physical expression results from a series of events channeling from one to the other as they open onto the body's surface from a spiritually interior and visually clandestine site. At that concealed site, an impression on the soul (affect) was thought to give rise to a sensation within the body. The sensation (feeling) seeks release by emerging in outward movement (gesture). Dance formalized this tripartite process by casting music as the so-called impression, a corresponding emotional state as the sensation, and dancing itself as the expression. Duncan's project of successive movements reacting unconsciously to prior movements, however, portrays the channel from interior to exterior as circulatory. When the dancer reintrojects her own dancing as if to incorporate new affect, her dancing appears auto-affected: It is caught in the rotating torque of a return upon itself.[36] When expression theory thus catches itself by the tail, a deferment of gesture's delineated connotations ensues. The semiosis of femininity becomes circular rather than outwardly addressed. When "each movement retains the strength to engender another" the dancer's personality becomes subordinate to a dancing self radically identified with natural process, but is also split or decentered within that very process. The dancing self hosts a nonexpressive communication between outer and inner.

Auto-affection or recycled expression is another facet of depsychologized movement: It transforms personality into nature, nature into dance. Or it could simply be perceived as a sexual provocation. The dancer "responding" to herself or reveling in her own dance reproduces the patriarchal myth of the

Figure 2. Drawing of Duncan
by Walkowitz from *The Masses*
(September 1917).

feminine body's closeness-to-itself.[37] It is not productive, but reproductive. The dancer does not, therefore, participate in the public sphere of productive labor, but typifies instead bourgeois privacy-as-subjectivity already firmly established by late-nineteenth-century capitalism. The dancer moves in the "natural realm of the self," having no public, impersonal language.[38] Yet the split of a return from the outside as constitutive of interiority lays claim to a certain outside as constitutive of inwardness.

Duncan's essentialism, despite pre-Raphaelite and post-symbolist resonances, is consonant with spiritual aspects of the modernist art project.[39] For example, natural dance has striking analogies with the color essentialism of Kandinsky, Klee, Malevich, and Mondrian.[40] Nevertheless, modernist rejection of subjectivism resulting in depersonalized emotion conflicts with Duncan's ostensible social impact. Despite her social militancy and avant-garde attempt to bring art and life together, essentialist metaphors and syllogisms insulate her performance from social reality. This is the double bind of the female soloist in historical modern dance: The female soloist's personality and the modernist subject's self-effacement coalesce aesthetically but conflict politically.

The beginnings of historical modern dance are often explained as an American reaction against European formalisms. This view implies that the modern dancer wrested her decision-making from the tyranny of culturally entrenched physical techniques. According to this narrative, her political position is unequivocal. Her revolt facilitated a reappropriation of her own movement and, by extension, that of the feminine body. But if we reimagine Duncan's dream of involuntary choreography not as an escape from outmoded formal constraints but as an abdication of individual will before nature—"a series of movements without my volition, but as the unconscious reaction"—the Duncan issue begs reformulation. How fulfill the social mission to represent feminine subjectivity while abjuring all voluntarism? Duncan enters social history as an imitator of all nature—Mother Nature—a transcendental signifier that only secondarily happens to be woman, or better, that can only be "a" woman when raised to this metaphysical level. Her solo, "Mother," for example, illustrates how the play of idol and fetish becomes activated in the service of an essentialized female role. Her embrace of the absent offspring is always followed by an opening of her arms and a distancing of her gaze as they move off into an ever-increasing distance. Her performance of embrace closes Duncan off from the outside: We see a self-embracing figure but also a self-effacing figure. By contrast, the open and reaching postures are statements of a mother's loss and anxiety, but also of motherhood itself as that which had instituted closeness. Duncan's presence to an audience is realized through her character's statement of loss whereas her enactment of emotional totality is perceived paradoxically as a withdrawal or self-obscurement. Nevertheless, she did intend to embody feminine subjectivity in public space as a rejection of woman's place in the private sphere.

> 1903: "She [the dancer] will realize the mission of woman's body and the holiness of all of its parts." —Isadora Duncan[41]

Duncan's concern was for the female body and the (female) child's body exclusively, and never, except as a vaguely democratic gesture, for the male body. According to Floyd Dell, simply by expressing "the goodness of the whole body," Duncan gave further impetus to the women's movement of the late nineteenth century.[42] Indeed, her demonstration of physical vitality flatly contradicted the late-nineteenth-century cult of invalidism and anorexia nervosa leading to "the consumptive sublime."[43] Yet, despite her public rejection of marriage, Duncan's personal and artistic fascination with children stressed the "inevitable continuity [that] women and children formed"[44] in patriarchalism. Consequently, Duncan's "somatic utopianism," as Evan Alderson has called it, can be apprehended in a feminist, socialist, and biologically essentialist light.[45] She transferred the idea of a soul in physical form to the syllogism: female body=nature, nature=dance, therefore: female body=dance. To paraphrase Thierry de Duve, the dancer's signifier (her body) became the metaphorical essence of woman's nature, woman-as-nature.[46] Duncan's dancing presented woman as close to nature, emotion, and the unconscious while also enshrining nature in the solar plexus, *her* solar plexus. This reversibility of the female body and nature led in turn to a paradoxical effect whereby Duncan, although scantily clad, nevertheless appeared to many chaste and distant. "The endowing of interior sensory events with a metaphysical referent," in the words of Elaine Scarry, occluded radical exposure.[47] This ambiguity cuts two ways: On the one hand, Duncan occupies space without taking an oppositional role within it; on the other, she equates the creative act of dancing with procreation and thereby reiterates the artistic strategy of New Woman novelists who "equate writing with mothering in an effort to reconceptualize the relationship between public and private spheres, cultural and biological labor."[48] The question I am leading to is this: Can we say that Duncan represents the contradiction "constitutive of the female subject of feminism," in the terms of Teresa de Lauretis?[49] Or, how can we explain that Duncan managed to occupy a subject position without positioning her subjectivity in space?

EXPRESSING THE INEXPRESSIBLE

1887: "The idea of absolute calm and repose of the immortal soul, possessing infinite capacity for expression, but at the same time giving no definite expression except that of capacity and power in reserve."   —*Genevieve Stebbins*[50]

In ways resembling the Delsartism of Genevieve Stebbins, Duncan did not express feminine subjectivity, she staged its "power in reserve."[51] Stebbins had opposed the expressive posing of the physical culture movement, advocating artistic statue-posing as an alternative. Whereas expressive posing allowed for conveying thoughts and feelings, artistic statue-posing "maintained beauty of form and proportion, but without expression."[52] In rejecting the expressive aspect of posing, Stebbins sought to picture human "capacity for expression" without its particular realization.[53] Stebbins sought a state of utter receptivity, an openness to all impressions but a privileging only of what she thought to be a universal of perfected form. Similarly, Duncan wished to shape dance from within sensation. Like Stebbins, Duncan aimed for a pre-expressive performance level, a state conditional for expression but not committed to its actual emergence.

For director Eugenio Barba, the pre-expressive level involves invisible energy that "refers to something intimate, something which pulses in immobility and silence, a retained power which flows in time without spreading through space."[54] Stebbins emulated statuesque figures to evoke states of inconclusive receptivity. Duncan's visits to the British Museum in 1899 led her to imagine a moving statue which she also referred to as "the quality of repose in motion."[55] Motion was Duncan's solution to the problem, already posed by Stebbins, of subduing expressive outwardness while maintaining sensate inwardness. Duncan staged herself as a subject of expression, not an expressive subject.[56]

1908: "Often I thought to myself, what a mistake to call me a dancer. I am the magnetic centre to convey the emotional expression of the Orchestra. From my soul sprang fiery rays to connect me with my trembling, vibrating Orchestra."   —*Isadora Duncan*[57]

Duncan places her concerns at the origin of movement where *sensation* is ignited. The catalyst of that sensation is the orchestra whose vibrations are conducted through Duncan's body to the spectator. Even the term "magnetic centre" suggests her will to draw expression back to impression, or to wed both in a median center not formally displayed but rather "indicated" by her performance. ("I do not fulfill it, I only indicate it.")[58] When Duncan locates sensation in the solar plexus, calling it "the temporal home of the soul," she implies that the two liminal terms of expression theory—impression and expression—converge in that part of her body. Sensation is the result of a movement from inner impression outward, but, in Duncan's dancing, it also magnetizes the audience "inward" toward the connector, the forcibly *magnetic* center of sensation. The woman in diaphanous veils moving on an empty stage against blue drapery is not the emblem of that expressive process; rather, she is the ground connecting orchestra and Idea. She is Mallarmé's hymen. As Robert Greer Cohn notes of Mallarmé's writing on dance, this joining function is "that of the ritual whereby a crowd is joined to the all by an intermediary, that of the 'hymen' between audience and nature with the impersonal dancer as go-between."[59] There is no expressional product emanating from her body: Hers is a dance of feeling as embodied sensation, not of expressive reaction to sensation.[60] Duncan's dancing maintained a deferred, one could also say a private, relationship to public space.

Charles Taylor uses the term public space rather than communication to speak of expression as symbolic activity.[61] The space between us organizes the perception of what is between us, "the space of things which are objects for us together."[62] Space becomes "public" as the events in it mold apprehension, producing social meaning. Dance can organize space to configure or reconfigure the relationships of bodies in just such an ephemeral, but also public, manner. Historical modern dance, in particular, is "art *in* society," in Richard Sennett's terms, "aesthetic work intrinsic to social processes themselves."[63] Extremes of aesthetic assessment in Duncan's audience point to such a negotiation in performance between the dancer's body and the spectator's body, a relationship which, in many cases, is also between a female and a male body.[64]

D. W. Winnicott's notion of potential space further nuances the processual and dynamic aspects of Taylor's concept. Based on his observation of children's play in which an alien outside is experienced, Winnicott posited that "cultural experience is in potential space."[65] Potential space designates the sort of play in which same-dominated, "me-extensions" of the subjectively perceived object are confronted with other-oriented, "not-me" perceptions of "the object objectively perceived."[66] Although Winnicott's contact is more developmental than Taylor's, it speaks to iconoclastic dance as a spectacle of bodies that, more often than not, are "not-me" in a significant variety of ways. Winnicott's notion of play offers a conceptual framework to imagine how Duncan might have induced her audience to meld their same-dominated vision of a disappearing feminine body with a "not-me" perception of feminine subjectivity coming into focus.

Figure 3. Duncan in *The Blessed Spirit*. (Courtesy of Isadora Duncan Collection, San Francisco Performing Arts Library and Museum)

If Duncan's movement issued from a closed, interiorized space, Gaston Bachelard's theory of space as a dialectics of inside and outside articulates Taylor's "public" with Winnicott's "potential" space: "Outside and inside are both intimate—they are always ready to be reversed, to exchange their hostility."[67] Such reversibility, already discussed in the process of im-pressive reincorporation of expressive movement, founded Duncan's political force in the aesthetic sphere. Recall that expressive dancing was iconostatic: it signaled meaning as an absent essence. Recall also that Duncan's solar plexus was fetishized as her own connection to her self—her inner nature with all of its dizzying metaphorical slide—standing forth as her own body. I want to argue that Duncan's politics—her danced politics—reside in a reversibility of loss through which she becomes her own missing other (soul). Her body becomes interchangeable with her soul, her presence with her absence. Reversibility maintains that "interiority is always an 'introjection' of the exterior or, more precisely, a dispersion or exteriorization of the interior."[68] The mutual porousness of inner and outer is the passivity of closure itself.[69] Duncan displaces powerful binaries such as inner/outer and private/public but also female/male, nature/culture, labor/capital. The subordinate term of each binary is neither productive nor reproductive but, rather, like a wound through which both are constitutionally in excess with regard to each other.[70] The benefit of this theory is to avoid choreographing Duncan as victim of her own historical limits. What I am proposing is a deconstructive reading of Duncan that can also be realized through a comparison with Valentine de Saint-Point, to whom I shall turn at the end of this chapter. Duncan's own otherness is revealed in Saint-Point's very differences with her. Saint-Point will thus serve to check the analysis from a different direction.

1887: "The dancer is not a woman who dances for the juxtaposed reasons that she is not a woman but a metaphor."
—Stéphane Mallarmé[71]

For Mallarmé, Loie Fuller, Duncan's forerunner in certain respects, did not dance but wrote with her body, suggesting the corporeal equivalent of a poem. The dancer was, in Mary Lewis Shaw's formulation, "an unwritten body writing."[72] Fuller skillfully manipulated light and colored silken veils to produce visual metaphor. Duncan extended Fuller's technological innovations in theater craft to the organic spectacle of "woman's body and the holiness of all of its parts." That is, Duncan's deployment of metaphor reveals processes similar to Fuller's at work.

In the terminology of metaphor theory, the female soloist was the ground connecting the vehicle (dance) with the tenor (nature). Duncan's ground is analogous to expression theory's equally invisible middle term: sensation. In metaphor, the ground is never manifested lexically because that trope derives its prestigious compression from abridging the comparison that founds it. The ground is the invisible assumption grounding the metaphorical assertion that two diverse things are identical. One could say that in the middle "ground" of sensation, wherein Duncan's lyricism is enacted, woman is expressively displayed only to vanish in the production of metaphor. She is an unwritten body, but one could also say that sensation is the portal through which impressions travel in both directions. To the "unwritten" nature of this body corresponds expression withheld as the material of new sensation. But the unwritten body also corresponds to sensation itself as the passivity of closure and self-identity. Although the power of dance to suggest the "presence-in-absence" of a literary text was quite independent of the "woman as nature" trope, both recur in the spectacle of sensation as something we can see but that does not really happen before us. "For the dancer," wrote Mallarmé's disciple Valéry in his description of La Argentina,

> is in another world; no longer the world that takes color from our gaze, but one that she weaves with her steps and builds with her gestures. And in that world acts have no outward aim; there is no object to grasp, to attain, to repulse or run away from, no object which puts a precise end to an action and gives movements first an outward direction and co-ordination, then a clear and definite conclusion.[73]

The distance thereby created is also, paradoxically, a communication rendering inside and outside mutually porous. The world indicated by steps and gestures is a world rewritten as movement. Valéry's point is that the dance outside the world derealizes itself precisely so that it might rewrite the world from its position of passive externality, that it might propose the gestural tropes of a new public space.

Despite obvious differences in self-presentation, Fuller could be said to have proposed a theatrical model for Duncan. Frank Kermode has linked Duncan with Fuller's symbolist choreography.[74] If in Kermode's terms, Fuller achieved "impersonality at a stroke"[75] by manipulating fabric under light and thus writing with her body, Duncan achieved impersonality through the extended metaphor of her own dancing. Expression theory was Duncan's fabric, so to speak, and metaphor her play of light. The theatrical vehicle connecting the impression of Nature (music) to the expression of Dance (movement) and occupying the mediating portals of sensation is Woman. To engender motions of the self is to gender that self as female. Metaphor, however, was triangulated: "Dance is woman" is conditional on "woman is nature," which depends in turn on "nature as the source of all dance." The freedom of woman was not in the public sphere of the outer world of events. Rather, it was as though veiled within the membrane of sensation that divides inner listening from outer response. Duncan's abdication of will—her choreographic dream—actually resides in the endless circulation of metaphor, in the prodigious abridgment of its sliding syllogisms producing the meaning of her works and closing woman off from public space: She is outside the world but also inside the dance. This is how I would understand Duncan's performance poetic,

as distinct from the impact of her public persona. The effect of her performance, however, was to situate her audience with her on the "inside," which
was, in fact, a critically positioned "outside."

In stressing the non-self-expressive quality of Duncan's expression, I do
not mean to deny her charisma, the historical fact that she spurred enthusiasm and excited audiences. I focus, in fact, on the deferral of her personality
precisely to delineate that charisma's intensity. Duncan described it as light. It
conformed to her natural aesthetic by traveling in waves,[76] and replicated her
expressive process itself when her body felt like "a fount of light."[77] Indeed,
light is the single term Duncan employed in which form and content, model
and response, feeling and vision attain the desired equipoise. It was an impetus, a channel, and a visual result. Yet light was also another depersonalization
trope. Modern dance seems to have been invented at the theatrical site of a
vanishing female body about to be reborn. "Dancing," writes Dierdre Pridden,
"destroys the movement which has just been executed and yet is not the attitude about to be formed, and therefore it is eternally in the present."[78] The
present, however, signals lapse, the receding wave, or an afterglow: an inside
within an outside. Her light threw no shadow.

Duncan's dance was meant to suggest, indeed, to instaure through suggestive practice, a new sort of social relation to the feminine body as an altered public space. Consider that affectivity was traditionally sequestered with
family and sexuality in the private sphere. In view of this, Duncan's containment of affectivity within what I have called sensation can also be interpreted
politically. That is, Duncan's rejection of an overtly delineated affectivity, which
I have been calling expression, is likewise a refusal to credit the inner/outer or
female/male binary by occupying, literally dancing on, its boundary. Neither
within nor without, Duncan critiques such binaries. In viewing reconstructions, it is frequently difficult to ascertain whether she dances a woman about
to emerge or about to recede, as her body wafts in the direction of the spectator only to recede to the back of the stage, accentuates the militant weightedness
of her poses as in *Revolutionary Etude*, or elides itself in a self-enclosed mass
on the floor as in *Mother* or many of Jean Grandjouan's drawings of Duncan
in performance.

At the risk of exaggerating her historical possibilities, this double vision
constitutes Duncan's postmodernity. "The subject that I see emerging . . .
within feminism," writes Teresa de Lauretis, "is one that is at the same time
inside *and* outside the ideology of gender, and conscious of being so, conscious of that twofold pull, of that division, that doubled vision."[79] Duncan's
dance materializes the possibility of being "at once within and without representation."[80] To say that the female soloist is in a double bind, to say that her
dancing extinguishes personality (expression) in order to configure subjectivity (sensation) and render it present as body (choreography), is to say "the
female subject of feminism is in both places at once."[81] The only problem with
applying such recent theory to Duncan is that being without representation
(outside ideology) is, for Duncan, being "within" sensation (the body as re-

ceptor of feeling). This discrepancy, however, is not anachronistic in that "without" and "within" are both rhetorical figures of an elsewhere, an unproclaimed subjectivity. The sensitive body can disrupt a reading of sensation as metaphor of domesticity and denial of agency, even though there is a structural relationship between these two insides, the discontinuous and the communicative.

THE CHORUS AND DISINDIVIDUATION

1905: "Dancing is the Dionysian ecstasy which carries away all."
*   —Isadora Duncan*[82]

Let us recall that Duncan's founding moment was also an educational moment: "It was from this discovery that was born the theory on which I founded my school." But the idea of a school did not derive simply from a disinterested belief in education. Rather, the school was destined in Duncan's mind to produce an essential element of her choreographic vision: the chorus.

> If I had only visioned the dance as a Solo, my way would have been quite simple. . . . But, alas! I was possessed by the idea of a school—a vast ensemble—dancing the Ninth Symphony of Beethoven. At night, I had only to shut my eyes and these figures danced through my brain in mighty array, calling on me to bring them to life.[83]

Dancing the Maenad or Bacchante was part of Duncan's lifelong project to recreate the Greek chorus by staging a "Dionysion." It was responsible for her statement "I have never danced alone."[84] Before the possibility of training other dancers presented itself, however, Duncan had already danced the chorus single-handedly. She reported of her production of Aeschylus' *The Suppliants*: "I found it very difficult to express, in my slight figure, the emotions of fifty maidens all at once, but I had the feeling of multiple oneness."[85] In this production, Duncan tried to be everyone and everywhere at once. In her own words, the experience of a multiple and divided self joined her body to a hallucinated and intoxicating community: "In the golden lights of the stage I saw the white supple forms of my companions; sinewy arms, tossing heads, vibrant bodies, swift limbs environed me. . . . When I finally fell, in a paroxysm of joyous abandon, I saw them."[86] The chorus represented the loss of self in community, a desubjectification in the interest of *Gemeinschaft* as presence.

> *1927: "From the beginning I conceived of the dance as a chorus or community expression."*   —*Isadora Duncan*[87]

The sense in which community enabled disindividuation was perhaps fantasmatic but nonetheless defining for Duncan's Hellenism. Community had connotations both of impersonality or abstraction and embeddedness in image-making, of both Dionysus and Apollo. "The great impersonality of its [the chorus'] moved soul"[88] allowed dancers to transcend tragic personalities that enacted the drama and become "interpretors of the abstract."[89] Yet, at the same time, the chorus' very possibility of emergence relied on its grounding in the community of related arts—poetry, drama, music, and architecture—that constituted a body for which dance was the "sensational conscience." From its embeddedness in the community of arts, the chorus derived the "public" support enabling its emergence as pure symbol.[90] As Duncan conceived it, the most ambitious project of modern dance was to reinvent the choral entity organically embedded in community. "I don't mean to copy it, to imitate it, but to be inspired by it, to recreate it in myself with personal inspiration; to take its beauty with me toward the future."[91] By sacrificing the expression of her personality to the reinterpretation of past art, Duncan is typically modernist in Eliot's sense.

Duncan's double sense of community also infers the familiar paradigm of expressive self-regeneration already analyzed with reference to choreography: The dance rejoins the community of arts in a real space (most properly, the theater of Dionysus) in order to sacrifice its specificity to the postlyrical state of disindividuation. Dance—the abstract symbol in its concrete essence—subsides back into the spatial, linguistic, and sonorous community of arts it had momentarily transcended and which supports its swooning body.

> Date unknown: "One can dance in two ways: 1. One can penetrate the spirit of Dance: to dance the thing itself, Dionysus. 2. One can contemplate the spirit of Dance and dance like someone who would be telling its story, Apollo."   —Isadora Duncan[92]

In the Dionysian vision, the dancer is the site of rapture. In this Nietzschean state of being rather than showing, telling, or contemplating, Duncan suggests that Dionysian engagement makes dance more fully present. It escapes from the ground of sensation and all the essentialist ties of that position. In the chorus, dancing beyond volition gained a different interpretation. Rather than dancing "before personality," the chorus danced "after personality" in a postexpressive state of ego dissolution where Maenads undergo the loss of ego boundaries. Whereas lyrical pre-expressive gesture had maintained subjective agency intact even as it attempted to transcend volition, the merging of the individual with the choral mass absorbed agency into a new, involuntary physical symbol. To dance in Nietzsche's treatment of the Apollo-Dionysus duality was to surrender subjectivity to forces inducing disindividuated intoxication. It was an experience beyond conscious design in which subject and object, artist and art, merged.[93] Duncan called it dancing "the thing itself." But even in her Apollonian lyricism, the blurring of woman with nature had already taken place: Disindividuation is a more emphatically theatrical form of this depersonalizing metaphor. The "pre" of her feminism transmutes into the "post" of her socialism. Nature is that which, apart from its adherence to the

Figure 4. Duncan in a Dionysian mode. (Courtesy of Isadora Duncan Collection, San Francisco Performing Arts Library and Museum)

private, can also be a signifier of the social and, specifically, of a utopian socialism. Duncan's Hellenism pictures socialist community as located between the private and the public spheres whose most provocative moment is the "post": the demystification of loss as an event of the "inside." The chorus demonstrates that loss is produced on the outside as a social experience rather than on the inside as a religious allegory. The differences between Duncan's lyricism and her Hellenism reveal a repressed direction of American social thought.[94]

> 1927: "*The Greeks in all their painting, sculpture, architecture, literature, dance and tragedy evolved their movements from the movement of nature.*"   —Isadora Duncan[95]

Duncan had always articulated a continuity between the pre-expressive Apollonian dreamer whose images, although danced, are never imparted in explicitly formal outline, and the postlyrical state that eradicated self-awareness and self-fashioning. Her writings also interpret the Dionysian order as an intensification of Apollonian Delsartism. Her contemplation of nature culminated in the wave figure: "The wave was the great foundation movement of Nature," and "all free, natural movements conform to the law of wave movement."[96] Yet, the "bacchic shiver" was also a movement derived from the natural wave:

> The "sub-motif" of this gesture is in all of nature. Animals, in a bacchic movement, throw their head back; in tropical countries at night, elephants throw back their head; dogs barking in moonlight, lions, tigers do the same. It is the universal dionysian movement. The waves of the ocean in tempest also create that line as do trees in storms.[97]

Dionysian frenzy is pictured here as an intensification of contemplative flow. Yet the bacchic shiver essays a radically different approach to feminine presence. Dionysian movement shatters the encasing membrane of sensation and possesses public space more directly. This occurs through the experience of feminine community staged in the Dionysion, in which the individual merges with myriad absent others, ultimately collapsing in exhaustion. The collapse is a moment of new departure for the material body.

To question whether Duncan's version of ancient Greece was authentic, whether her research into quattrocento art qualified as real scholarship, or whether her interest in classical antiquity did not flagrantly contradict her burnished image as modernist innovator, are pointedly irrelevant.[98] Such approaches to dance history fail to perceive the very dialectical relationship of the past and the future to the present in Duncan's choreography.

"THE SUBLIME ANDROGYNE OF DREAM AND ACTION"[99]

Although she represents no competitively "strong" moment in dance history, French dancer/choreographer Valentine de Saint-Point (1875-1953) takes the final step possible to early modernism in de-essentializing the feminine. Saint-Point was the only female futurist and thus uneasily aligned with the most overtly masculinist of avant-garde movements in the 1920s.[100] Certainly futurism, but also much avant-garde production, developed masculinist bodily aesthetics that implicitly critiqued Duncan.[101] While Saint-Point was an artist of multiple talents, her choreographic output was apparently limited to the *Metachorus*, performed in Paris in 1913 and in New York in 1917. Her thinking on the transition between pre- and post-expressive movement is sufficiently dialectical to warrant our attention here. *Metachorus* demonstrates how Saint-Point mediated the gender gulf of aesthetic modernism and, by taking the chorus to a metachoric level, further specified the chorus's depersonalizing, desubjectifying work.

Reading Saint-Point requires a navigation between two topics: gender (the futurist woman) and dance (the metachorus). "Manifesto of the Futurist Woman" responds to Marinetti's "Manifesto of the Futurist Dance," in which the futurist leader had lumped Duncan with Saint-Point:

> Valentine de Saint-Point conceived an abstract metaphysical dance that was supposed to embody pure thought without sentimentality or sexual excitement . . . abstractions danced but static, arid, cold, emotionless.[102]

In response to Marinetti's futurist dance project glorifying machines and violence, Saint-Point ventured no apology for or reinterpretation of *Metachorus*. Rather, its aesthetic goals are subtly reaffirmed in a discussion of modern gender identity.

Saint-Point rejects biological identity as a criterion of gender identity. As in Aristophanes' speech on the androgyne in Plato's *Symposium*, she postulates masculine and feminine principles in all people: "IT IS ABSURD TO DIVIDE HUMANITY INTO WOMEN AND MEN; humanity is composed only of FEMININITY and MASCULINITY."[103] Having severed gender identity from the gendered body, Saint-Point advocates that women adopt a new, albeit age-old, cultural policy: They should become "Amazons." She both qualifies masculinity as brutally violent and favors the universal rebalancing of gender traits toward the masculine pole whose energy has been lost to both sexes. War, as Marinetti suggests, recovers an essentially male aggressivity. Saint-Point wishes to restaure the same resources in women.

The raw aggression of the male character renders it essentially nonreflective and destructive, whereas the feminine extreme is characterized as intuitive and imaginative, qualities that can be woman's strength or weakness. When weak, they lead to wisdom, pacifism, and goodness. Saint-Point holds that the latent genius of femininity resides in cruelty and injustice. She calls therefore for a splintering of sentimental relations between men and women. If woman is to revivify the original force of femininity, she must adopt the roles of mother or lover in a very particular sense: as the mother who creates children without bonding or as the lover dedicating herself to the projection of vice and desire. These two roles—played simultaneously by Duncan with entirely different interpretations—cannot be performed by the same person for Saint-Point. Therefore, she calls feminism "a political error."[104] Saint-Point's position is to liberate women from all moral constraints but also to condemn them to nurture and support male heroes by engendering or desiring them without sentimentality or passionate involvement. Only thus can they become cruel and unjust again.

Saint-Point's choreography dramatizes none of these transgressive positions. She presents herself in *Metachorus* as both genders and neither. Dressed as a warrior, her face veiled and thus permanently absent from the dance, she "conceived an abstract, metaphysical dance that was supposed to embody pure thought without sentimentality or sexual excitement."[105] Sentimentalism and sexual ardor are traits that "The Manifesto of the Futurist Woman" admonishes women to abandon. Rather than mimic the universal cruelty of a world having violently redistributed its sexual economy, Saint-Point's dance presents the tenets of her cultural policy "coldly," nonmimetically. "A geometrical figure that signifies something, an atmosphere, a costume, a veiled face, a voice issuing from an invisible chest, precise movements, rigorous attitudes . . . all of that means something."[106] Resolutely anti-expressive (far from "sensations" and "psychology"), Saint-Point's metachorus rejects gender norms and eludes the mimetic quality of dance depending on music as an analogy for women depending on men.

One reason for Saint-Point's very un-Artaudian strategy resides in her need to establish an absolute in dance that could be distinguished from Duncan's physical essences. The most obvious demarcation lies in Saint-Point's rejection of music, which she considers to render dance contingent, obedient, and slavish: Music is an aestheticization of sentimentality. "The dance, then," she wrote, "is but a plastic art—an exoteric materialization, a bodily rhythm, instinctive or conventional [for example, in terms either of 'artistic dance' or classical dance]—of music."[107] Furthermore, the traditional dependency of dance on music reflects the old-fashioned and mutually weakening interdependency of the two sexes. Reminiscent of Mallarmé's description of Loïe Fuller, Saint-Point unsexes herself to gain direct access to the Idea.

Saint-Point enacts the uncoupling of a male-gendered music from a female-gendered dance by removing the connecting term: sensation or feeling (sentiment or passion). Dancing to music was not devoid of ideas, but Saint-Point wishes more direct and unmediated access to them:

> Music has always depended upon an idea; there never existed, and today less than ever does there exist, any music without some indicative title, a sort of ideistic theme which the composer transcribes and develops. . . . The dance, then, is merely a material part, an accessory of music."[108]

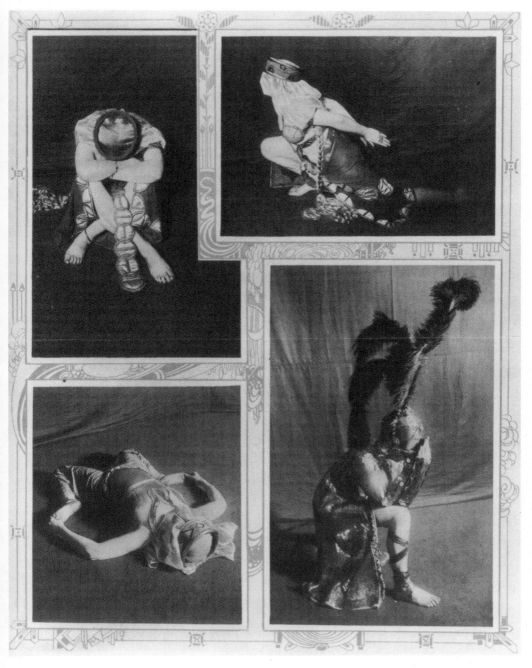

Figure 5. "Mme. Valentine de Saint-Point giving futurist dances at the Poirier Theatre, Paris," from *The Sketch Supplement* (January 7, 1914). (Courtesy of the Dance Collection, the New York Public Library for the Performing Arts, Astor, Lenox, and Tilden Foundations)

Saint-Point attempted to reverse this paradigm in which music stood for the mind and dance for the body, sound for the concept and movement for its shadowy illustration.

> There appeared to me calling for affirmation an ideistic dance, one suggested cerebrally by an idea, a vision, a definite theme to be interpreted; nothing vague, uncertain or disarranged.[109]

The intellect is thus opposed to "bodily rhythms" and, through a double bind by now familiar in Saint-Point's thinking, the feminine body performs the abstract dance of the intellect. Saint-Point calls for a materialization of the idea in its primacy across the ground of the female, but also androgynous, body.

Saint-Point sets up two parallel series of reflections. In her discourse on woman, the male and female oppose yet also permeate each other, allowing humankind to slide across a continuum of sexual difference. She disparages traditional images of male and female. Nevertheless, the male ideal to be expropriated by women embodies force, lasciviousness (*luxure* or *lussuria*), will, and brute energy, all goals to which the futurist woman should aspire.

In her discourse on dance, the mind/body dichotomy is invoked also in terms of a past/future dialectic. The old dance of the past is merely an adjunct of music: mimetic and illustrative. It typifies the body's shortcomings as secondary, derivative, and contingent. The autonomy of futurist dance from music renders dance highly conceptual: The body enables a direct access to the idea of which it is hardly even the intermediary. Like woman with regard to masculinity, the body expropriates the idea. In the metachorus the female soloist adopts the position of mind (traditionally gendered as male) just as in the arena of sexual politics she expropriates male energy. Across the sexual and choreographic paradigms, masculinity invests the traditionally feminine preserve of the body with its own brutal identity. Saint-Point creates mind out of matter by expropriating the sexual aspects of the male gendered mind and reinvesting them in a woman without a body, or more precisely, in a woman whose body is divorced from sensation (feeling). I would argue that, in this way, Saint-Point arrives at presence—the body's material signification—as a post-expressive movement of subjectivity toward the inside.

If Duncan presented dancing as an idea of woman (the woman of the future), Saint-Point presented woman as a dance of the idea (the futurist woman). Saint-Point's sublimation of woman to idea is tantamount to the erasure of feminine difference in the futurist woman's sexuality. The metachorus may be another face of the female soloist's double bind. The idea of Woman (Duncan) and woman as Idea (Saint-Point) can both be thought of as variations on presence-in-absence, but also as aesthetic-theoretical *embodiments* of social confrontation in modernist terms.

TWO

Bodies of Radical Will

Mechanical impulse and primitive urge dance as one
and forget, in their frenzy, the light of creation.
Could the wheel but unlearn its conformity
it might sing with the herd of horses, untrammeled,
and should a flame scorch the frozen agendas,
all heaven would flee from the tumult of windows.
—Federico García Lorca, *Poet in New York*

NEW THEATRE AND THE REVOLUTIONARY DANCE MOVEMENT

The thirties, especially in New York, was a decade of great cultural centrality for dance. Whereas theater, film, fiction, and cultural critique all underwent change during that decade, the imprint of radicalism on American modern dance was probably more seminal than for any other art. Yet, as if appreciably more than sixty years had passed since then, the reasons for dance's former cultural centrality have become obscured. Little magazines of the early thirties reveal a socialist avant-garde attempting to redefine culture and politics through bodies mobilized into action.

Although the recognized "trailblazers" of modern dance—Doris Humphrey and Charles Weidman, Martha Graham, Hanya Holm—were artistically innovative, radical publications hosted a debate over whether their aesthetic forms were adequate to the more radical mission of expressing socially revolutionary sentiments. This chapter attempts to outline the dance theory of a cultural milieu more politically radical than individuals later canonized as the aesthetic radicals.

Revolutionary dance, as it was called in the early thirties, was part of intellectual socialist production with roots in a long Anglo-American tradition of radicalism. American intellectual radicalism prior to the thirties had "been largely isolated from its traditional constituency, the proletariat, and, perhaps more importantly, from the working-class party."[1] One of the effects of the Great Depression was to create an increasingly self-identified working class. The misery and deprivation of the Depression era engendered performance that continues to be, with respect to its energy, seminal for dance and theater alike.[2] In the case of dance, the move of young, radical artists away from the modernists of modern dance was mediated by left cultural critique in which some dancers themselves also found a voice. The class consciousness of American radical politics would give explicit content (social relevance) to the aesthetic revolution of modern dance. This content was already implied in Isadora Duncan's radical leanings, but was somewhat muddled by the founder's reputed paganism as well as by subsequent second-generation attempts to formalize and codify new movement discoveries.

The revolutionary dance movement was nurtured by the Workers Dance League, an organization sponsoring joint concerts by its member groups. In January 1934, The W.D.L. presented the first revolutionary dance concert, including the New Dance Group, the Theatre Union Dance Group, the Jack London Rebel Dancers of Newark, the Red Dancers, the Nature Friends Dance Group, the Modern Negro Dance Group, and the New Duncan Dancers.[3] In 1934, according to dance critic Edna Ocko, the W.D.L. boasted eight hundred dues-paying members, twelve amateur groups in addition to the performing groups, and over fifty classes.[4] The organization gave specific attention to the development of black dance and to the need for encouraging men to dance.

New Theatre, a journal founded in 1933 but never subjected to serious analysis by modern dance historians, promoted but also documented the revolutionary dance movement.[5] The energetic and precise if intensely sectarian dance writing in *New Theatre* was the work of critics (and often dancers) who imagined modern dance's potential to stimulate social change. As a critical as well as a choreographic project, revolutionary dance aimed to create an avant-garde that could reconfigure social relations and/or choreograph their moribund stagnation, thus hastening the advent of socialist revolution. Modern dance vocabularies, although not inherited from nineteenth-century bourgeois culture, were still considered tainted by negative bourgeois thinking either in the guise of escapism or fascination with decay. The revolutionary artists—primarily the young students and company members of Hanya Holm's group and later of Martha Graham and Doris Humphrey, the first generation to have been trained by those aesthetic innovators—were exhorted to look beyond them or, short of that, to abandon their formalist concerns. Heavily influenced by the work of their mentors in a still-developing field, the fledgling choreographers wished to redirect modern dance forms to socially relevant themes as mediated by left cultural critique. Thus, the class consciousness of American radical politics set about to endow the aesthetic revolution of modern dance with politically revolutionary content, or to create a second revolution in modern dance that would politicize aesthetics. Philosophically justified by Isadora Duncan's radical tendencies, this revisionism was a corrective to modern dance that had strayed from Duncan's radical if ill-defined mission and foundered in a sterile formalism.

In an essay titled "Diagnosis of the Dance," Emanuel Eisenberg called for a revolutionary style that would displace modernist formalism:

> When they [choreographers] acquire a new body style that is directly related to the literal physical functions and the general psychological background of

the workers of the world . . . then the revolutionary dance movement will begin to take on meaning.[6]

Edna Ocko also called for a politicized aesthetics in innovative ways of moving:

> The revolutionary dance can emerge only after the significant (revolutionary) emotion and the mode of expression have moved together for so long a time and have interpenetrated the composition to such an extent that *the very movement of the dancers has revolutionary implications* and the very idea arises not from casual inspiration, but from a living with and a thinking for the proletariat. It must be so subtle a welding together of manner and matter, of emotional content and dynamic ideational form, that it can, at its best and greatest agitational heights, commandeer revolutionary mass feelings of the profoundest and most stirring sort, and project proletarian ideas of vast implications on the one hand, or specific everyday class issues on the other.[7]

The revolutionary dance exerted pressure on dance modernists by demanding that modern dance address social problems. Modern dance aesthetics became subject to pointed, perhaps unprecedented, critical inquiry and cultural critique. When potentially radical choreographers faltered in the project of "building on the old technique," and fell back on the easier task of "putting up a structure of this old technique," radical critics renewed their call for entirely new vocabularies.[8] Despite the fact that their emphasis on specificity appears from today's perspective entirely unimaginative, only newness for many radical critics could be truly consonant with negative culture. In radical dance, experimentalism and realism were not wholly contradictory values.

New Theatre polemics mirrored contemporaneous debates over radical literature. The fundamental issues, as noted by James Burkhart Gilbert, were "the relation between bourgeois and proletarian art, the question of reconciling form with content, and the conflict between art and propaganda."[9] Although the issue of agit-prop dance (dance of agitational propaganda) did arise, it was easily disposed of as undesirable. By far, the most hotly contended issues of left-wing dance criticism were form versus content and heritage versus innovation. Surprisingly, classical ballet was not an entirely dead issue for two reasons: No modern dance had emerged in the Soviet Union, which was viewed in radical circles as a utopia on earth,[10] and Lincoln Kirstein was a vocal advocate of classical technique in radical journals, albeit with unrepentant sophistry.[11] Kirstein employed all the catch phrases of radical polemics to support conservative aesthetics. Left-wing rhetoric was clearly the language of the day.

The issues of form versus content and heritage versus innovation were intertwined. As with radical literary criticism, radical dance observers preferred relevant subject matter to any preoccupation with form. Nevertheless, they urged the choreographer to abandon movement vocabularies at her disposal and, if possible, to invent entirely new ones. There was a desire, especially in the writing of Edna Ocko, to see content as welded to form.[12] To disparage formal questions in and of themselves did not preclude a demand for innovation. Formal questions were rehearsed occasionally with respect to choreographic conventions but arose inevitably when it came to technique. The danger of relying on Graham technique, for example, was that by redeploying Graham's so-called bourgeois heritage the younger choreographer unwittingly reiterated the bourgeois ideology subtending it.

To ask how to create revolutionary dance was to ask how to choreograph revolution by engendering an avant-garde, "the product of true proletarian culture."[13] As Ocko pointed out, "Working class ideology, no matter how thinly sketched, cannot be a superficial integument slipped on to any skeleton of a dance technic."[14] Eisenberg observed that a body well trained in the techniques of Wigman, Graham, Duncan, Humphrey, Weidman, or Tamiris was not automatically adaptable "to choreograph depictions of hunger, oppression, charity, hypocrisy, uprising, strike, collectivism, [or] racial fraternity."[15] He derided as delusory the expectation that revolutionary dance would materialize simply "through a sudden intensification of energetic movements, a glow of red in the costume, a brief but hearty session of practice at clenching the fists."[16] "The trouble with most of our revolutionary dancers," wrote Irving Ignatin, "is that they become 'revolutionary' too suddenly."[17] Precisely because of their technical status, established dance techniques of however recent date militated against the new historical realities that begged for artistic expression. They had been transported as already existent procedures from a world about to expire into a world about to be born. The essential critical concept was that revolutionary dancers should already have entered a revolutionary culture that could not yet have existed. This was the impulse behind revolutionary dance thinking that remade modern dance into an avant-garde project rather than an artistic manifestation of social protest. Only from a progressivist viewpoint was revolutionary dance a form of social protest. From a radical viewpoint, it was a discourse of desire bringing social action into being: The theory of revolutionary dance makes it a truly rehearsive act. It rehearses revolution.

Nonetheless, the precipitous abandonment of all technique was, as Paul Douglas pointed out, "completely undialectical because it overlooks the fundamental truism that content and form in any art medium are inseparable."[18] Ezra Freedman argued,

> To discard even the valuable contributions to the dance of the bourgeois schools would be comparable to the folly of a Soviet automobile factory abolishing the belt method of mass production merely because Henry Ford, a member of the hated capitalist class, originated it. . . . Only as our ideology improves will the need for new technique spur creative work in this field.[19]

Despite all critical urging, the problem was momentarily insoluble because critical discourse had outpaced creative activity. Eisenberg was in favor of greater choreographic precision:

Constructively, then: how shall the revolution be choreographically conveyed? . . . When they [the dancers] rise, it must be unmistakably against someone, not merely out of the depths. When they mass together, it must be in a representative demanding body, not merely as an electrified group that is aspiring somewhere or other. . . . Anything else is dreary bourgeois emotionalism and involves no more than an audacious superimposition of neo-revolutionary gestures on a decayed, juiceless and deceptively earnest body.[20]

One way around the pitfalls of technique, both of movement and of dance-making, was the study of mass dance. Jane Dudley, a dancer with Holm and later in Graham's company, wrote a piece for *New Theatre* in 1934 titled "The Mass Dance." Dudley described the process of creating mass dance in the classroom as a study in revolutionary action:

In order to give the members of the class an understanding of what it means to move together as a group, a few simple exercises should be given, such as standing together and swaying from side to side, walking together backwards and forwards, sinking down and rising up. These are exercises purely on a movement basis. It is possible to color the exercise by adding meaning to the movement, e.g., the group should go towards a point as though asking for something, demanding something. What must be remembered is the goal— *achieving a group sense in the class.*[21]

Dudley recommends the class begin with the simplest of movements both because of participants' lack of formal training and because the resulting dance should not carry any unwanted ideological residue:

The simple, fundamental steps—the walk, the run—are the most useful and effective. Think of the possibilities in the walk—marching, creeping, hesitating, rushing forward, being thrown back, the group splitting apart, scattered in all directions, uniting, coming forward, backing away, being thrown down, rising up. For this one does not need "steps," *bas de basque [sic], tour jete,* etc. All that is important is the movement of the group in space.[22]

To start with the basics such as walking and running was an approach already used by earlier modern dance innovators such as Duncan and Graham. Yet the simplicity of approach here was intended to bypass specialization and to institute an aesthetic education in the revolutionary act. It was not a matter of discovering new forms but of developing new intents that would transform the appearance of those forms. Dancer Ruth Allerhand also developed a procedure for mass dance class whose affect on the dancer was to make him or her a better revolutionary. Having experienced the exercises Allerhand recommended, the worker-dancer becomes acutely aware of "the simplicity, directness and elemental quality of all movement":

Now, well balanced and eager, his horizon broadened, he turns from his introspective gropings toward a relationship with the world around him. He is

drawn into moving forward. He actively cuts into space, using his body impulsively, he runs, leaps, turns, he creates and composes within space. From
all directions, others approach, galvanized by the same forces within themselves, the result of the same development through which he has just come.
They appear to him myriad reflections of himself. Spontaneously reaching
toward them he is absorbed into the group.[23]

Through mass dance, the worker-dancer sheds all remnants of bourgeois subjectivity and becomes *social woman*. Eisenberg's critique of choreography for the
group was thus answered by abandoning the dichotomy between life and performance that technique and training imposed. As Edith Segal noted: "The theme
or subject-matter of the group dance is therefore not the private property of the
director, or even of the group, but that of the audience, of society."[24]

A solution to the ideological dilemma of the bourgeois dance heritage
was arrived at less easily in the case of the female soloist. In 1935 the W.D.L.
presented soloist and small group works featuring Lillian Mehlman, Miriam
Blecher, Nadia Chilkovsky, Sophie Maslow, Anna Sokolow, Jane Dudley, and
Edith Segal.[25] The first performance of revolutionary dance soloists took place
at New York City's Civic Repertory on November 25, 1934.[26] In February
1935, an article titled "Ladies of the Revolutionary Dance" attacked the new
soloists as "bourgeois ladies" indulging in the "soul-expression" of the "spiritual-intellectual Lady."[27]

> The romantic dream-obsessed Lady, with a "free" (though sometimes mus-
> cularly disciplined) body, and a Mind unfettered enough to explore the
> profoundest recesses of her Soul, is surely the ideal standard figure which the
> predominantly middle-class culture of the last forty or fifty years has pro-
> duced and has handed over with necessary intactness to the revolutionary
> dance movement.[28]

Eisenberg's critique centers again on those qualities of modern dance which
are insufficiently specific and therefore only deceptively adaptable to the needs
of the avant-garde: "Their wide-eyed stepping Toward the Light is psychological-aspirational and so unspecific as to be interpretable by any vision one
selects."[29] This time, however, "bourgeois emotionalism" is gendered as feminine. Eisenberg seems to propose that the body lose its gendered specificity to
gain revolutionary specificity. Yet he does not propose that revolutionary dance
be exclusively danced by men. In branding modern dance as both bourgeois-
emotional and feminine, he contents himself with attacking the congenital
ambiguity of the female modern dance soloist through the sexist charge of
emotionalism. In 1929, Michael Gold belittled Duncan for similar reasons.

Nathaniel Buchwald countered by accusing Eisenberg's wholesale rejection of bourgeois forms as "extreme 'leftism'": "In developing a given field of
revolutionary art we start not from technique, not from a revolt against bourgeois forms, but from content, from a revolt against bourgeois ideology."[30]
Eisenberg persisted, however, in maintaining that "the dance must start abso-

Figure 6. "Soloists of Workers Dance League" (left top to right bottom): Anna Sokolow; Jane Dudley; Edith Segal; Miriam Blecher; Lillian Mehlman; Nadia Chilkovsky; Sokolow, Sophie Maslow, and Mehlman; and Maslow.

lutely fresh—or it must return to folk-patterns and the periods preceding the decades of what we understand as bourgeois culture."[31]

Although emotion was disparaged when it lacked political focus, it still emerged as an essential ingredient of revolutionary dance. The reason was probably that emotion bridged the pre- to post-revolutionary gap. For modern dance to be politically revolutionary, it had to produce revolution as well as reflect revolutionary culture to come. It needed to catalyze unrest but also reaffirm the inevitability of change. In other words, the revolutionary dancing body was under two contradictory mandates: to be a body of desire and a body of power. For its pre-revolutionary theme, it could dance about oppression and arouse sympathy and indignation, as well as demonstrate "revolutionary and militant verve."[32] For its post-revolutionary theme, it could dance revolutionary culture itself. Both phases were ideally collapsed into one dance wedding absence-in-presence (desire) to presence-in-absence (power). For this merging to come about, a new and inherently dialectical vocabulary was needed. Realism was being pushed into a performance "of the future" that would coax new culture into becoming.

Despite this double bind, a general critical consensus that strong but passionately lyrical flow should be the physical criterion of revolutionary dance was negotiated, notwithstanding disputes as to which choreographers best realized that aim. For example, Paul Douglas believed that the desired revolutionary aesthetic had been initiated by Duncan in her "erect affirmative stance and . . . free use of every part of the body."[33] He named Tamiris Duncan's heir: "Her [Tamiris's] refusal to adopt bourgeois dance forms is a dialectic negation and in this sense she is the only dancer who is carrying forward the positive tradition of Isadora Duncan."[34] Tamiris ostensibly achieved her edge with "a full use of her entire body in flowing rhythm" and an avoidance of "subjectivism or abstraction."[35] "The space through which she moves," asserted Douglas, "seems limitless."[36] Ignatin saw the potential for a truly avant-garde art in Graham, although her "technic will undergo modification with the increase of revolutionary subject matter—it will have to become more joyful, conscious of power . . ."[37] The issue subtly shifted from how to transform modern dance into revolutionary dance as "a real weapon for the emancipation of culture," to that of who should receive the laurels of aesthetic or political correctness.[38]

Emotion transmitted in movement's flow and the implication of self-conscious power worked as a glue, allowing dance to simultaneously address pre- to post-revolutionary situations. Ocko said revolutionary dance needed to go beyond "body-service to the movement" toward "the depiction of kinesthetically-realized emotional states" or "emotional crystallizations."[39] Movement took second place to intent verifiable by emotional tone only. Similarly, Harry Elion recommended that "the seeming contradictions between improved technique and lack of clarity in expression" could be overcome only by "becoming more dramatic."[40] From a different perspective, Blanche Evan argued: "If a dance attempts to convert . . . [it] must carry its message by a more emotional ideology."[41] Despite disagreement about the use of the modernist heritage, left-wing writers agreed that revolutionary dance should distinguish itself from

Figure 7. Cartoon of a radical dancer from *New Masses* (Nov. 3, 1937).

a purely formal break with formalism on the one hand (such as had been undertaken by second generation artists such as Graham, Humphrey, et al.), and
also embody revolutionary ardor and energy through an aggressive occupa-
tion of space and an energetic acknowledgment of the body's right to flow. But
this could be convincingly performed only by those who truly grasped its message, those for whom dance was a revolutionary activity. Despite a denial of
introspection and private personality in the name of collective action, emotion
was essential in the thirties to the political energy of dance.

The theory could be formulated as follows: without emotion, no revolution. The dialectical body would ultimately elaborate physical techniques of
political desire through which emotion moved others into action. "Emotional
crystallizations," in Ocko's terms, "must be compounded of not only 'sympathy' for the working-class movement, but a thorough intellectual grasp of
Marxian dialectics as well."[42] Radical dance was clearly anti-modernist in its
reliance on personal emotional power.

FROM A CONVERSATION WITH EDNA OCKO

Edna Ocko was active as a dance critic, dancer, publicist, and organizer
of left-wing modern dance between approximately 1928 and 1946. Some of
her writing appeared under the following pseudonyms: Elizabeth Skrip in the
Daily Worker, Francis Steuben in *New Masses*, and Eve Stebbins in *Cue*. Much
of her writing in the first two publications, however, was signed Edna Ocko.
What follows are excerpts from a conversation between Edna Ocko and the
author (October 7, 1993).

Figure 8. Anna Sokolow in *Dances for Spain* (1939). (Courtesy of the
Billy Rose Theater Collection, the New York Public Library for the
Performing Arts, Astor, Lenox, and Tilden Foundations)

EO: I earned my living when I was going to college playing piano for dancers. This was in the twenties. I was able to be a pretty good accompanist (my brother was a musician). I saw a lot of dances and it was a conceit of mine that "I can do it too." So, in exchange for playing the piano, I took dancing lessons with Bird Larson, then with Hanya (Holm). I was a very free-floating, free-thinking individual.

MF: There must have been a point at which your interest in radical politics in American life of the early thirties made a connection with your interest in dance.

EO: My father was a cigar-maker and a radical too. So I had some feeling about justice for the poor and the downtrodden. So it wasn't strange to me to read, or see, or think of ideas that these people called "left-wing" later on but that in the beginning were connected to the downtrodden and the poor. And then I was a reader, I was an English major in college which was why I was able to write, and I read the *Communist Manifesto* in the Forty-Second Street Library reading room because I had heard so much about it, and it moved me to tears. I remember I was embarrassed crying in the reading room of the public library, but no one noticed it. It was so true. I had a feeling of its truth. So it wasn't difficult for me to slide into thinking that the dance was an expression of people, expression of feeling, and of feelings about the downtrodden and the poor.

MF: And then did you feel that taking place around you, that other people were making these connections?

EO: I don't know how conscious I was at that time. But I was very aware that there was a "left-wing" movement. In any case, everything flowed without any conscious effort on my part. I was one of the founders of the New Dance Group. There was great support for dancing. First of all, people loved to go to dance recitals. It made no demands on their intellect, so to speak; it made a certain demand on their affection for girls that move around. And boys too. So dance recitals were very popular. And when we would go out to trade unions and to labor unions we were bringing the dance to them. They didn't have to come to us. They didn't have to pay for it. They were not necessarily very fond of our serious revolutionary qualities. But we were dancing for nothing, they were seeing us for nothing, and it in some way tied in with what they knew. They liked seeing dance.[43]

MF: I am fascinated with the way in which the audience that you people cultivated at that time, which was as you say a working-class audience that was very receptive, developed (this is my theory) a strong audience for modern dance, in a way created that audience that later became the modern dance audience in a broader sense, which allowed modern dance to survive through the Second World War.

EO: First of all, we brought the dance to them. We didn't make them pay a quarter. Secondly, the subject matter appealed to them. Thirdly, we were mainly young females, and I won't eliminate that aspect of it because there we were expressing ourselves in subject matter that *they* were interested in, that presented *their* concerns. And we were going out to Brooklyn to do it and it didn't cost them anything. So, just from a practical point of view, you can see why they were the audience. So if we gave a concert in one of the Broadway theaters, which is what we did on Sunday evenings when there was no show, the people from Brooklyn and the people from the Bronx, the labor unions, came to see us. So we reached out to the new audience.

MF: Was the audience reading *New Theatre*? Did they follow its debates on dance?

EO: I don't know who read it. But I do remember that in intermission some of the dancers went down in the audience and sold copies of *New Theatre*. It was ten cents a copy. I remember there was a dance at the end of which we held up copies of *New Theatre*. There was an audience to buy the magazine.

MF: Were you conscious at that point of the degree to which you and the people you were working with were really organizing an audience for dance?

EO: No. We weren't philosophical about it. We were just excited about performing, excited about the applause that we got, excited about being able to have an audience. So we had no awareness of it being significant, but the fact is we enlarged the audience for dance. There was a kind of enthusiasm that took place in that period.

MF: You alluded to the way that modern dancers not directly involved in the Communist movement wanted to perform for these audiences.

EO: We gave them an audience. We filled their houses. When Graham danced on Sunday night at the Guild Theater, let's say, she never filled the house per se by her audience. As soon as we got the left wing interested it was jam-packed. She had a new audience, and they were loyal. The left wing was a tremendous influence in all the arts. It corresponded with the needs of people to have their interests expressed. They couldn't get it from the Hollywood movies, they couldn't get it from the ballet dancers. . . . Graham was not truly a radical. But she knew where her interests lay, and I don't mean that in a negative sense. She knew that we were the audience; we were not uncultured in a certain sense in the dance, and many of her own dancers were radical.

MF: It was at the moment that radicalism became emptied of its earlier meaning that Martha Graham became the darling of the radical set.

EO: Because there was a thing called the popular front. And the enemy had become not the capitalist class, but fascism. The important thing was to unite everybody against fascism, not against capitalism. Remember that the rise of fascism was a very frightening experience. The popular front united everyone against fascism, and that's why it was called the *popular* front, because it united many forces that otherwise might have been antagonistic. And since we were radical we also took a stand publicly. We helped the people that didn't want to take a stand publicly, who were embarrassed about it. We fronted for them. We stood on the street corners. You had to protest. We were there to do the protesting. We didn't only represent ourselves, we represented those people who didn't want to take a public position.

MF: Before the popular front, a lot of left-wing writers said that the dance would trigger political change.

EO: Well, we thought so. We wanted to believe it. It was important to believe that what you're doing is important. Of course, a lot of the dancing, if you saw it today, would be very unsophisticated, very agit-prop. At that time we even divided ourselves between new dance and agit-prop dance. I would never say it in so many words. They carried banners saying "Working Class," or wore working class clothes, or banners that said "Black and White Unite and Fight."

MF: What were some immediate signs of agit-prop in dance?

EO: Technique became pantomime instead of it being dance movement. It was literal.

MF: So there is a subtle distinction between when dance becomes content-laden in a good sense, but not literal in a bad sense.

EO: Look, it can't be "content-laden," it can't be so burdened down by content that it doesn't move.

MF: Having made the distinction between agit-prop work which you didn't favor, how do you justify the pressure put on Graham to be more literal?

EO: No, not literalism. Because actually, dance is danced ideas too. Isadora Duncan danced ideas, and as a matter of fact, she also did the first agit-prop dancing. We did not want them to do agit-prop dancing but we thought that if it were done on the high quality of a real dancer, it would be more meaningful. . . . Direct engagement is not necessarily artistic, that's one of the problems.

MF: It's almost a kind of contradiction.

EO: It's very easy to dance a dance called "Anguish." It's another thing to do a dance called "Elegy for a Departed Worker." You could do "Anguish" in a general, abstract way and people might interpret the anguish as the death of a worker. So, it could be done. But you have to be a good dancer and you have to have movements that are expressive without being literal.

MF: There's a constant delicate balance. Did you ever feel that you put people in a double bind?

EO: No. I thought I could push them in that way. But it was the audience that put the pressure on. It was important to get the audience to understand what they were looking at, but also to raise their standards.

MF: It seems to me that what you wanted was to bring together revolutionary form and revolutionary content.

EO: When people are revolutionary they are passionate.

MF: If there were one thing you could bring into the present and keep with you from those experiences and that time, what would it be?

EO: Passion.

THREE

Emotivist Movement and Histories of Modernism

The Case of Martha Graham

"No emotion—cold design—but it may convey emotion through its tensions."
—Louis Horst, quoted in Horst and Russell, Modern
Dance Forms in Relation to the Other Modern Arts

"One after the other. Hatred, ecstasy, rage, compassion! Anything was possible once the body was disciplined."[1] Thus Bette Davis described Martha Graham's teaching circa 1928. Davis would later incorporate Graham's stage walk in *Now, Voyager* (1942) and credit the dancer with showing her how staircases could be negotiated to dramatic effect.[2] Above all, Davis retained from Graham's teaching the image of a keen ability to communicate emotional meaning. "She would with a single thrust of her weight convey anguish," Davis wrote. "Then in an anchored lift that made her ten feet tall, she became all joy."[3]

Understandably, Davis's own interest in movement was expressive, not formal; as an actress Davis apprehended movement as a tool of theatrical and cinematic characterization. Her impressions could only have been gleaned, however, from Graham's charisma as pedagogue. For as Margaret Lloyd has established, by 1928, the year Davis studied with her, Graham had begun to redefine dance movement as non-narrative and, in this regard, self-referential.[4]

Graham's experiments with absolute dance maintained a certain philosophical continuity with the goals of predecessors Isadora Duncan and Ruth St. Denis, whose work had already dignified dance as an autonomous art. Graham's initiative, however, did more than identify the independence of dance from the fine arts that had excluded it; she also posited dance as an autonomous form of knowledge. "Dance is an absolute," wrote Graham. "It is not knowledge about something, but is knowledge itself."[5] Critic John Martin fittingly noted: "There is no literature, to speak of, in English on the subject [of modern dance] . . . and the only source of enlightenment has been the actual performances of the dancers themselves."[6] With Martin, as with others, dance theory set out to create itself at the site of performance. This was an exciting period for American dance culture and New York became its center.

By the 1960s, Graham's modern dance no longer had the "absolute" look; by the 1970s, critics implied that Graham's aesthetic had been emotivist from the very beginning. Such revisionist tendencies were recalled in a recent debate in which Sally Banes asserted that "Graham's choreography is not 're-flexive' and therefore not relevant to a discussion of modernism as it emerged in the dance world under the influence of the Greenbergian gallery aesthetic."[7] Clement Greenberg's definition of modernism subsumes it to a theory of minimalism, stipulating that art become its own subject matter and thereby relinquish all reference to the external world. It is based on an earlier theory of the avant-garde as productive of an artistic absolute.[8]

Banes justifies taking Greenberg as a starting point by asserting that "modern" dance knew no true modernism until the sixties.[9] And she holds that American dance modernism—understood as dance focused reflexively on its own medium—occurs only with the advent of minimalist Judson Church choreographers.[10] Susan Manning has responded that dance modernism is found throughout the twentieth century, and notably in the choreography of Mary Wigman and Martha Graham.[11] Graham's case arises in the Manning/Banes exchange as one in which emotion and ambiguity are problematized relative to modernism. Let me rephrase the problem for my own purposes in this way: How can a modernist aesthetic characterized by the disjunction of form and content depend entirely upon emotional impulses of a unique self (emotivism)? In other terms, I want to argue that thirties modern dance did not lack a modernist moment. What it did lack was a formalist critical witness to articulate its modernism in words.[12]

The issue of Graham's aesthetics during the Great Depression was noteworthy for its interpretive challenges. What content might be ascribed to Graham's dances such that her politics would emerge from her modernist ambiguity? The debate over Graham's formalism has since been buried and forgotten although the so-called emotionlessness of her work was, at the time, argued vehemently. Indeed, we can reconstruct Graham's modernism in part because radical journalism called her so vigorously to task for it. I propose that we assess Graham's aesthetic by reading right- and left-wing critics in tandem, each as containing the other's missing supplement.

MODERNISM IN EARLY GRAHAM

I do not reject the Greenbergian model in order to claim that Graham practiced a Cold War formalism in the late twenties and early thirties. But it would be equally distorted to ignore the ambiguity she did cultivate. The contraction, a scooping movement rendering the spine concave, could suggest sorrow or joy, but could also remain fundamentally obscure and even thoroughly abstract. Ambiguity in movement was a key to Graham's formalism of the thirties.[13] By the forties, a coherent yet evolving movement vocabulary told all stories, fit all moods. Furthermore, in some late Graham works, such as *Adorations* (1975) or *Acts of Light* (1981), choreography became the site of a demonstration of Graham technique, but these later formalisms have eclipsed the crucial earlier one. We might think of Graham in the early thirties in Greenbergian terms as analogous to Arshile Gorky and Milton Avery in modern American painting. Following Donald Kuspit on Greenberg, we could say that Graham "prepared the way for modernist reduction to the medium" through a "personal, almost radically subjective" abstraction.[14] Only much later in Graham's career did formalism come to signify a standardized movement code.[15] At the beginning, however, Graham engaged in a search for subjective form.

Given her three successive formalisms just outlined, Graham's modernism should not be evaluated against criteria so specific to the sixties. Should not Graham's earliest work rather be evaluated in the light of its own artistic, cultural, and political contexts? And should not her later work be evaluated in light of her earlier work and changing historical contexts? Graham's choreographic career, after all, does span a sixty-five-year period. I would argue that aesthetic causality could be established from relevant contemporary theories of modernism. During the first thirteen years of her choreographic career (1926–1939), the developing New York modern dance establishment shaped a discourse significantly influenced by left-wing opposition to Graham's formalism and emotional impassivity. The tendency of the right was to deny her formalism and to enlist her in an emotivist and dramatic project.

By the 1980s, Graham's historical importance became misplaced between turn of the century "natural" dance and sixties "objective" dance.[16] Nancy Ruyter has identified the philosophical basis of first-generation American modern dance as an antiformalism derived from democratic principles. Thus, Isadora Duncan, Ruth St. Denis, and Ted Shawn reacted against European formalism in theatrical dancing and physical culture by opposing it with a "natural" dance.[17] Emotivism easily fits into natural dance as a motivating force, the source of antiformalist form. Toward the end of her career, Graham was frequently lumped with this set. Banes describes the mission of sixties avant-gardists as "the purging and melioration of historical modern dance, which had made certain promises in respect to the use of the body and the social and artistic function of dance that had not been fulfilled."[18] Reacting against the founders of modern dance, choreographers in the wake of Cunningham devised new pretexts and procedures, enacting a noncharismatic return to antiformalism. As the oldest active member of the second generation, Graham was scapegoated by sixties avant-gardists for embodying bankrupt emotivism. As Yvonne Rainer noted in 1966, "In the case of Graham, it is hardly possible to relate her work to anything outside of theatre, since it was usually dramatic and psychological necessity that determined it."[19] Unlike Duncan, however, Graham had significantly departed from the ideology of natural gesture.[20] Her dance may have been natural to her own body, but it did not provide a natural image for other bodies. Graham was antiformalist as regards old forms, but also anti-emotivist as regards new ones. Her primitivism betrayed no enthrallment with emotion, but rather a new fascination with form.

In reconstituting Graham's early aesthetic, it will be helpful to consult contemporary critics of her work: John Martin, first dance critic of the *New York Times*, appointed in 1927; Edwin Denby, dancer and poet whose writing appeared chiefly in *Modern Music* and the *New York Herald Tribune*; Stark Young, theater critic for the *New Republic* until 1947; and left-wing critics such as Edna Ocko, Edith Segal, Blanche Evan, and Michael Gold publishing in *New Theatre*, *New Masses*, the *Daily Worker*, and occasionally the *Dance Observer*. The impact of this last group has been all but stricken from the historical record of modern dance history.

Martin envisioned Graham's subjective search as the foundation of "expressional" dance. But giving the cue to later critics, Martin only allowed for the emotional nature of subjectivity. Formal acts, in the words of Paul Goodman, a Graham contemporary in the thirties, "express the nature of the . . . bodies involved," not necessarily what they are feeling.[21] Martin's term "expressional" practically obscures the body's sentient primacy in early Graham. Martin's awareness of the uncertain relationship between formalism and emotionalism leads him to deny any theoretical dimension to Graham's thinking: "Though she herself has spoken and written eloquently of it [her dance], she has never been able to formulate any objective theory for it, for the simple reason that it has none."[22] Martin's stance against theory and for emotional expression genders his analysis. In his words, Graham's famous search for theatrical economy is her masculine trait, whereas her discovery of the raw material of choreographic analysis is her feminine trait.[23] Martin pictures Graham in equilibrium between two dynamic "inner forces": her "dissipating tendencies" are pejorative representations of the feminine nature—its "inherent emotionalism" and "Dionysian indulgence"—whereas her ability to formalize these drives, her "integrating force," "gives her movement its character and shapes its contours."[24] The ability to "integrate" form with content, to substitute exchange-value for use-value, would be typically rational and therefore reputedly masculine. For Martin, Graham's artistic evolution resulted from "the growth of this power to hold in check a veritable menadic strain which is instinct with destruction."[25] Martin explains Graham's artistic power as an inherently masculine "restraint" endowing the destructive feminine drives of self-expression and improvisation with coherent form, albeit without narrative. He speaks therefore to the theoretical cogency of her work only with reference to its so-called masculinity. In Martin's discourse, Graham begins to sound like the "newly evolved woman" Paul Strand thought he had discovered in the painter Georgia O'Keeffe: "O'Keeffe," wrote Strand in 1924, "works from the unconscious to the conscious, from within out."[26]

The rhetoric of expressivism as influenced by aesthetic Freudianism in the twenties and thirties suggested that the body in the service of the unconscious was the reputed domain of female artists. Such bringing to consciousness of unconscious material was stylistically concomitant with a process of abstraction. Had Graham herself not adopted a "male" position on formal abstraction quite early, she could have been accused, as was O'Keeffe, of being an unconscious subject; that is, of being "woman."[27] From such inadequate critical concepts arose the "natural growth" metaphor and the impossibility of theoretical interpretations applied to an artist whose masculine principle seeks to master its unfathomable feminine inspiration.[28] Nevertheless, Martin introduced a new inflection by picturing the masculine principle as lodged within the feminine subject. Judging from similar ideas in her own writing, it appears likely that Graham and, as we shall see, Louis Horst prompted some of Martin's critical language.

HORST'S TENSION AND DESIGN

At this time an exchange of ideas went on between Graham and her mentor, composer, and teacher Louis Horst. Horst's teaching notes (ca. 1943) outline a modernist duality that recalls Martin's analysis of Graham. Horst theorizes two functions of modernism in modern dance: the psychological function of introspection or looking inward and the cerebral function of abstraction as related to the machine. These poles are placed in dialectical relationship and are actualized in Graham's work as an interplay of physical tension and choreographic design.

According to Horst, "The Twentieth Century looks 'inward.' In dancing, this absorption in inner emotions causes a twist in the body."[29] He also writes: "Modern dancers must be absorbed in all aspects of every movement—What Martha Graham calls 'complete physical awareness.' This movement tension will produce dissonance, but not necessarily distortion."[30] Horst envisioned "theatrical emotionalism" as decadent because it came with "ease," "grace," and technical skill given a natural appearance; dissonance, on the other hand, was a sign of psychological introspection necessary to the forging of new dance. Horst's design criterion was thus highly antithetical to introspection because design imposed lines and planes on the twisted and dissonant body ("body broken into planal surfaces and divisions").[31] In the spirit of design, Horst required "a scrupulousness bordering on stiffness—rigid uniformity—lack of sensualism—temperance—measured discipline—hieratic—formal."[32] Somewhat paradoxically, this repressive tension was meant to render a sense of "inner quality."[33] Graham's technique, as described by Horst, evolved from a marriage between affect and discipline, the feminine and masculine traits Martin had proposed.

Yet Horst was troubled by the theory of this union. His teaching notes reflect a certain anxiety about the balance between physical tension and visual design:

Machine theory is static. . . . Formal order and design replacing expression of personal emotion and records of emotive fragments. Danger of losing itself in remoteness and inhumanity or being tied down to mechanical formulae. Purism—nothing as impure as emotional patterns permitted.[34]

As Horst explored ways to merge abstraction and emotion, the mechanical and the introspective, Graham choreographed the union of sexual polarities in *Appalachian Spring* (1944). In this work, the mechanical or generally stolid male settler is married to the organic, introspective frontier woman who celebrates the spring of her youth with an air of reminiscence. Two secondary roles echo this gendered opposition: The pioneer woman is nostalgic and self-absorbed; the preacher is fanatic and rigidly mechanical. *Appalachian Spring* is constructed from a collage of narrative fragments out of which emerges a more abstract reflection on female and male, organism and mechanism, tension and design. The issues of tension and design are also found between 1926 and 1937, when Graham was still focused almost exclusively on the female body and created non-narrative works.

That art emanating from woman, particularly from her own body in movement, could be an expression of virility (cold design rather than unconscious instinct), even if that "virility" were provisionally divorced from her person and attributed to an aesthetic, is a bold critical stance to have taken in the 1920s. O'Keeffe, another American artist whose reputation was closely associated with the presentation of her body and the first American female visual artist to gain notoriety in the late teens and twenties, was promoted by art critics as a woman remarkably in touch with her feminine, and therefore sexual, nature.[35] Physical expression unconnected to labor was thought to be feminine by many male critics, and therefore dance became a realm of modern art only too "naturally" inhabited by women. The parallels between O'Keeffe and Graham are indeed striking: Both drew inspiration from the landscape of the American Southwest, both became entangled in sexual rhetoric that promoted even as it imprisoned their careers, both were understood to create—moreover, to incarnate—metaphors for the feminine, the unconscious, and an unrecognized America. Although O'Keeffe fought long and hard to dispel the sexual connotations her work as a female modernist evoked among critics, Graham attempted to elude this kind of assessment by associating her physical appearance from the beginning with strength and economy. Whereas O'Keeffe withdrew from sexual identity, opting for an androgynous relationship to her work, Graham occasionally inflected her movement with masculinized and/or mechanized traits.

The unresolved contradictions to be confronted in Graham's choreography can also be encountered in her early statements. "The machine is a natural phenomena of life" (1936), for example, or, "Virile gestures are evocative of the only true beauty" (1928).[36] Apart from her late autobiography, Graham authored two articles and gave a number of public lectures.[37] Her other statements were collected from disparate remarks in interviews; choreographic notes have also been published.[38]

Martin speaks of Graham's art as a "purely personal emanation . . . [based] on the principle that nobody can think another's thoughts, feel another's emotions, experience another's reactions, or express his own intuitions and convictions in another's terms."[39] Such a denial of communication over a common expressional ground is, indeed, a precise definition of subjectivity in early Graham. But for Graham, formalism is a way around the limitations of sexist emotivism, the cornerstone of "expressional" dance. That is, without a certain formalism, Graham could not attain the requisite subjectivity because her work would be dismissed as self-indulgent. Thus, Graham was formalist in this very particular sense, which leads to the issue of abstraction. Her early work stands out against other contemporaneous dancing as mercilessly reductive, that is, dehumanized or mechanized with regard to expectations of the dancing figure as a body in expressive flow acknowledging its own sexuality. In 1935, one critic asked whether the "mono-sexual" makeup of Graham's company did not result in "intense abstractedness."[40] They saw Graham's art "entirely depersonalizing and in a deep sense un-sexing the body." Although admitting that this situation is entirely appropriate to some of Graham's work because "the group and the soloist are abstract unknowns in a poignantly organic formula," a warning is issued against its dangers to Graham's development: "exaggerated psychological self-involvement" and "esthetical formalism."[41] This viewpoint is encountered throughout thirties criticism; what critics failed to see, however, is that Graham was *not* emotivist precisely because she *was* feminist and purposefully avoided identification with the feminine as powerless. I suggest we locate Graham's politics in the necessary ambiguity of this position.

PRIMITIVISM AND ABSTRACTION

Banes argues the need for contextualization in dance history but does not acknowledge the interest many modern artists of the twenties had in the trinity of primitivism, cubism, and abstraction.[42] Yve-Alain Bois has shown that these dominant trends in the visual arts of the 1920s imbued human morphology with a quality of "psychological absence."[43] Graham's mask-like visage, ubiquitous in photographs of her early work, and her refusal to equate dance with the connectedness of movement bespeak a parallel formalism that is substantiated by contemporary sources.[44] "At this time," wrote Margaret Lloyd, an eyewitness of the thirties, "Martha's dance was movement for movement's sake. She eschewed all literary entanglements, all drama save what was movement's own. The face was rapt, immobile; the hands were stiff, the costumes stark."[45] Jane Dudley, who danced for Graham from 1935 to 1946, said: "Onstage, you never felt she was acting. She had a sense of remoteness around her."[46] Edwin Denby read Graham's early style as physically unorganic: "She allows her dance to unfold only on a dictatorially determined level. I have the impression that [she] would like to keep a dance constantly at the tension of a picture. She seems to be, especially in her solo dances, clinging to visual definition."[47] Using Duncan's fluid "humanity" as a point of comparison, Denby described Graham's "unremitting tautness," her rejection of flow

Figure 9. *Appalachian Spring* (1944) with Graham and Hawkins.
Photo: Arnold Eagle. (Courtesy of the photographer)

or its limitation to the quality Laban called bound flow, as the "difficult" aspect of her choreography.[48] Denby also cited Graham's "acute sense of the downward pull of gravity and of balance, and an acute sense, too, of where the center of pressure of a gesture is."[49] Weight, tension, and angularity were the hallmarks of Graham's early work, to the virtual exclusion of flow. She herself qualified her early period as "an extreme of movement asceticism" necessary for "intensification" and "simplification" of her choreographic statement.[50] Reducing flow is tantamount to removing the link that renders weight, tension, and angularity organic, emotional, and conventionally human for many spectators. The creation of a new aesthetic adequate to the modern age thus risked alienating segments of the audience unwilling to receive affect through geometry, the impersonality of forms.

Human action in early Graham was materialistic to the point of seeming despecified, generative of a formal physical geometry. For these reasons, Graham's early choreography pursued what Bois calls the "refusal of psychological depth" at the level of the individual.[51] In *Lamentation* (1930), for example, a woman enshrouded in a tube of stretchy fabric pulls, twists, and rocks her body from seated and, occasionally, standing positions. While the successive collapsing and lateral pulls of Graham's swathed figure suggest mourning, these movements also draw attention to their own formal quali-

Figure 10. Graham's impassive visage of the thirties. Photo: Ed Moeller.
(Courtesy of the San Francisco Performing Arts Library and Museum)

ties.[52] Graham withholds facial expressivity throughout the piece: Her lips remain slightly parted, her eyes but half open in an unfocused, upward glance. It is as though she wished to convey emotion only after reducing it to formal design. Here again, formalism derives from the nature of the body involved. The choreographic material of *Lamentation* is the physical material of grief, not its emotional effects.[53] Such modernism was decried by a left sensibility that demanded art translate its own social critique: "When millions are compelled to suffer crushing miseries," wrote one critic, "she can find in the lamentation idea nothing beyond a stylized, rhythmical decoration devoid of communicative emotion!"[54]

Horst's teaching notes identify modernist formalism with a theory of the archaic: "In an Archaic period there is a *Conscious* absorption in the *Material* of ritual."[55] Consciousness of materials is the hallmark of modernism, whose spirit Horst sets between the primitive and the classical: "It is the birth of aesthetic comprehension; the artist breaking through the ritual. The complete concern with this awakening led to the intense absorption with design, often two-dimensional."[56] Bound flow is motivated by design rather than by emotional complexes: "This great absorption in the Materials of any art brings with it *tension* (as implied in the word at-tention)."[57] Moreover, the archaic also has the advantage of explaining Horst's design aesthetic: "Since the interest focussed on line, such art therefore becomes two dimensional and planal."[58] Horst's theory of the archaic outlines a Greenbergian reflexivity before the fact.

Inasmuch as Graham's early work abstracted from emotion, it seemed to renounce the temporality involved in viewing it, as do the visual arts. The air of timelessness associated with ritual, out of which the "archaic" modern artist was thought by Horst and Graham to emerge, affected the theatrical pacing of dance. Elizabeth Kendall has written of the way Graham's teacher, Ruth St. Denis, "slow(ed) dancing down" in order to establish its independence from high-impact vaudeville performance. A focused absorption in a singular mood performed in an elastic time frame established early modern dance as a visually distinct art form.[59] Graham allowed, in fact, a non-narrative time to unfold in which modern dance most aptly laid claim to its indigenous brand of theatrical communication, its autonomy or "absolute." The new flexibility of time introduced by St. Denis fostered a climate favorable to Graham's reduction of flow. One could fill time with less and less movement. Moreover, Graham's architectural use of space—geometrical patterning and angular facings in the group works—also complemented the self-referentiality of time. Time became a function of design in space rather than of dramatic pacing.

DANCE AS SEMIOTIC FETISH

The "tableau vivant" style Graham used in her early group works illustrates how expressive moments were consistently displaced by a formalist choreographic practice. In *Primitive Mysteries* (1931), the soloist Graham interacts with eleven choristers who confront her frequently in smaller groupings. The numerous four-figure compositions around Graham awakened the expectation of meaningful gesture while remaining, nevertheless, consistently ambiguous.[60] Graham's deliberate avoidance of emotionally motivated sequences of movement corresponded both to the rootedness of the dancers and the identical energy level of each group entrance and exit. Internally, each section projected images dominated by iconic stasis. As Horst noted, "The dancer cannot just 'turn,' but must move in planes. 'The room must seem to turn with you.'"[61] The patterned quality of the "tableau vivant" seemed designed to suggest a symbolic context even as any unequivocal readings of that context were intention-

Figure 11. Graham in *Lamentation*. Photo: Soichi Sunami.
(Courtesy of the photographer's estate)

ally evacuated. Those few gestures that did have recognizable meaning—the agonized pressing of flattened palm to forehead by the chorus or the "joyful" kick of a bent leg in the air by the soloist—emerged in isolation. Such "emotional decontextualization" underlined how emotion and psychological depth could be separated.[62] One does not see emotion developed over time in the work; instead, one sees emotion as if stranded within the time of the work. The flash of meaning conveyed, which so impressed Bette Davis, is actually bereft of psychological dimension when used to such choreographic ends.[63]

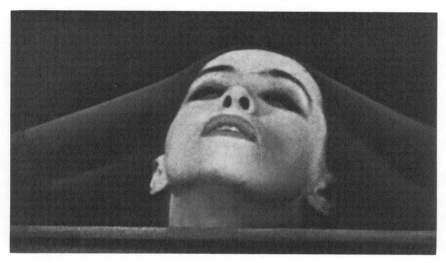

Figure 12. Close-up of Graham in *Lamentation*. (Courtesy of
the Dance Collection, the New York Public Library for the
Performing Arts, Astor, Lenox, and Tilden Foundations)

Thus, *Primitive Mysteries* was an exercise in the creation of choreographic
meaning rather than the articulation of any particular meaning in choreography.[64] In sculptural terms, one could say that Graham's expressive movement
lacked modeling of the mass in the individual form, giving instead, to use Bois's
words, an "instantaneous impression of volume."[65] The imitative gestures and,
above all, the signifying of ritual itself by processional entrances and exits that
framed each of the dance's three sections—all potentially dramatic aspects of
the choreography—provided instead a foil for the ambiguous or "primitive"
material as such.[66] Although recognizable mimetic details allowed for a momentarily expressivist reading, they remained isolated from the work as an entirety, unmotivated by the fabric of the surrounding dance. That fabric was
destined to thematize dance itself as primitive with regard to form and mysteri-
ous with regard to content.

Quite by accident, Bette Davis's homage to Graham mirrors a critical
tendency of the seventies and eighties to boil down Graham's complex artistic
evolution to a single emotivist period. Establishing Graham as the great
emotivist of modern dance explains multiple revolts after the fact: first that of
Merce Cunningham, but much later those of the post-Cunningham or Judson
choreographers. This reading of dance history frames continuities as largely
dichotomous because it presents modernism in modern dance proceeding
through a series of conscious rejections at the expense of subtle transforma-
tions. By dramatizing conscious breaks, the concerns of history and theory
become partisan debates. A failure to historicize Graham's aesthetic radical-
ness is cited by dance historian Susan Manning as an unfortunate confusion

of the ends of criticism and history.[67] The promotional ends of criticism are likely to dislocate, at least temporarily, something called historical sensibility because they reduce the artistic landscape to the aesthetic vitality of a present moment, that of live performance as a site of uncritical newness. Denying Graham's modernism has been one way for contemporary critics to argue the historical originality of later avant-gardes.[68]

Thus, for example, a profile of Merce Cunningham by Richard Kostelanetz in 1975 contains the statement that Cunningham's predecessors used "typical gestures" serving to "mime identifiable emotions or feelings."[69] In a similar vein, Susan Sontag clarified the objectives of postmodern choreographer Lucinda Childs by contrast with Graham's work, which she characterized as "heavy with descriptive intentions based, above all, on ideas about the primitive, the authentic, both in movement and feeling."[70] This sort of assessment, frequently written in the 1970s and 1980s, induced an image of Graham's dance theater as, in Nietzschean terms, exclusively operatic. It was assumed that Graham's history was uniform, that she had always subscribed to a rational rhetoric of the passions.[71] I respond that Graham's early choreography proposed a different way to present passion on the stage. Much, if not all, of Graham's experimental work in the late twenties and early thirties attempted to redefine human presence in purely bodily terms.[72] Thus, a historicity is needed that counters the place assigned an artist in linear and progressive (modernist) history. We need especially to examine how a dialectic of dance's historicity interrupts the linear chronicle of modernist dance history.

One essential means of Graham's redefinition of human presence was the concerted use of ambiguity, the physical hallmarks of which were weight and discontinuity. By restricting or eliminating flow, extending time, and accentuating the body's architectural presence in space, Graham stymied the easy assignation of emotional meaning to dance. She later characterized her approach as "a new plasticity, emotional and physical."[73] Although her concern was not to rid dance of emotion, expectations of emotionality in movement were displaced in favor of what physical and emotional materials could accomplish in and by themselves, outside the services of narrative, typical gestures, and descriptive intentions.[74]

Then, her work was labeled severe and uncompromising. There was, and still is, something irritating about the convergence and concentration of social and psychic concerns into the body which characterizes thirties modern dance. The body becomes a "whole" whose relevance to a totalizing array of concerns is indicated paradoxically by the rigid reduction of dancing to physical presence, its elimination of narrative, and paring down to movement "essentials."[75] It was as if the more the body were confined within these minimalist, ascetic limits, the more it might conduct a totality of "naked" significance. In order to open itself to this semiotization, the body must become "de-subjectivized." That is, the body as a material object, the body as such, by reducing itself to its own physical limitations, embodied values of a religious, social, aesthetic, and political nature all at once.

Only well after the thirties did Graham's work become emotivist, or operatic in the Nietzschean sense, when an expressive veneer became applied to its formulaic vocabulary. This was brought about by changes in Graham's personal performance style that were calculated to supplement her declining technical prowess. In the late 1950s and early 1960s, she accentuated the emotional quality of her own performance to deflect attention from a diminishing technical facility. By the 1970s, a new generation of dancers was able and willing to imitate the emotional throes of an aged Graham in technically sophisticated formalizations of her highly personal style. But to label Graham uniformly emotivist for this reason blurs the progress in her early thinking from the initial stage, which I will call materialist (1926-33), to the dramaturgical (1934-45).

AMERICA AND ITS DOUBLE

In 1926, Graham's choreographic project seemed motivated by a quest for the primitive. As she declared: "We must first determine what is for us the Primitive—that expression of its [America's] psyche only possible to a supremely cultured and integrated people."[76] From the start, the primitive was inextricably linked to her perception of Americanness: "For we, as a nation, are primitive also—primitive in the sense that we are forming a *new* culture."[77] In one respect, Graham's rhetoric squares with a typically modernist conflation of archaism and newness in which the immediate past is rejected along with earlier classical influences. What is ultimately rejected is history itself, so that the primitive becomes a state that cannot write itself, that rejects representation. "Primitive means the beginning."[78] Determining "what is for us the Primitive," when "us" designates "a supremely cultured and integrated people," implies that archaic and machine culture are recursive steps in a developmental process that uncovers its own origins. When Graham quotes Wolfgang Paalen's *Totem Art* in her notes for *Dark Meadow of the Soul* (1946), she sets primitivism in a temporal frame between extremes of emotion and abstraction:

> In order to pass from emotion to abstraction, man is obliged, in the maturation of each individual, to pass through the ancestral stratifications of thought, analogously to the evolutionary stages of the species that must be traversed in the maternal womb.[79]

Graham transcribed this text in 1946. Her postwar, neomodernist sources of inspiration were cultural anthropology, myth, and depth psychology. In the early thirties, they had been social reaction, machine culture, and ritual. Although Graham did not create explicitly machinic dances (she identified sentimentality for the machine as European rather than American), machine culture was responsible for "a characteristic time beat, a different speed, an accent, sharp, clear, staccato" in her work.[80] These are precisely the qualities that limit flow. In neither her modernist nor her neomodernist stage, however, is emotion conclusively expressivist. Instead, she conceived emotion as the vestige of an earlier evolutionary stage—as Paalen expressed it—rendered obsolete by machine culture. In other words, Graham's early group works throw light on the way machine culture afforded the rediscovery of the primal as aesthetic dehumanization.

Graham's materialist approach has emotional force precisely because it is prior to and beyond personality; emotion is presented dispassionately in its very "mechanism." In displacing time as a cumulative order of culture, Graham's materialism displaces the history of the passions and substitutes dispassionate spatial orientations that suggest how behavior can be defined as movement. The inner/outer duality of expression theory is distanced from the subject-body and reconfigured as hyperbolic depth (the unconscious) and hyperbolic surface (the machine). Graham's modern dance reconfigures emotional depth as primal energy manifested in the abstract design qualities imposed on human form and movement by machines. Thus, the mechanized quality of bodily movement is functionally archaic but also aesthetically modern.

In her search for the primitive, Graham traveled closer to home than her European counterparts. She looked instead to the Indian culture of the American Southwest and Mexico. The primitive other that contained secrets masked by Western civilization was to be discovered in non-European cultures. Graham sought primitiveness within the geographical boundaries of the American continent, and even within America itself. Unlike many of her contemporaries, she attempted to identify her otherness *as* American rather than her otherness *from* the American.[81] She identified with the American Indian, a male figure in her thinking since he was a figure of "integration."[82] The "other," primitive space was an esoteric or uncanny space structuring a physical environment called "America" that awaited theatrical discovery. Thus, we could say Graham posited two Americas: one known and one unknown, one false and one true, an America and its double. America was endowed with an unconscious. The true America was secreted in the body. In this reading of modernism, the invention of modern dance entails formalizing the hidden American "psyche" in physical terms and from a certain exotic yet internal site. At the same time, given the reductive aspect of her early formalism, the primitive played a double role: It acted as a theatrical clue to her reductivist intent, and, more importantly, it replaced a quantum of feeling that had been formally excised by movement asceticism. That is to say, emotion was not encoded in the work, but in the audience's reception of the work. In this respect, the primitive look of formal reduction invited the spectator to reinject emotion whenever that reduction suggested abstraction as another face of the profound or universal statement. Thus, an idealized signified becomes legible in Graham's formal experimentation as primitivism cashes in formalism for a remote humanism. This is an effect of spectatorship.

Graham's movement bore the traces of the effort expended to discover and hone it. Her primitivism implied that space was a neutral field in which a

Figure 13. Graham and company in *Primitive Mysteries*. (Courtesy of the San Francisco Performing Arts Library and Museum)

hitherto unrecognized self could be organized. No familiar emotional reaction could be foreseen, yet the very decontextualization of feeling through movement suggested the provocative possibility of a different emotional response to American space, that "monstrous architecture."[83] Movement was fashioned from the interaction of an unconscious or socially unacknowledged self with a topography. Americans were thus physically and psychically molded by the spatial characteristics of their geographical and social world.[84]

Graham reflected the humanist tradition of the 1930s that saw "man" as an end in himself: "Power," she wrote, "means to become what one *is*."[85] One's naive and powerful self-discovery of personhood was an allegory for the creation of the dancing self strictly out of one's own body. In fact, Graham qualified modern dance as a uniquely subjective act ("there is only one of you in all of time")[86] and as a response to social reality ("a direct relationship to the blood flow of the time and country that nourishes it").[87] The modern body as "self" was not purely solipsistic. Graham's primitivism implied as corollary to self an outer space that erected inwardness: "The dance form is governed by social conditions. . . . The history of the dance is the social history of the world."[88] Space—the American topography—preexisted as a conditioning reality for the inner self. In the historical and topographical senses, this space was the American plains. On the other hand, social space, fundamentally "urban and not pastoral,"[89] was characterized by accelerated rhythms of the machine and social action ("a focus directly upon movement"/"this is a time of action").[90] Graham's references to the land as "divine machinery" seem to conflate these topographical and social codes in her writing.

One could almost call American space a formal influence. Urban action drew its justification from the thinly veiled primitive space of a recent past on top of which modern society was built. Yet whereas the choreography implied a program for social action, closer scrutiny dissolved activism into an aesthetic reflection on national physiognomy. Graham's modernism was a vehicle for her "political apoliticism."[91] Like the tension between the formal and emotional elements in her work, the aesthetic and the political infused one another with undetermined meaning. The term of that infusion was a body gendered female and the advantage of such indeterminacy was adherence to an essentially invisible feminist stance.

Graham's solo *Frontier* (1935) was about American space as a vessel for the courageous, pioneering body and the impress of space on that body. A lone woman in a long dress looks out from a bit of fence anchoring two ropes that ascend outward in a V-shape. She is the focal point from which the V ascends, but also the source of another vision of space in which we find her.[92] Looking outward, dance was a metaphor for America; looking inward, America was a metaphor for modern dance. She discovers with her gaze, explores with her movement, and dominates with her gesture. She measures space in a quadrant by traversing square patterns, and dances within it by emphasizing the circular spiral of her own kinesphere. This self, however, so easily identifiable with an American primitive as political radical, contained areas of ambiguity: It was feminine, and it was a dancer. It was defined, that is, in bodily rather than discursive terms.[93]

Stark Young was troubled by the "stubborn elimination" of feeling he found in Graham's early ascetic work.[94] Denby also had misgivings about Graham's "unrelaxed determination."[95] Even for the most acute observers, pervasive ideas about the body's naturalness may have numbed sensitivity to Graham's iconoclasm.[96] The Americanness she sought to discover/embody at this early stage of her choreographic career was a paradoxical construct: both "primitive" and "supremely cultured" or "integrated," both fetish and design for living, both female and male. Graham's modern dance flaunted primitivism not only as an experienced mode of being (dancing as "complete physical awareness"), but also as a cultural construct to be acknowledged critically (wo/man).[97] As Martin noted, "She does the unforgivable for a dancer—she makes you think."[98] Graham's dance resulted from a double and reciprocal fashioning of the body and space. By appealing alternately to essentialist reductionism and national identity, she was able both to explore abstraction and imply cultural critique. How else could the soul be assimilated to an "inner landscape" even as the model for that landscape was fetishized as America?

In 1933, Graham wrote: "Since the dance form is governed by social conditions, so the American rhythm is sharp and angular, stripped of unessentials. It is something related only to itself, not laid on, but of a piece with that spirit which was willing to face a pioneer country."[99] Here, Graham gives formal-

Figure 14. Graham in the Southwest. (Courtesy of the Dance Collection, the New York Public Library for the Performing Arts, Astor, Lenox, and Tilden Foundations)

ism a moral tone and informs abstraction with social relevance. She envisioned the essential character of American dance as unadorned, but also and more importantly as nonimitative. Representation of emotion came with imitation. Unmitigated presence was formulated as a theatrical goal of modern dance, suggested both by idealized ("of a piece with that spirit") and socially determined ("governed by social conditions") images of America.[100]

Graham's writing during this period also embroils imitation (to be avoided) and unique presence (to be fostered) in a convoluted symbolism of male and female roles. Seeking the indigenously American, Graham was led to eschew imitative dance, which she linked to European ballet and its reputation for effeminacy. "America is cradling an art that is destined to be a ruler," she wrote, "in that its urge is *masculine* and *creative* rather than *imitative*."[101] Marianna Torgovnick has shown how the primitive can furnish an access to the essential and, in most modernist practices, to masculine identity.[102] Graham presented a simulacrum of masculine identity, but her virility marks a locus of an other feminine. Effeminacy in dance was therefore linked in

Graham's mind to imitation or miming. Miming has the negative connotations of mimesis as derived from classical dance, and also suggests the imitation of "superior" work by male artists.[103] "Movement comes from the body itself," she wrote, "not the movement of the body trying to adapt itself to a foreign element."[104] This statement was quite radical for its time and sounds in fact not so very different from Cunningham's rhetoric since the fifties. Graham, in other words, has been cast in the role of emotivist ever since Cunningham's declaration of independence from her, and dance history of the early thirties has become obscured by critical response to the sixties. In a parallel manner, Graham's revolt against the classical tradition seemed to be a revolt against an artificial "feminine" in the name of an essential "masculine." Yet, her rhetoric allows a third term to show through in which the feminine is recuperated: an imaginary feminine masculinity. There is thus a double consciousness through which Graham articulates her own experience in male terms, but also reintroduces the feminine.[105]

Dance for Graham was not imitative precisely to the degree that "it is the affirmation of life through movement."[106] Here we can understand reflexivity as the integration of dance into a holistic philosophy of the body that is not blatantly expressive.[107] Elizabeth Kendall has remarked that "in one sense, American modern dance emerged from . . . late nineteenth-century women's anxious ideas of their physical selves: their supposed condition of chronic disease was the background; the search for renewed health was the impetus."[108] Each new modern technique stemming from Graham rehearses the effects of natural forces such as gravity, flow, or chance on the body. By implication, those techniques integrate the dancing subject with inevitable principles. The body and flow, for example, become interacting wholes. This could be demonstrated in the work of Erick Hawkins, and even idiosyncratically, yet fittingly, in Cunningham.[109] Such choreographic agendas promote the body as a living enactment rather than a pantomimic objectification of natural processes.

Graham also wrote of dance not as a "mirror," but as "participation;" not as "reaction," but as "action." These terms undercut emotion as description, proposing emotion rather as an untranslatable way of being in the moment's present. The intention of her work was to remain at the origin of its own presence, not at the origin of meaning. Graham's writings show that she developed a theory of choreography in which dance was closer to life than were other forms of theatrical mimesis. (This stance recalls Jackson Pollack's later rejection of "illustration" in favor of "equivalents" in a practice of abstract art that nonetheless has a subject.)[110] The rejection of an imitative role for dance was linked to Graham's refusal to derive dance from anything other than the experience of being an urban American woman in the "rhythm" of her time. In her work, even gender became detached from its conventional traits: Graham shunned any typical femininity in dance. Representing the American spirit required presenting strength and virility bordering on ugliness: "The dance must be strong."[111] Nevertheless, as already noted, Graham's interest in the primitive pointed indirectly to her involvement with the feminine. Her frequent references to the masculinity of modern dance can be misleading: Until 1938, only she herself and other women danced her company work. Graham's vision of the "virile" feminine is behind her quest for primitive otherness. Her modern dance reintroduced the feminist paradigm that had been written out of early modernism after 1900. Graham's gendered modernism suggests that her primitivism might, in Hal Foster's terms, "be thought disruptively, not recuperated abstractly."[112]

GRAHAM IN THE PROLETARIAN MOMENT

Code words of radical political culture circulate within Graham's statements of her personal poetic in the 1930s. Proletarian artists uncovering previously ignored American social realities were called "discoverers of the real America."[113] "The submerged American continent" with its "new barbarous English" constituted an artistic domain of twenties and early thirties literary radicalism in New York.[114] Like Graham's vision of America as "monstrous vital rhythms, crude, glowing colors," lack of obvious cultivation was the sign of an unrecognized culture she sought to capture in a "dynamic economy of gesture."[115] Graham's proposal to understand the primitive was thus attuned to contemporaneous radical outlooks.

By the early thirties, Graham had earned recognition in the New York press as a new American dancer of superior technical ability, the inheritor of Isadora Duncan's mantle. But she also became a controversial figure in politically radical publications. The challenge posed to Graham by the left-wing press was initially one of political correctness in that it assumed that the relation between art and politics could be known in advance of their articulation. But it quickly accelerated into a debate within the left as well as between the right and the left over her formalism. This debate can be reconstructed from articles in *New Theatre* and *New Masses*, publications until recently never mentioned by dance scholars. Indeed, there has been a general unwillingness to explore the impact of social pressures on Graham's artistic development. Biographer Don McDonagh handles the situation in one paragraph:

> Graham's pre-eminence and moral fiber proved an immoderate attraction for causists in the 1930's. But where they wanted political commentary, she provided moral parables. Her vision was directed to unlocking the fetters that bound the spirit, not those twisting the social fabric.[116]

McDonagh's explanation ignores the point that Graham's feminist sensibility comes with its own political awareness. The issue to grasp is how Graham's apparent apoliticism articulates her feminism.

Graham's choreography appeared to elaborate an *aesthetics* of social struggle that left-wing writers found both tantalizing and frustrating from a *political* viewpoint. Her titles indicated a potentially radical orientation: *Re-*

volt (1927), *Immigrant: Steerage, Strike* (1928), *Sketches from the People* (1929). "Steps in the Street," a section from *Chronicle* (1936), was interpreted by a critic of the *New York Sun* (1936) as picturing "the unemployed shuffling along the avenues, now and then bursting forth in rebellious movements."[117] Jane Dudley remarked of the "Strike" section of *Immigrant*: "I remember 'Strike' particularly because the light came in on one side of the stage, on a standing light so with her [Graham's] face high it just lit one part of her, and it was very stark and very militant and very angry."[118] Such dances pursued the formal concerns of modernism while also thematizing labor by underlining the physical effort involved in some modern dancing. Unlike Duncan, whose body proposed the figurability of a somatized nature, Graham somatized effort. Of her style at this time, critic Edna Ocko wrote: "When the body stands it seems immovable. The body in motion is belligerent and defiant. It seems almost impossible to do meaningless dances with this equipment."[119] Yet, Graham was repeatedly reproached for aloofness from the social struggles of her own period.

The 1930s debate over Graham's artistic and social values mirrors the Lukacs/Bloch debate on expressionism in contemporaneous German Marxism.[120] Long submerged by a "social amnesia" resulting from fifties blacklisting, the "Realist/Modernist" debate in American modern dance is only now coming to light.[121] That Graham forged her choreographic identity in its crucible enables a corrective to the ahistorical distortions of seventies and eighties criticism. Thirties critics subjected Graham's output to a dissecting gaze, a morbidly precise and exacting scrutiny weighing its balance of formalism and social protest. In attending to Graham's politics, one grasps how her work could have been perceived by a large segment of her audience as formalist and passionless, which is precisely what recent criticism has wanted to deny.

There were two critical camps within left-wing criticism: Those who felt Graham was the last of a line of decadent bourgeois dancers and others who subscribed to her growing solidarity with the radical left. Emanuel Eisenberg faulted female modern dance soloists for "body manipulation" based on "obscure foreign symbols from a romantic-individualist world."[122]

> The movements of rebellion and protest are absolute parallels to those romantically circular and inspirationally upward-straining gestures of "release" which characterize bourgeois nonconformity and individualism.[123]

As Richard Sennett has noted, "a revolt against repression which is not a revolt against personality in public is not a revolt."[124] In a similar vein, Paul Douglas called Graham "the most developed bourgeois dancer since Isadora Duncan."[125]

> The perfection of Martha Graham's dancing is limited to her own ideology. She will be remembered as the greatest dance exponent of the last stages of capitalism struggling in its final agonies to salvage something out of its chaotic and decaying torment.[126]

Partially at issue here was Graham's artistic influence over her dancers—Anna Sokolow, Sophie Maslow, Jane Dudley, Lily Mehlman, Lillian Shapero, Sophia Delza, and others—whose own choreography already showed commitment to the worker's movement.[127] Graham's influence over young "revolutionary" dancers was primarily technical; still, it raised the question of whether her vocabulary was suited to their revolutionary themes. A propos of a collective concert of Graham's students, Edna Ocko remarked: "There is a danger in the continual reduction of militancy to an abstraction."[128] This problem was typically laid at Graham's feet. Her formalism was interpreted as inhibiting, even literally arresting, the radical content of her acolytes' creativity. In his "Change the World" column for the *Daily Worker*, Michael Gold asked, "Why should our proletarian dancers who have something new and different to say, follow her [Graham's] technique so slavishly?"[129] Curiously, none of Graham's critics observed that her work's radical potential was largely attributable to the fact that it was inhabited by politically radical young women.

What were the limitations of Graham's technique from a political standpoint? As Blanche Evan explained, the very idea of a fixed vocabulary militated against politically radical aspirations for modern dance:

> Why cannot we apply Martha Graham's command over physical movement to the expression of vital ideas? Why must movement be used meaninglessly as padding in a dance? The modern dance revolted from the ballet because it wanted to go beyond virtuosity, it wanted to express ideas and emotions in movement, through movement. It is sophisticated these days to pooh-pooh Duncan. It might be a good check on modern dancers to return periodically to her "Art of the Dance" and to recall the raison-d'etre of the modern dance.[130]

Although Graham's technical command of movement was a model to be emulated, the vocabulary through which that command manifested itself was suspect. The notion of formal movement technique came increasingly under fire for its absence of flow. In a 1934 review, Stanley Burnshaw observed:

> One thinks of her idiom as the cinematographic counterpart of body-motion: here is no flowing from posture to posture but a series of momentarily arrested stills. Yet each still is a composition balanced with severe care, even to the toes, fingers, and hair.[131]

Radical critics, dancers, and bourgeois critics alike faulted Graham for her elimination of flow, but they did so for different reasons. Burnshaw went on to demonstrate how Graham's montage eliminates emotion:

> After an entire Graham evening one thinks of Emerson's "Line in nature is not found," because of its application in reverse: Curve in Graham is not found. And this absence of lyric quality is both the source of her original contribution and its limitation for revolutionary artists. While conferring freshness on her treatment of commonplace dance themes, it takes its toll in passionlessness. There is no abandon in her, she never allows her body to be

run away by an overpowering impulsion. Figuratively speaking, she never flies off the ground. Always a subduing intellect cerebralizes the materials of passion—the fire becomes a frozen flame.[132]

The *Dance Observer* responded to Burnshaw point for point: Paul Love explained the hidden continuities of Graham's angularity and fragmentation, in short, the value of her aesthetic modernism:

> Previously her movement, presenting only essential segments of the complete line, and depending on its abruptness and force to make the spectator carry over to its conclusion, needed two or three repetitions before one could definitely characterize the dance. This has usually been called her percussive method. That is, if the dance required a circular arm movement, she found that if she presented it in its entirety there would be an inclination to lyrical softness which was not in accord with the emotion she wished to convey; and that if she presented a fraction of it the eye of the spectator would naturally supply the rest in imagination and at the same time perceive the emotional impact she desired.[133]

The *Dance Observer* had one year's worth of left-wing publication on dance to catch up with. As of 1934, its writers more often than not defended Graham's modernism against charges of life-alienating form by appealing to the notion of an absolute:

> Her dancing is not a commentary on any material fact such as war or peace or plenty, but is in itself the fact, the actuality, the essence and therefore not translatable in any terms except the visual one of movement into which she puts it.[134]

According to this argument, the body endures abstraction only to become more "immediate." That is, its self-referential absoluteness makes it a part of the world because when dissociated from social reality, it is self-speaking. Yet, despite such arguments, even politically conservative critics preferred flow to montage. Having vindicated her rejection of lyricism, Love could still write:

> Now she [Graham] is presenting movement which is much freer, much more continuous, and much more lyrical. It has far less of the intellectualization of the former. It comes closer at present to the term "physical," which means that the body as simply body is more predominant.[135]

Of Graham's *Celebration* (1934), Douglas remarked "a greater use of space and more elevation indicates the influence of some of her students, who from an ideological viewpoint are more advanced than Graham herself."[136] Her students were thought to be ahead of Graham precisely in their antiformalism. Blanche Evan asserted: "As a modern dancer, I object to *having* such a dictionary [Graham technique], even though the movement words *are* vigorous, direct, concise."[137] Graham's technique presented a paradox: It embodied an ideological insight that was absent from, yet still of necessity circulating within, her choreography. Ocko said:

> Whatever confusions exist in the work of Martha Graham, this much is true: her technic has elements which make it ideal for depiction of militant evaluations of society, her dances more and more approach realistic social documentation, and her verbal sympathies are avowedly one with the revolutionary dance.[138]

On the basis of an intensive course with Graham in 1935, however, Evan depicted the choreographer as a divided self:

> There is a strong conflict in Martha Graham. The sources for her approach to the dance seem to spring from two opposing poles. In one sense she is a realist. She often makes reference to the "new race" which, she says, must be direct, concise, unsentimental. On other occasions, she appears the perfect mystic.[139]

Despite left-wing critiques, viable alternatives to Graham's aesthetic did not come easily to mind. "The counteragent to bourgeois training," wrote Eisenberg, "is scarcely a hurling of oneself groundward on all fours and an extravagant series of simian faces in the name of political art as identity of the revolution or the proletariat; yet this would appear the alternative to so dreary, juiceless and outmoded a figure as the Lady [the female soloist]"[140] In search of more emotional equivalents to the dance of Graham, Wigman, and Duncan, Eisenberg still rejected emotional primitivism. Yet as long as the female soloist remained a "lady," she could have no revolutionary force. Anna Sokolow's lecture "The Revolutionary Dance," presented at the New School for Social Research in 1936, made peace with this contradiction. As reported by Marjorie Church, Sokolow

> started from the premise that all modern dance is revolutionary, in the sense that it has broken from the classic, using new techniques, new forms, new subject matter. However, she said, those working in the revolutionary dance movement place another meaning to the term: that of a movement which allies itself with the point of view of the revolutionary class itself—which, today, is the working class. She stated also that there was as yet no form which could be called "revolutionary." . . . As to body technique, the revolutionary dance is concerned not so much with building a new system as with making use of the excellent equipment provided in systems now being taught."[141]

Left-wing partisans of Graham, however, envisioned the possibility that her formalism could become socially relevant: "Far from being 'the dance exponent of the last stages of capitalism,' Martha Graham's genius is related to and instinctively strains towards the revolutionary forces in modern society."[142] Ocko presented a range of opinions on Graham's politics. Reproaching the choreographer in 1934 with flying "from this palpable, real, aching-to-be-interpreted world to past periods, lost civilizations, and ancient or medieval forms," Ocko commended Graham's *Chronicle* (1937) for protecting "the right and ability of the modern dance to deal with contemporary social material."[143] Yet she still accused Graham of "icebound formalism" in 1937: "This passionate devotion to the technique of form, and this preoccupation with pure, non-correlative symbolism destroyed all hope for any semblance of social realism."[144] Even when focused on "relevant" subject matter, Graham was unable "or unwilling," in Ocko's words, "to embrace the humanity and passion of its theme in human and passionate terms."[145] Such double-edged criticism implies that whereas Graham's vocabulary was suited to realism, it was not executed in the spirit of realism. Without emotion, no politics. The semiotics of revolutionary politics required a body projected energetically into space, neither aspirationally released nor formalistically rooted. These polemics may well have exerted pressure on Graham to define technique and emotion distinctly from one another.

In 1930, Graham articulated emotion as *extrinsic* to the technical formalities of movement: "The dance has two sides—one is the science of movement, the technique which is a cold exact science and has to be learned very carefully—and the other is the distortion of those principles, the use of that technique impelled by an emotion."[146] Since Horst had asserted Graham favored dissonance but not distortion, her statement almost reads as an apology for having eliminated affect. Bodily techniques did not embody emotion; rather, they stood open to its infusions. Technique was not posited as instrumental to the emotions; it was merely instrumental to form. In this way, emotion entered her choreographic theory as a by-product of subjectivity rather than as a goal of technique. Graham viewed emotion as the injection of primary processes into a formalized use of space. Rather than imposing emotional typologies on the body, Graham saw the dancer as the producer of autonomous action that is open, in equal yet separate measure, to technical refinement and emotional inflection.[147] "There is a vitality, a life-force, an energy, a quickening that is translated through you into action and because there is only one of you in all of time, this expression is unique."[148] Emotional inflection can also be derived by the narrative contextualization of a dance. Evan Alderson has shown that "it is almost a principle of [Graham's] dance that the expressiveness of the steps is given a more specific but still not explicit range of reference by their context, so that they metaphorically enlarge the given meanings."[149] Blanche Evan saw this ambiguity as a definite limitation:

> Already I have seen Martha, and her students both, take these exercises and put them *in toto* into dances to express anything or nothing. This is the inevitable result when the forms of technique become an end in themselves, when no clear relationship is made between technical theory and technical practise, *and* when no bridge is drawn between technical practise and creative technique.[150]

Graham's 1930 essay "Seeking an American Art of Dance" appeared in *Revolt in the Arts*. In the editor's introduction to this volume, Oliver M. Saylor wrote: "Esthetic revolt is the concomitant of social revolt, just as esthetic traditionalism is the companion of social order."[151] His position was progressivist, not radical: "Both the avoidance and the mitigation of unrestrained revolution are difficult—but possible," he wrote.[152] Even though Graham never joined the Communist party (Agnes De Mille notes that the pressure on her to do so was "extravagant"),[153] Graham's aesthetic goals cannot be separated from the influence of the American left and its rejection of bourgeois art: The will to begin with embryonic form, the search for a style appropriate to an epoch and to native traditions, the apprehension of individuality as a social phenomenon, the evocation of human potentiality realized, the frequent choreographic use of the mass within an aesthetic context evoking urbanism and machine culture—all these are signs of progressive, if not radical, political culture. Although unequivocal political meaning is not found in Graham's statements, she did court a left-wing audience, and her dances did contain revolutionary fantasies.[154] Her emotional ambiguity, however, was apprehended by the left as political evasiveness.

When examining the dynamics of Graham's growing reputation in the thirties, one is struck by how left-wing involvement in modern dance accrued to her advantage. *New Theatre* weighted dance equally in importance with theater and film, thus bringing her to the attention of a working-class audience avid for performance. Pressures exerted on Graham to express greater solidarity with that audience may have been motivated by the memory of Duncan's emotionalism. The left's own position on Duncan, however, is marked by a sexual politics that illuminates the rationale for Graham's restraint.

In the first article on modern dance to appear in *New Masses* (1929), Michael Gold praised Duncan's autobiography as a revolutionary document: "The old sex standard, based on private property," wrote Gold, "is breaking down in this revolutionary day. . . . Love is respectable now."[155] Duncan's freedom, however, also stirred Gold's anxiety:

> Sometimes I suspect Isadora is the first woman who has written down what every woman actually feels about Love. If this is true, the future is a black one for males. The day will come when the human female will devour the male in the moment of Love, exactly like a female spider or locust.[156]

For Gold, Duncan's class politics become submerged in the sexual politics of her emotion: "She was a Red, but not a real revolutionist. It was all emotion with her, glorious and erratic."[157] Gold expresses more than a belief that the previous generation's radicalism had been confused. His masculinist bias exhibits the double bind of the female soloist as revolutionary artist who was exhorted to privilege content over form and employ emotion to configure a body of political desire which would stir the masses. Yet whereas, for reasons of political effectiveness, she was expected to exude emotion, affect demonstrated the reputed weakness of her sex. "Emotion," writes Ann L. Ardis, "was presumed to constitute 'a female domain of knowledge' in the nineteenth century."[158] So it was, too, in the twentieth.

I argue that Graham understood this critical bias inherited from the Victorian age and therefore recoiled from emotional, flowing, and curvilinear movement. Although her work inevitably demonstrated some insensitivity to issues of class, she fashioned a political response to sexism in aesthetic terms. Graham's history reveals the dual politics of American modern dance: feminist on the one hand and politically radical on the other. Political radicalism was put into question by a nascent feminism that, in Graham's case, took refuge in modernism. The drama of the 1930s for Graham was to solidify her reputation by gradually adapting her choreography to theatricalized emotion that would not compromise her sexual politics. Although the political events of the thirties rendered her position increasingly untenable, unforeseen factors led to her triumph.

Left-wing critical pressure for modern dance to speak to the masses also induced female soloists to devise work for large groups. "Now the individualism must give place," wrote Graham in 1930. "The universal is being made manifest through employment of the mass."[159]

MASS DANCE

"It is with movement, rather than with steps, that it [modern dance] is concerned."[160] Once "steps" (studied and disingenuous instruments of translation) are eliminated, the body can reclaim its massiveness. By shedding an artificial division of labor according to which the legs locomote, the arms imitate, the head rules, etc., the "massive" body asserts a different aesthetic of weight, angle, and balance. The denial of locomotion in *Lamentation*, for example, favored a sense of the solo figure as a mass, accentuated by the tube of jersey from within which Graham's torso appeared to expand with each new gesture.[161] And just as certainly, the meaning of mourning in *Lamentation* transcended the individual, and sought a universal or depersonalized meaning. The term mass became increasingly integrated into Graham's aesthetic pronouncements: "We build in mass and are built in mass, spiritually and physically."[162] She used the term "mass" to sustain an image of the body as a socially collective entity: "Through its dancers so brilliantly springing to life and talent throughout the country will come the great mass drama that is the American Dance."[163] It would appear that this drama was class conflict, but that is not spelled out. Graham grafted her modernist aesthetic of the massive body onto the social mass which is the group, thereby deftly folding a modernist aesthetic into socially activist choreography. "Mass" can point to the importance of weight and space in Graham's dance, but "mass" also betokens the precedence of choreography for the group over that for the soloist. "Our greatest dance form will eventually be an orchestration of various physical rhythms and spiritual melodies in mass movement."[164] The notion of mass

The Graham Concert Group   *Vandamm*

Martha Graham - Dances in Two Worlds By EDNA OCKO

IN times like these, when revolutionary art is the banner for a class marching into power, the artist must work against time. He must wrest from incipient Fascist censors whatever he realizes is valuable for the perpetuation of his art, and his works must be rich in content since he speaks for and to a rising social class, and realizes that he must be the crystallizer and organizer of their feelings. This places an enormous responsibility upon him, particularly when the field in which he works is limited, since he must constantly guard and proclaim the interests of the class he champions.

In the modern dance, the task is less simple than one at first believes. There are so few great dancers in the world today that the temptation to make a mechanical and arbitrary division between revolutionary and bourgeois dancer is difficult to avoid. And it is to skirt this danger that one considers Martha Graham not only as the high point of the bourgeois dance, but also as an artist whose work, while still encircled, is drawing closer and closer to the belief in and expression of a new social order.

At the close of the dance season of 1935, Martha Graham stands almost unquestionably as the greatest dancer America has produced since Isadora Duncan, and as one of the outstanding exponents of the modern dance in the world. We must determine then, the philosophy by which she creates and through which she interprets social phenomena, since, in her position as leader, she is a determining influence upon a vast number of disciples. As a performer, her sincerity and integrity is unquestioned. She has never

consciously catered to Philistine art-lovers, nor casually succumbed to the blandishments of a financially tantalizing Broadway. As a technician, she has, Picasso-like, shifted styles. This year, however, her efforts have crystallized. Hers is the closest approach to a *system* of dance technic which is basic, transferable, and capable of infinite variation. She has developed a science of modern dance movement which seems remarkably suited to make the body a fit instrument for expression. And this rigorous training presents itself to me, at least, as an admirable technic for the revolutionary dance. It has, above all, strength and endurance; it permits of amazing gradations in dynamics; it embodies dramatic elements of militance and courage. Its most delicate moments are fraught with latent power. When the body stands, it seems immovable. The body in motion is belligerent and defiant. It seems almost impossible to do meaningless dances with this equipment. In training, the pupil is told to be strong, "strong enough to destroy barriers," that her body must surmount all physical difficulties, must be "energy on the move," creating and recreating strength and change within itself. This technic has produced dancers definitely aligned to the militant working-class movement whose merits as directors, teachers, and soloists, cannot be gainsaid. Anna Sokolow, and her Dance Unit in *Anti-War Cycle*, and *Strange American Funeral*, Lily Mehlman, Sophie Maslow,—all show to advantage the results of this training. The Graham Concert Group has reached a high technical standard, and its presence on a stage literally surcharges the air with energy and militance. There is no ques-

tion that Martha Graham has succeeded in founding a school of the dance that is a major influence throughout America.

It would be absurd at this time to assume that Miss Graham, as a creator, is concerned with the expression of personal vagaries, that her thinking is haphazard, wilful, uncharted. Tracing the course of Miss Graham's dances would be charting an Odyssiad. At times she drew close to a welcoming realistic shore, then the tenuous siren songs of mysticism, abstraction, purism, drew her out of her path into strange, unfrequented waters. We assume that this pilgrimage is ended, that she has dropped anchor in the rich harbor of social realism. What are her dances, then, of social content?

IN 1929, the year of the stock crash, of the collapse of bourgeois security, the following dances comprised, among others, Miss Graham's program: *Vision of the Apocalypse*, in which a figure views the suffering and miseries of an enslaved humanity; *Sketches of the People*, which, according to a reviewer at that time, proclaimed "social revolution"; *Immigrant*, composed of *Steerage* and *Strike*; *Heretic; Poems of 1917* in two parts; *Song behind the Lines; Dance of Death*, the latter anti-war dances. These were presented at a time when most performers were doing isolated sketches on a variety of unrelated, superficial topics.

There was, in the years following, a definite tangent shot away from this realistic direction. The works of Martha Graham became mystic, Mexican, Hellenic, Medieval (*Ave, Salve, Cere-*

Figure 15. An article on Graham by Edna Ocko
with a photo of *Celebration*. (*New Theatre*, July 1935)

drama begs a question by suggesting a plural, submerged or unindividuated subject. The mass subject is not a "primitive other" but a "public everyperson."

Graham's growing interest in the mass took her into Americanist themes. One can detect in the phrase "the great mass drama that is the American Dance" a relinquishing of the feminist project (the "discovery" of America) in deference to an ideologically tinged project glorifying America's history. The term "mass" contains the germ of Graham's own deradicalization as a modernist. Her social relevance, however, did not come into immediate focus. Of the 1935 *Course*, Stanley Burnshaw wrote:

> It teases by hints of broader social meanings. Is there any significance—however tenuous—in the careful division of "characters" into "Three in Green," "Two in Red," "Two in Blue"—groups that preserve identity throughout the development? Is there sociological implication in the separate pursuits of these color-groups, racing in competition of a kind, to the impulsions of driving, relentless music? Or is it no more than a superb choreographic design flowing in rich and brilliant color with genuinely thrilling instants? If "Course" is a new departure, Miss Graham has not clearly communicated her meaning.[165]

By 1935, public feeling grew increasingly antifascist rather than anticapitalist, pro-democratic rather than pro-worker. Thus, even as Graham was beginning to modify her uncompromising modernism, the evaluative criteria of left-wing aesthetics were also mutating. Social awareness was becoming inseparable from nationalism. At first, *New Theatre* rejected this chauvinistic trend in modern dance as artistically mannered and politically dangerous. In "The Star Spangled Dance," Blanche Evan charged the *Dance Observer* with initiating this trend:

> What is left of the American this-and-that in modern dance? It is obvious that the desire to be American and to express America is being used as a pretext to promote the idea of chauvinistic art—and for no other purpose. Since the modern dance has had its only significant development in America and Germany, the insinuation is unmistakable: "Down with German methods, German dance art, artists, teachers."[166]

Popular front politics reduced class/gender contradictions within the left. Having maligned Duncan in 1929, Michael Gold reconsidered her from a purely antifascist perspective in 1937:

> Do our young revolutionary dancers and poets create such images of a new human beauty toward which the race may strive in socialism? To my old-fashioned mind, some of them need to go back to such American democratic sources as Walt Whitman and Isadora Duncan, not to imitate, but to learn an ultimate faith in the body and spirit of man. Emerson had it, but T.S. Eliot does not have it, and it has led him, as all such fear and hatred of the masses must lead, to the last negation called fascism.[167]

Graham began her Americana cycle at the advent of the popular front in 1935. At this time, broader antifascist coalitions were being embraced by international communism. Once Stalin adopted the credo of socialism in one country, which precluded the spread of revolution, to be communist in America was to be nationalist. If Graham had been unable or unwilling to address the class issues of the Great Depression, she solicited good grades from the left by taking a courageous stance on race: In 1936, she refused Hitler's invitation to appear at the Berlin Olympic games because many of her dancers were Jewish.[168] This surely enhanced the willingness of left critics to perceive the growing emotionality they craved in her work. *Panorama* (1935) and *Chronicle* (1936) apparently demonstrated Graham's increasing sympathy with the left at a time when such solidarity was gaining wider popular approval as indigenously American. Of *Chronicle*, Owen Burke wrote in *New Masses*:

> The patterns are abstract; there is no miming. Program notes might clarify and save the audience the need to puzzle over subtleties in meaning, of intention. But although the ideas of the dancer are obscured in the overabundance of choreographic movement, *the emotional overtones* carry through, and with them the meaning of the composition and its significance.[169]

Later in the same year, Burke said the revised version of *Chronicle* was "brilliantly and stirringly anti-war, anti-fascist."[170] He also hailed the publication of Merle Armitage's book on Graham in terms that officially erased the critical standoff between Graham and the left-wing press:

> For twelve years Martha Graham has pointed the direction of the modern dance, and the best of our younger revolutionary dancers carry on through the technique she has taught them.[171]

Among others of radical persuasion, only Blanche Evan resisted the perception of a substantive difference in Graham's relation to social realities. In "Her Chosen Theme" (1938), Evan asserted:

> There is an increasing number of anti-war and anti-fascist dances. But the creative process of movement has not changed. *An American Lyric*, for instance, Martha Graham's newest group composition, boasts a fine *base* for a dance script. "This dance has as its theme the basic American right—freedom of assembly"—so reads the program note. But again, the *movement symbols* employed in the dance are not symbols expressive of the theme. They are movements from the composer's pre-determined category of pure "kinesthetic," detached and abstract and purely physical. The audience seems to remain emotionally unmoved and intellectually unsatisfied.[172]

Graham's tributes to anti-Franco Spain, *Deep Song* (1936) and *Immediate Tragedy* (1937), however, marked the total capitulation of left-wing criticism to her aesthetic. In their themes and their emotionalism, these dances were

unequivocally aligned with the popular front, which no longer required anyone to take a socially radical stance. An enthusiastic Henry Gilfond in the
Dance Observer saw the opportunity to cut the Gordian knot by melding the
idea of absolute dance with that of social progressiveness:

> Here is a divorcing of the dance completely from the representational. Here
> are no simple pictures, no pictorial view, but statement, the statement of the
> artist's relationship to the contemporary scene.[173]

In Gilfond's view, Graham transcended the demands of specificity and formalism alike. Having reconciled Graham's conflict between politics and aesthetics, Gilfond continues in a vein mimicking left-wing enthusiasm:

> Dancers have a duty to their people, as well as themselves. The dance, and
> Martha Graham, move towards what might be called social realism. The dance
> and Martha Graham move forward.[174]

Graham's move from modernism to political radicalism encompassed a move
toward populism. Burke's review of *Deep Song* attributes to that work "an emotional drive that might profitably find its way more frequently into classic contemporary dancing."[175] More important, *New Masses* sponsored the premiere of
Graham's *American Document* (1938), Graham's first work to include a male
dancer and a spoken text.[176] This ultimate reconciliation is symbolized by a
Hirschfeld caricature of Graham on the cover of *New Masses* for October 18,
1938.[177] Thus, Graham became socially relevant at the very historical moment
when radicalism expired, when revolution became despecified as antifascism.

In her recent biography of Graham, Agnes De Mille attempts to maintain
the purity of Graham's modernism by stressing the choreographer's disdain
for communists and her absorption throughout this period in high modernists
such as Henry Moore, Pablo Picasso (himself at one time a member of the
Communist party), and Paul Klee.[178] It can nevertheless not be denied that
Graham's gradually evolving social radicalism in the early thirties set the stage
for *the* political triumph of her career: a dramatic homecoming of the fellow
traveller into the arms of the popular front.

INTO THE EMOTIVIST MAINSTREAM

As noted earlier, Graham's political acculturation of the late thirties is marked
by her relinquishing feminist problematics.[179] The choreography of the late
thirties and early forties alluded increasingly to American history in ways that
made her materialism take a back seat to nationalism. With the coming of
war and the death of radicalism, Graham was not alone in seeking the high
ground of American identity.[180]

Having originally sought national identity in more experimental and he-
retical personae, Graham could have found herself aesthetically displaced in

Figure 16. "The employment of mass" in Graham's terms. A 1993 performance of Graham's *Panorama* (1935) reconstructed by the Martha Graham Dance Company. © Jack Vartoogian, New York.

American Document, out of step with dance which, as Denby wrote, showed her too subtle to play this game effectively: "One can see that Miss Graham's intentions were to make the movement open plain and buoyant. Perhaps it is her own natural subtlety that defeated her. The movement turned out to be inelastic, it strikes poses, and it pounds downward."[181] Lloyd, however, remembers how the devout patriotism of *American Document* "won the country" on Graham's third national tour in 1939. She also states that the work was "almost too explicit."[182] *New Masses* saw "a new directness" in *American Document* "that might well be imitated not only by the older dancers, stemming from the bourgeoisie, but also and particularly by the younger dancers who are earnestly seeking broad audiences among the trade unions and other mass organizations."[183] *American Document* does show a development from Graham's essentialist and geographical definition of America to a more truly multicultural one. "Its episodes," wrote Lincoln Kirstein, "commenced with an introductory duet, a preamble for a grave circus. . . . There followed an Indians' lament for the spirit of the land they had lost, then a statement of Puritan fury and tenderness, an elegy of the emancipated Negro slaves, and a finale of contemporary self-accusation, a praise of our rights, and a challenge to our own powers to persist as a democracy."[184]

Graham's Americana work strove in general to consolidate her reputation as a theatrical communicator. Through more traditional uses of the American theme than previously employed, she sought choreographic formats theatrical

Figure 17. *New Masses* cover
publicizing the premiere of Graham's
American Document (1938).
(Courtesy of Albert Hirschfeld)

enough to render her vocabulary more accessible and less esoteric. To this end, she had "apprenticed" herself to actress Katharine Cornell as a choreographer and movement coach.[185] Cornell's physical stylization in performance, more derivative of naturalism than modernism, indicated the way toward dramatic impact without rendering dance literal.[186] Graham's close association with Cornell is partially responsible for her apparent shift from modernist to mainstream emotivist. In the iconography of photographs and, to some extent also, of the stage, this change is signaled by the abandonment of the static frontality of the figure in such works as *Primitive Mysteries* and *Lamentation* and the adoption of the sculpted profile, chin jutting forward, eyes somewhat extinguished, which would later become her—and was already Cornell's—stylistic signature.

By 1936, we also find a marked shift in Graham's writing from formalism to a conscious molding of emotional signifiers through dance: "The artist," she then wrote, "can objectify and make apparent what we all feel," implying thereby two things: (1) feelings can acquire easily recognizable outer form in dance, and (2) subjectivity, although inherent in the creative process, need

Figure 18. The move into drama: Graham in *Letter to the World* (1940) with Jane Dudley. Photo: Arnold Eagle. (Courtesy of the photographer)

nevertheless not mar theatrical communication.[187] Dance may be the voicing of "hidden" emotions deriving from "something deep within you," but emotions inhabiting dance transcend personal difference to become shared, legible, socialized. Graham seemed to be casting herself as "social woman" whose role no longer was to explore autonomous subjectivity but to reflect solidarity with "what we all feel." This is the period invoked by most critics of the emotivist or psycho-dramatic persuasion that has significantly distorted Graham's historical identity.

In 1940, Graham had achieved legibility in the eyes of her harshest critics just as a changed political agenda altered their expectations of her work. Both the critical and creative agendas had shifted. "*Every Soul Is a Circus*," wrote Owen Burke, "is new for Martha Graham and for contemporary dance. It moves in novel and broadening forms, developing the use of pantomime in dance structure. It plays with psychological study and brings pathos to the dance theater as has rarely been done before."[188] In a parallel manner, Graham's own prose reflected a turn toward representational clarity: "My dancing is just dancing," had yielded to "the basis of all dancing is something deep within you."[189] The dance of "being" now sought its source in "appearance": emotion and "strong feeling."[190]

A still later development of modern dance, one that would compromise the conceit of inwardness as Graham originally had, I would paraphrase as: "Something deep within you is just dancing." Graham would leave that for Cunningham to say.[191] Yet, Graham's early insistence on expression as a by-product, rather than a source, of movement influenced him. Of his work with Graham, Cunningham has said:

> That was what I really didn't like about working with Martha Graham—the idea that was always being given to you that a particular movement meant something specific. I thought that was nonsense. And, you know, I really think Martha felt it was, too. Once, when we were rehearsing *Appalachian Spring* [1944], I had a passage that Martha said had to do with fear, or maybe with ecstasy—she wasn't sure which—and she said why didn't I go and work on it and see what I came up with. I did, and she was delighted; she even said it has solved some of her other problems. It's always seemed to me that Martha's followers make her ideas much more rigid and specific than they really are with her, and that Martha herself has a basic respect for the ambiguity in all dance movement.[192]

By recognizing the blurring of fear and ecstasy in movement, Cunningham leads us to reflect again on Bette Davis's series of cameo moments: "One after the other. Hatred, ecstasy, rage, compassion!" Unlike Davis, Cunningham does not envision Graham's emotions as discrete units of a semantic code parsed by movement. Rather, the uncertain definition of fear and ecstasy, or of ecstasy as fear, suggests an emotionally ambiguous body in which Graham's and Cunningham's work can be seen to share.

Figures 19 and 20. Martha Graham in a study from *Herodiade* (1941) and Katharine Cornell in a studio portrait. The cameo of physical, but not ocular, proximity to surface textures yields a privileged, "interior" moment. (Courtesy of the Dance Collection and the Billy Rose Theater Collection, the New York Public Library for the Performing Arts, Astor, Lenox, and Tilden Foundations)

Figures 21 and 22. Cornell's and Graham's similar profile signatures. (Courtesy of the Theater Collection and the Dance Collection, the New York Public Library for the Performing Arts, Astor, Lenox, and Tilden Foundations)

FOUR

Expressivism and Chance Procedure

The Future of an Emotion

Since the "Cunningham revolution," two critical positions have emerged on expressivity.[1] Dance critic Marcia Siegel argues for a return to the expressive values lost since Cunningham and post-Cunningham work.[2] In particular, Siegel would like expression to be snatched back from the dangers that theory represents. In her view, theory contaminates the practices of criticism, history and choreography alike. Conversely, an overwhelming prejudice against expressivity in our century has led philosopher Francis Sparshott to discount its historical existence and purpose. He dismisses expressivity as a topic of philosophical investigation because it is not theoretically cogent. I will argue against Sparshott that expression is endowed with its own theory,[3] and against Siegel that even those elements in performance which seem the most "intuitive, visceral and preverbal" can be profitably discussed in theoretical terms. Cunningham's work did not originally dismiss expressivity as much as it sought to redefine it.[4] As long as Cunningham was actively putting expressivity into question, he manipulated the expressive model in new ways.

THE CHANCE OF EXPRESSION

Early modernist expressivity was nourished by classical expression theory. Expression theory makes emotion a stimulus of dance movement. In so doing, it divides emotions into discrete events impinging on the inner consciousness of the subject. Consider that theory in the concise formulation of early twentieth-century modern dancer Loie Fuller. Working backward from motion to emotion, Fuller called motion "the expression of a sensation" and sensation "the reverberation that the body receives when an impression strikes the mind."[5] For the actor, it could be charted as follows:

Impression $\longrightarrow$ Sensation $\longrightarrow$ Expression

Impression is an inner realization, sensation the feeling engendered by the impression, expression the crystallization of an outer reaction. Expression responds outwardly to sensation through a physical displacement dissipating sensation's indwelling reverberation. When extended to dance, expression theory allows that music be the initial impression whose impact on the soul (sensation) is translated into the physical movement of dance. For the dancer it could be charted:

$$Music \longrightarrow Feeling \longrightarrow Dance$$

When applied to dance, classical expression theory holds that feeling attains outward expression in reaction to the harmony of music.

Although it did receive much attention in the 1870s, as Francis Sparshott suggests, the tenets of expression theory precede Loie Fuller by at least four hundred years.[6] In 1463, Italian dancing master Guglielmo Ebreo da Pesaro wrote that we respond to harmony as we are "moved to perform certain demonstrative external movements, signifying what we feel within."[7] Seventeenth-century French librettist and theorist Guillaume Colletet attributes the imitation of a passion, such as joy, in dancing to "the impressions which the soul makes naturally on the body."[8] According to this view, the impression of harmony on the soul indirectly causes the body to move:

> The soul takes such pleasure in harmony that it would voluntarily leave itself to join harmony more perfectly. But, though there are obstacles preventing it from returning to that natural felicity in its present state, the soul can still oblige the body which constrains it to imitate harmony through dance; dance can be called a conformity of the body to the soul and of the soul to movement.[9]

In this quote, Colletet clarifies that the sensations of the soul can only be acted upon, as it were, by the body as a proxy. Thus, at its theoretical root, the concept of imitation is never far from that of expressivity. In moving joyfully, the dancer cannot help but represent the joyful movement of the soul: Dancing is by its nature secondary because it is derivative of a spiritual reality which it represents. The body is not responding directly to its own sensations of harmony but rather imitating those of the soul, which cannot move of itself. For classical expression theory, the body does not move in a way that could characterize its unique nature as a body. This is because dancing *imitates* the euphoria of the soul's sympathy with the impression music makes upon it. In this view, dance translates an unobserved, "spiritual" experience. In a like manner, eighteenth-century theorist Johann Jacob Engel pictured physical expression as the representation of the soul's thoughts: "Expression is simply the palpable *representation* of the soul's propensity to think, and of the feeling with which its perception is affected, that is to say, the state in which it is placed by the object of its present contemplation."[10] Once expression is understood as part of the process of representation it is clearly open to theoretical reflection.

While expressivity has been practiced and reflected on in dance since the Italian Renaissance, it has also played a role in twentieth-century modernist projects where we least expect to encounter it. Consider its presence in the work of Merce Cunningham. Although his earliest choreography in the 1940s was expressive in the traditional sense, by the early fifties it distinguished itself by the dissociation of dance and music.[11] In Cunningham's choreography, music and dance functioned together yet were not a unit; no inner rhythmic correspondences allying bodily movement to meter were premeditated. "The two co-exist," he wrote, "as sight and sound do in our daily lives."[12] Cunningham accomplished this by applying John Cage's ideas on chance procedure to his choreographic vocabulary. Chance procedure involves the charting of all possible movement options prior to their arrangement. Thus, chance dictates the combinations of known variables, each of whose possible appearances has been foreseen. What is unforseen, and still left to chance, is the sequence of the combinations. "When I choreograph a piece by tossing pennies—by chance, that is—I am finding my resources in that play, which is not the product of *my* will."[13]

Cunningham applied chance procedure to composition in order to eliminate his own intention as a choreographer. This would ensure that music and dance would not reinforce one another emotionally unless it happened by accident. He dissociated dance from music to the degree that the latter might no longer furnish the animus for dance. Chance procedure was meant to ensure that no inflection of movement, no intentional allusiveness, would creep into dance. At issue were both how a dance was produced and how it was received. Cunningham's approach to composition and the presentation of dances necessarily rejects more than a conventional image of "dancing to music"; it assails the classical expression theory on which that image is founded. Expression theory sees movement as rooted initially in emotional sensation, just as talking is initially rooted in the meaning that conscience bestows on words. In fact, talking is the closest thing in language to expressive movement in dance. Music and dance, thought and words, form organic wholes in expression theory despite their functional distinction. When Cunningham dissociates music from dance, he does intentional violence to expression theory: He effectively pries physical sensation loose from the emotional impression that purportedly caused it. To sever the traditional contact between music and dance is to sever the continuity between feeling and the body's theatrical presence. Thus, physical movement would no longer "force out" (*express*, or press "ex"—outward), that is, no longer manifest subjective states outwardly. Nevertheless, his view of dance does not preclude subjectivity, the existence of a particular inner self. I will argue that Cunningham's dissociative practices have come to be interpreted as a far more radical alternative to expression theory than his writing and performances actually indicate. I will suggest that chance procedure as used by Cunningham, until a certain point in his career, purveys expressivist values, albeit in an original way.[14]

Consider what he himself has said. Cunningham seems to relate what happens in his dances to his personal experience of the world. Referring to the flashing lights of *Winterbranch*, Cunningham reflected, "Where do those lights come from in my experience? I thought about this a long time, and one of the

Figure 23. Merce Cunningham working with facial expression in the first of his works
to employ chance procedure, *Sixteen Dances for Soloist and Company of Three*
(1952). Photo: Gerda Peterich. (Courtesy of the Dance Collection, the New York
Public Library for the Performing Arts, Astor, Lenox, and Tilden Foundations)

things it could have been is that we toured so often in a Volkswagen bus, driv-
ing at night, at two in the morning and seeing lights from on-coming cars illu-
minating something, a person, a tree, or whatever, constantly changing."[15] In
other words, things that are an expression of his life—even if only coinciden-
tally—find their way into his dances.

Because he hasn't put his own intentions in the work, he is able to claim
that it means whatever the audience sees in it. In a 1970 interview, Cunningham
spoke of his audience's violent reaction to *Winterbranch*.[16] Because the piece
produced a diverse yet extreme audience reaction, the choreographer stated
that *Winterbranch* may have been about violence, or may have displayed violence convincingly to the audience. Although it was not his professed intent to
express violence, he nevertheless noted the prevalence of violence in contemporary American life as a corollary to the adequacy of this interpretation. The
artistic intent that one might presuppose in a more conventionally expressive
choreographer is here assigned to the realm of the artist's unconscious motiva-
tion. Yet the audience's instinctual reaction furnishes the communicative rap-

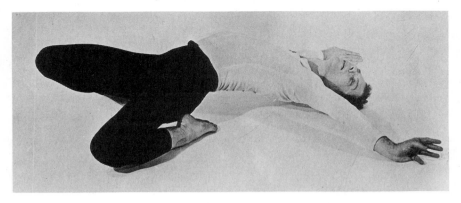

Figure 24. Merce Cunningham in *Lavish Escapade* (1956), one of the "strange, seemingly psychologically oriented, solo works," according to composer Earle Brown in James Klosty, *Merce Cunningham*, p. 76. Photo: Louis Stevenson. (Courtesy of the Dance Collection, the New York Public Library for the Performing Arts, Astor, Lenox, and Tilden Foundations)

port presupposed by expression theory. The "sensation" resulting from the "impression" may no longer be located in the artist's soul. Indeed, it is now "out there," in the world of commonly shared experience. But all can feel it— that is, are its victims or observers—and construe its "expression" accordingly. However questionable this commentary about his own work might be, Cunningham is still grappling with the same issues that exist in expression theory. Instead of saying, "We are sensitive souls whose physical movements reflect what we feel within," his dancers work at dissociating themselves from stimuli. In fact, Cunningham's dances are often meant to show disjunction, just as classical theater represented feelings that, however disturbing, unified experience.

With regard to other works, Cunningham has evoked stimuli such as the new ways information is received in the modern world, the interruptive experience of television, the quality of contemporary life, and the nature of scientific discovery. His reception theory could be charted as follows: ·

Information $\longrightarrow$ Contemporary Receptivity $\longrightarrow$ Movement

Contemporary receptivity should be understood as a willingness to acknowledge feeling without the need to internalize it and subsequently manifest it outwardly. This expressive formula no longer reflects the inner resonances of experience in the dancer, but experience is nevertheless essential to the production and the reception of any Cunningham piece, because the formula is not wholly fortuitous. That invisible entity that expression theory calls the "soul"—prime receptor of all impressions—is somewhere intact.

The early Cunningham work of the 1950s clearly resisted forms of emotivism associated with modern dance of the 1940s. While expressivity was present in Cunningham's work in the fifties and sixties, he shifted its locus from the dancer as transmitter of feelings to the movement itself. During those decades, Cunningham's work served indirectly to critique expression as a form of modernist hysteria. Expression, in his work, emerged from movement without any emotional overlay. In other words, his aesthetic did favor expression, though without intention. "I could see," he remarked to Susan Sontag in a 1986 interview, "who and what they [the dancers] were *through* what they were doing."[17]

In his conversations with Jacqueline Lesschaeve, Cunningham asserted that "movement comes from something, not from something expressive, but from some momentum or energy."[18] Although he thinks of movement as being only about itself, he does not go so far as to assert that movement generates itself. Cunningham's movement comes from energy, just as traditionally expressive movement comes from inner turmoil, euphoria, or some such "sensation" caused by an "impression." Movement is still a *reaction* to the hidden *action* of an impression. Yet, for Cunningham, it is in reaction to a physical rather than to a spiritual reality, to energy rather than to the soul. Because he affords dance movement an origin in the physical rather than the spiritual, Cunningham secularizes expression theory, or aestheticizes it.

Cunningham also speaks of "the exhilarating moment that this exposing of the bare energy can give us."[19] Such moments experienced by the performer are equivalent to visual moments for the audience. They stand forth from the continuum of movement as aesthetic summations, recognized kinesthetically and imprinted on the gaze as memorable. Roland Barthes likens this "pregnant moment" to Lessing's aesthetic of painting in *Laocoön*. "Painting can use only a single moment of an action," writes Lessing, "and must therefore choose the one which is most suggestive and from which the preceding and succeeding actions are most easily comprehensible."[20] In this view, painting should depict a summation of moments which encapsulates in contiguous space what is usually only evident over time. In a similar manner, Cunningham calls those dancing moments exhilarating which sum up, as it were, an invisible energy source in a cognitive flash: In that moment, the energy source of dancing is as good as expressed. In other words, Cunningham denies the expressive model even as he conserves that model's theoretical profile. Indeed, he links energy to feeling when he calls it "a source from which passion or anger may issue in a particular form, the source of energy out of which may be channeled the energy that goes into the various emotional behaviors."[21] This is to say, it seems to me, that the body can have a direct rather than imitative rapport with emotional behaviors as long as it attends to something more fundamental than emotion, while just as differentiated. In Cunningham's view, different forms of energy are as differentiated as forms of emotion. In his fundamentalism, he is still concerned with correlating an outer manifestation to an inner essence. "Lack of fullness in a particular movement," he adds, "or exaggeration of a movement outside the particular limits of its own shape and rhythm produces mannerism, I should think."[22] One could not apply such aesthetic criteria without some covert, or even unconscious, notion of correlating an outer manifestation to an inner source.[23]

AN AESTHETICS OF INDIFFERENCE

A viewing of Cunningham's company in 1990 reveals that the project, which emerged in the fifties, is still fully intact. Yet, the apparent *modus operandi* of that project has subtly altered: The Cunningham dancer of the eighties and early nineties does not manifest the detached subjectivity in the way his or her predecessors did.[24] Let me flesh out this point by describing a work of the mid-sixties that contained symptoms of both the "pre-" and the "post-revolution" performance styles.

In 1966, John Cage recited anecdotes to Merce Cunningham's choreography in *How to Pass, Kick, Fall and Run*, eliciting supercilious titters from the audience.[25] Despite the broad appeal of Cage's text, the choreography it accompanied was not intended humorously and showed formal continuity with Cunningham's earlier work; indeed, it asserted random structure as vigorously as had the 1953 *Suite by Chance*.[26] Thus, more than a decade after Cunningham's most radically experimental period, he continued to keep the structure of his compositions palpably arbitrary. In the fifties, audiences gave vent to shocked outrage at these experiments.[27] In contrast, audiences of the sixties showed a complacency in response to choreographic randomness. Had Cunningham's audience come of age, or had his work taken on the character of an accepted and elaborate in-joke?

It was at approximately this time that the doctrinaire aspect of Cunningham's work, the so-called "Cunningham revolution," took shape in the media. This surely coincided with the first federal government funding of modern dance and the first modern dance festival on Broadway, funded by the Ford Foundation and the New York State Council on the Arts in 1968. At the time of this increased public attention, Cunningham was identified as one of the five "major" modern dance choreographers.[28] Yet, from a retrospective point of view, the "revolution" was more a media event than an authentic description of Cunningham's art. Comparing his company's performance style in the fifties and early sixties with that of the eighties, one can weigh the negative impact of the "revolution," and the prestige it garnered, on the performance of his work.

Cunningham had resisted expressivist values in favor of movement that relied on a dancer's unique execution of it. This execution was not repeatable—in the sense of being transferable from one dancer to another—because, unlike choreography based on expression theory, it in no way relied on a fixed code of emotional values in movement. Only a particular dancer could convey a particular movement as meaningful and elicit a particular response. "Cunningham asked each dancer to move in conformity with his or her particular physical constitution."[29] This aesthetic has ultimately been manipulated and, I think, mutilated, by the dancer having become one who reflects chance procedure rather than one who copes with it.[30] The Cunningham dancer is now too frequently a body devoid of intention, agency, and interiority, a body primed to mirror the dictates of chance. Remembering the audience

Figure 25. A studio portrait of the Cunningham company in the fifties by Arnold
Eagle. Viola Farber is at far left. (Courtesy of the photographer)

reaction to *How to Pass, Kick, Fall and Run* in 1966, it is tempting to hold
them responsible for the effects of the Cunningham revolution. A subtle and
delicately balanced aesthetic stance was hardening into a choreographic dogma
of reduced flexibility and resonance.

Deborah Jowitt has suggested that since the seventies, "the widening age
gap between him [Cunningham] and the other dancers affected his relationship to them. Somehow, either it was harder for them to reveal their individuality through the steps he gave them, or harder for them to reveal to him the
individuality that would enlighten him when he was making up the steps."[31]
By the seventies, Cunningham may have become more distant from his dancers, growing more interested in technical uniformity at the expense of individuality. Yet it is difficult to say whether the differences I am describing here
are attributable to audience reception or qualities intrinsic to the work. This
is one of the most profound and nettling issues that dance history and theory
has to work out methodologically. Consider that Cunningham's choreography in the fifties read as both more and less shocking than it does today in the
nineties. It appeared more shocking in that it violated a context of expressivity
far more influential and pervasive in the fifties than at present. As Jill Johnston
wrote in her essay "The New American Modern Dance," "the modern dance
establishment of the 1950's apprehended Cunningham's depersonalized concentration as de-humanization."[32] Conversely, Cunningham's choreography
also appeared less shocking in the fifties because from that place, the motif of
incommunication could often be read as a statement on the community of

Figure 26. Merce Cunningham and John Cage in a performance of *How to Pass, Kick, Fall and Run* in Ann Arbor, Michigan, 1965. Photo: Martha Keller. (Courtesy of the Cunningham Foundation, Inc., with permission of the photographer)

absolute individuals. Which is to say that, in the fifties, the accidental concordances between dance and music that chance procedure afforded were actually the point of the performance, rather than the *intention* categorically to avoid them in the name of an ideology of disunity. "Cunningham's philosophy," wrote composer Pauline Oliveros, "allows a natural rather than an imposed relationship to arise between the music and the dance."[33] Thus, the unpremeditated occurrence of an expressive fit between dance and music was of a higher natural order, indeed contained some message about a higher order beyond individual control. Yet, at the same time, it also expressed the inviolability of individual privacy. There was no attempt on the part of the individual dancer to match or to control the social. Vernon Shetley has interpreted Cunningham's work as "an attempt to imagine a form of human society that reconciles individuality and community."[34] It would, indeed, seem that Cunningham restores the public/private split that Duncan had critiqued.[35] The issue of gender here arises in other manners as well because, as Ramsay Burt has pointed out, Cunningham's aesthetic neutrality carries with it "a seemingly indifferent stance toward gender."[36]

I take the loss of what seemed to happen of itself as a loss of the human factor in the equation. I assume that the loss of personality is a phenomenon of broader sociological origin wedded to particular instances of artistic choice.

In 1979, David Vaughan wrote that Cunningham had become more interested in "mass effects" and was creating pieces in which "individuals do not stand out even when everyone on stage is doing something different."[37] However, Vaughan's claim that "Cunningham does in fact want 'character' from his individuals in their way of moving primarily" begs the very question I am raising here.[38] For I argue that a qualitative difference, produced over time, occurs in Cunningham's particular concept of expressivity. There can be no doubt that Vaughan thinks of individuality in a radically reduced field of relative differences, while the desideratum of character from movement seems entirely contrary to Cunningham's philosophy, according to which it emerged naturally. This could be considered a minor issue only by those who undervalue the fact of performance.

Indeed, the performance qualities that enabled Cunningham's choreography to achieve its original impact are too quickly forgotten. What distinguished Cunningham's earlier work was the inner intensity with which seemingly arbitrary acts were danced. At that time, his dancers seemed to move on the borders of a volatile sensitivity. This arresting contrast between the way a piece was structured and the quality of the acts constituting it—particularly in Carolyn Brown, at other times in Viola Farber, and, less overtly, in Cunningham himself—gave that work its unique imprint. Marcia Siegel has remarked that Cunningham wasn't originally "aiming for any standard company veneer or attitude, which is one reason his older works are so hard to revive. Neither he nor anyone else can seem to picture other people in Carolyn Brown's roles, or Viola Farber's or his own." Siegel goes on to associate, correctly I think, the unique presence of the dancers with dramatic intensity: "Because they don't play roles other than themselves, the drama of their movement experience is constantly in play on the Cunningham dancers' faces."[39] It was as if the choreography itself were the "impression" received by the dancers as they articulated it. They remained skeptical of allowing that "impression" to become sensate, withholding it from the movement. One may have seen expression without intention in the dancers' movement, as Cunningham claimed one might, but one also saw unexpressed intention in their faces. That is my point. Cunningham dancers, in their depersonalized concentration, were still people with intent. Because they did not play roles but remained resolutely themselves, Cunningham's dancers did appear as psychological and social agents. Nevertheless, in their performance they refrained from the demonstrative exercise of those capacities.

In her essays on dance, Cunningham dancer Carolyn Brown has stressed the dramatic impact on the performers themselves of Cunningham's early works, even of those based on chance procedure. Of *Untitled Solo* she writes, "though it is choreographed by chance procedures, the atmosphere is clearly and intensely dramatic."[40] What Cunningham had removed through chance procedure was the narrative circumstance rather than the subjectivity of the dancer. His dancers *did* impose their own imaginative order on the choreography in a very subtle way, even as they held their expressive selves in abeyance. That is, while imposing no predetermined forms on their choreographic tasks, they seemed to project a vigilance about how each task might correspond to their internal state. The choreography was not performed as much as tested or tried out with great expertise. They did not, in other terms, project what has since become a look of psychological "emptiness." Indeed, the quality of the dancer's gaze was an important element of the early style. That gaze was intent, at times smolderingly intense, while avoiding explicit dramatic statement. Agency and intent were present in the dancers, though they may have consciously withheld these qualities from their movements. Expression seemed to emanate inward rather than be manifested outwardly. The dancers assessed expressive process by their very enigmatic presence, rather than flatly opposing that process. They inferred a range of intentional objects without expressing them.[41]

Currently, Cunningham's performers appear visually homogeneous with the media's understanding of his "revolution" in what seems to be an attempt to eliminate expressivist values entirely. Their movement reveals nothing about who they are; their presence is both efficient and removed; their movement is in response to the "sensations" of arbitrariness. Cunningham's later work no longer calls expressivist values into question: It has become inexpressive rather than anti-expressivist.[42]

How to may have prefigured this change by diminishing the questions about dancer and subtext—movement and intention—which made the earlier work so provocative. In replacing music with talk in *How to*, Cage was merely switching dissociative practices. Indeed, using talk as if it were a musical accompaniment further stressed the independence of movement and sound. As in earlier work, any correspondences between talking and dancing in *How to* were accidental rather than intentional.[43] Further, correspondences between movement and articulated language were implicitly spoofed by the title, which implied instructions for organized, culturally programmed moves taken from football. The presence of champagne and Cage's drawling diction immediately belied a connection between himself and the athleticism of the dancers beside him on stage. Ironically, this piece failed in part because the audience insisted on understanding it on their own terms. As Richard Kostelanetz points out, "the dancers ineffectively compete with John Cage's compelling onstage rendition of funny one-minute anecdotes."[44] *How to* could not successfully maintain talking and dancing as independent entities as music and dancing could. Cage's recitation overpowered the dancers in part because the audience related solely and directly to the text.[45] Rather than attaining an independence from surrounding media, dancing appeared diminished by them. A later film of the work shows two speakers (John Cage and David Vaughan) instead of the original one. There, at moments, when their speech overlaps and the thread of meaning is lost, one is free to attend to the dancing and a more dynamic interplay between dance and text emerges.

The Cunningham revolution was to have done away with expressivist values and their tendency to impose psychological meaning on movement. Despite that, the dancer's subjectivity was still important in Cunningham's beginnings and is now reemerging as a choreographic issue. Yet the new ex-

Figure 27. Cunningham's *How to Pass, Kick, Fall and Run*.
Dancers: Carolyn Brown, Valda Setterfield, Peter Saul, Gus Solomons, Jr.,
Barbara Lloyd, Sandra Neels, Albert Reid. Photo: Nicholas Treatt.
(Courtesy of the Cunningham Dance Foundation)

Figure 28. Reacting to the onslaught of sensations with ironic abandon. Douglas
Dunn, Michael LaSalata, Jane Townsend, Susan Blankensop, and Grazia Della-Terza
in Dunn's *Wildwood* (1989). Photo: Beatriz Schiller. (Courtesy of the photographer)

pressionism is thoroughly different from what it would have been without Cunningham.[46]

THE AFFECT OF BODIES

In 1975, photographer James Klosty compiled a book of photos in tribute to Merce Cunningham. Many of Cunningham's collaborators—dancers, composers, and painters—wrote short essays or agreed to be interviewed. Dancer Douglas Dunn contributed a poem that can be read as an ironic blueprint for chance procedure:

> Talking is talking
> Dancing is dancing
>
> Not talking is not talking
> Not dancing is not dancing
>
> Talking is talking and not talking
> Dancing is dancing and not dancing
>
> Not talking is not talking and not not talking
> Not dancing is not dancing and not not dancing
>
> Talking is not dancing
> Dancing is not talking
>
> Not talking is not not dancing
> Not dancing is not not talking
>
> Not talking is not dancing
> Not dancing is not talking
>
> Talking is dancing
> Dancing is talking
>
> Dancing is talking
> Talking is dancing
>
> Not dancing is not talking
> Not talking is not dancing
>
> Dancing is talking and not talking
> Talking is dancing and not dancing
>
> Not dancing is not talking and not not talking
> Not talking is not dancing and not not dancing
>
> Dancing is not dancing
> Talking is not talking
>
> Not dancing is not not dancing
> Not talking is not not talking
>
> Not dancing is not dancing
> Not talking is not talking

> Dancing is dancing
> Talking is talking.[47]

This poem appears to chart the relations of opposition, contradiction, and contrariness between talk and dance. What starts out in the poem as a binary opposition between speech and movement, stressed by the tautological assertions that "talking is talking" and "dancing is dancing," is seen in the course of the poem to be mutually self-inclusive. Thus, the poem develops assertions such as dancing is and is not talking, and that dancing is not not talking. At the precise center of the poem talking and dancing are equated. The poem then works its way back out of that classical symmetry to reflect its initial polarization of talking and dancing in a mirror reversal. At the center, however, the poem suggests that somewhere along the spectrum of chance procedure, you will encounter expression theory. Indeed, it is at the precise center of all the dissociative options that expression theory itself materializes as an option. Whether or not it was originally intended to do so, Dunn's poem cleverly calls into question the reductive aspect of Cunningham's project. It envisions aleatory movement as already embodying its opposite: meaningful talk, and by extension, expression.

Intentionally or not, Dunn reflects on chance procedure formulas applied to a work such as *How to*. The refusal to see verbalized sense as the subtext of nonverbal action is, after all, at the heart of choreographic randomness. Without the tactic of chance, subjectivity closes in on movement, determining all its meanings and options. Without chance, dance becomes a form of talk, a conscious coping with meaning and communication. Dunn's poem has the earmarks of a grid analogous to the charts Cunningham prepared before applying chance procedure to the vocabulary of a dance. Options are playfully yet systematically charted for talking and dancing as if these two activities stood for a finite number of preselected choreographic phrases. More importantly, this poem reenacts chance procedure as it affects the audience of a Cunningham dance. It is clearly related to *How to* because that work placed talking and dancing in dissociated contiguity. Dunn's poem describes the effects of talking and dancing falling or not falling together, corresponding and not corresponding. It comments on chance procedure not by a random structure, but by recalling the logically structured series of options that precede the use of chance.

One can attribute this commentary to Dunn's parodic impulse, but it is also true that art critically involved with its own theory is invariably humorous. Perhaps the poem can throw light on Dunn's own choreographic project. His work of the late 1980s makes ironic comment on the conventions of expressivity from within the Cunningham tradition.[48] In his own solo in *Light, O Tease* (1987), in the concluding group dance for the five performers of *Matches* (1988), as well as scattered throughout the solo piece *Haole* (1988),[49] and to some degree throughout the group work *Sky Eye* (1989), Dunn develops an analytic—one might say somewhat self-parodic—but also critically self-conscious view of expression.[50]

Figures 29 and 30. Emotion emerging without gestural forms
to contain it in Douglas Dunn's solo from *Light, O Tease* (1987).
Photos: Beatriz Schiller. (Courtesy of the photographer)

In the solo of *Light, O Tease*, Dunn appears the site of emotional upheaval without narrative circumstance. That is, there are no actions following a logical pattern, there is just movement and anguished, though muted, vocalization. Through that movement, each emotion surfaces as a minor paroxysm, no sooner entertained than abandoned. Each instant is both saturated with "sensation" and short-circuited as expressive gesture. His body accommodates the eruption of sensations as momentary pangs, but never allows them a conclusive conduit toward the surface as correspondingly meaningful gesture. Dunn's body shudders and trembles in response to inner stimuli while never turning those stimuli into recognizable, culturally encoded gestures. What *is* recognizable is their channeling from an "inside" to an "outside" and their gradually increasing intensity. Dunn ends the solo by moving about fluttering his arms like wings, thereby suggesting humorously and self-parodically that we have just seen the hatching of an exquisitely sensitive, highly vulnerable bird. The humor of this moment tends to undercut the issue raised by the solo.

In Cunningham's early work, there was a tension between the dancer and the impersonalized choreographic task he or she performed. In contrast, Dunn conceived emotion itself as a choreographic task.[51] Cunningham's attempt to demystify the conventional rapport between music, feeling, and movement should be understood as a way to escape subjective closure. Dunn, on the other hand, questions that closure by reproducing the expressive fit rather than denying it. Nevertheless, none of the emotional "sensations" he seemed to experience were conveyed as expressive gesture *per se*. In Dunn, the drama of "sensation" has been divorced from expression. Like the Cunningham dancer, Dunn has no expressive intentionality. Unlike the Cunningham dancer, he appears to be the ready conduit of emotional impulse.

In the final segment of *Matches*, although there was occasional hissing suggesting the impersonation of dragons in keeping with the work's oriental motifs, no dominant expressive code—neither contemporary nor historical—organized the dancers' movement in reaction to sporadic "sensations." Those sensations that evidently imbued them were actualized histrionically without being "expressed" in any legible way. Nevertheless, the action of expulsing inner sensation was more pronounced, more dramatic, than in the earlier solo. *Matches* ended in a highly active effort on Dunn's part—subsequently joined by the other dancers—to exorcise "sensation" without expressing it. This was the work's final image. "Choreography," in the conventional sense of patterns of bodies moving in space, appeared abandoned as the dancers, standing fairly closely to one another and descending at times to their knees, flailed about while vocalizing in various semigrotesque postures.

In the examples just evoked, Dunn and his dancers pursued the task of emotion with considerable honesty and commitment. Its status as task was evidenced by the duration of the scenes: A real emotion might have exhausted its gestural gamut long before either of the scenes described came to a close. The realization of the passage of time accompanies another insight: An emotional state does not have to be viewed as motivated by sensitivity to "impressions." Once the audience is led past the first two options—"this is about

Figure 31. Dealing with intersubjectiviy at a formal remove. Douglas Dunn and
Grazia Della-Terza in Dunn's *Sky Eye* (1988).
Photo: Beatriz Schiller. (Courtesy of the photographer)

emotion," "this can no longer be about emotion"—that is, once their expectations of emotional process have lapsed, they are left to examine the tokens of emotional process. With the intentional uncoupling of time and feeling the audience is led toward a speculative reflection on the production of emotion itself. When the rapport of gesture to emotion no longer seems naturally inevitable, other expressive codes become logically possible. Dunn induces his audience to reflect on just such an unpredictable gesture not yet come to pass. His choreography presents it in a nascent state.

Dunn's choreographic strategy, in combination with his use of time, is particularly suggestive of a third, speculative moment according to which expressivity can be redefined rather than simply revived or denied. This recuperation of emotion effectively points beyond the ideological closure of opposites that determine the way we read emotionally charged movement. Classical expression theory defines emotional fields through polar opposites such as joy and sorrow, ecstasy and dejection, whereas Dunn eliminates gestures corresponding to such polar opposites even as he maintains their stimuli. In the terms of expression theory's model, the nature of Dunn's initial "impression" is unknowable because it is not complemented by a gestural counterpart. He opens movement and its emotional subtext to a range of intermediate possibilities. By focusing on the body as a conduit of "sensations," Dunn reinterprets expression theory in a nonreactive manner. In so doing, he reinterprets Cunningham's relation to expression theory by exploiting again its authentic connection to "sensation" but sidestepping the aporia of its negative moment, the reductionism to which it has led.

One could say that Dunn points to an unexplored theatrical organization of "sensation" by avoiding compelling expressive formations. Emotion may be present without including it in the gamut, or mapping it along the spectrum, of any particular semantic field such as joyful/sorrowful. Dunn depletes the recognition factor of emotions by overexposing their intensity without really subscribing to their form. His recent work has moments that put us in visceral contact with theory. Thus, it also demonstrates that expression need neither be rehabilitated by rejecting theory, as Siegel argues, nor discounted in the name of theory, as Sparshott claims.

FIVE

Where He Danced

In the current period of AIDS activism, the primary critical operation of gay studies has been the cultural analysis of homophobia.[1] Focusing on the poetics of disempowerment, this analysis recalls earlier feminist discourse. Like women, gay men are victimized by the projections of a "male gaze," but the issue of the eroticized versus the phobic investment of that gaze affects them differently. The feminist seeks to deny the erotic investment of the male gaze, to expose it as phobic, whereas the gay male exposes its ostensibly phobic quality as a screen for its eroticism. These two strategies—grossly oversimplified here—complement each other but also suggest, in their very complementarity, a theoretical impasse: Two such representations of the desiring male as adversary cancel each other out. As he moves between the feminist and the gay scenario, he is proved to be phantasmic, evicted from the shell of his generic sexual body as an actor who does what he does not mean or means what he does not do; or he merely actively hates, entirely misconstruing his own apparent loving or desiring. Theories of sexual otherness have psychically cross-dressed the anonymous male gazes, only to desert him in a wild "no man's land." Appropriately enough, the men's movement begins with wildness, utter displacement.

Deemphasizing theory, some gay scholars choose to understand homosexuality as a superior naturalism that happens to debunk patriarchy by revising the entangled rapport between homosexuality and patriarchy. The current ethos of gay discourse presses for uncompromising acceptance of gayness as a complex of sociosexual practices. To that end, a common strategy of recent scholarship has been to reinscribe homosexuality in the suppressed subtext of the dominant discourse, thereby naturalizing what that discourse labels unnatural.[2] Despite its aggressive sophistication, this strategy has its dangers. It could stamp gay identity as a historical by-product of male hegemony and thus suggest compulsory homosexuality.[3]

Is it possible that an enlarged concept of maleness is needed, one in which gayness partakes? Could the most radical objective for gay discourse now be to reconceptualize maleness in terms of neither the Feminine nor the ideologically Masculine? By moving onto the terrain of an amplified maleness, gay theory could disqualify, rather than merely subvert, the basis of phobia. This approach might involve relinquishing not the politics of representation but the constant infusion of that politics with figures of desire.

Feminist theory concerned with the specificity of the Feminine seeks a transerotic sense of identity. From Kate Millett to Luce Irigaray, feminism sought to denaturalize cultural assumptions about women while leaving the entity "woman" open to speculative configurations.[4] Alice Jardine, discussing feminisms in search of the specificity of woman, has pointed out that the development of theory tends to relinquish the energy of political activism. Further, what Jardine would call the most theoretical of feminisms, neofeminism, has dismantled biologically determined sexual identity as intrinsic to the structure of the Feminine. Instead of rejecting theory, Jardine argues for the utility of working through theory to establish a subject position. Most pertinently, she contends that

> as long as we do not recognize new kinds of artificial, symbolic constructions of the subject, representation, and (especially) experience, we will be engaging in what are ultimately conservative and dated polemics, not radical theory and practice. It becomes particularly tempting at times of extreme political crisis to abandon this challenge of our century and revert to a "natural view of things": reality is what I hear, see, and touch.[5]

The same dangers are present for gay scholarship, which also needs to place itself theoretically rather than merely to *dis*place, at a time of political crisis, the history of phobias that besiege it. Paradoxically, gay theory may remain a classically libertarian or egalitarian discourse with a twist, not a reasoning on otherness in the manner of speculative feminist theory.[6]

If feminist theory is increasingly the speculative site of a construction of the Feminine disentangled from any erotic subjugation, some gay studies seek quite differently to reveal homosexuality as everywhere already present beneath appearances. Thus, for example, Douglas Crimp divides the world's population into two groups: gay males and "those of us who have obeyed civilization's law of compulsive genital heterosexuality."[7] In this view, which eliminates the lesbian position entirely, male homosexuality is a hidden naturalism and heterosexuality the obedience to an artificially imposed law. Crimp chooses to present *praxis* as *techne*: the *techne* of pleasure. Some gay theory could, therefore, be characterized as an essentialism of desire, in that it partakes of the by-now familiar patriarchal claim to the status of the Natural.[8]

Placing the essence of homosexuality in an affirmation of desire may stem from a profound ambiguity in the position of the gay male: He experiences social otherness but biological sameness. That is, he is basically in a theatrical rather than a speculative rapport with his own nascent "identity" as other. He must always perform that identity, his difference, before he can think it through adequately and imagine cultural possibilities for its assimilation and acceptance. He expresses the affirmation of his unique and difficult subject position by parodying a secondary (or primary) other: woman. Parody, however, necessarily entails the theatrical impersonation of parody's target. And it is difficult for this performance, always a re-presentation, to suggest radical newness: Its theatricality is parasitic on already existent codes. The gay male wishes to exchange sameness for otherness, but he must do so in the very terms of the same. In short, it is more paradoxical for him to figure as a third gender than it is for the lesbian.[9] His difference, instead of redirecting others' performances, squanders its energy in a vortex of appearances, parodies, and ironies. Establishing the gay male *cogito* is an operation never performed foundationally, once and for all, but always one about to be reenacted for yet another first time.

In considering cross-dressing as a historical vehicle for the gay *cogito*, I analyze two performance texts: one pre-AIDS and one contemporaneous with the AIDS crisis. Jean Cocteau's 1926 essay on transvestism, "Une Leçon de Théâtre: Le Numéro Barbette," both proposes traditional gender roles as foils for androgyny and consigns the figure of the androgyne to a "no man's land" outside the tight sexual polarity from which it emerged. The space between life and death recurs significantly in Cocteau's *oeuvre* as a space of sexual difference. The 1988 performance piece *Suiren*, by the Butoh dancer Kazuo Ohno, provides an alternative to Cocteau's poetics of estrangement. An exemplar of difference within polarity, Ohno attempts simultaneously to perform and demystify cross-dressing. For Ohno, "no man's land" is the land of sexuality itself.

BARBETTE'S ACT

Cocteau describes a popular music-hall number performed at the Cirque Médrano by the American trapeze artist and female impersonator Barbette.[10] As the word *leçon* in the essay's title indicates, Cocteau views Barbette's work not as an excursion into camp, but rather as an allegory of theatrical anamorphism. In a set furnished only with a trapeze under the proscenium arch and a divan center stage, Barbette's act consisted of a series of high-wire stunts interspersed with female impersonation on the divan. According to Cocteau, the "scabrous little scene(s)" of impersonation were rhetorically linked to the acrobatic gyrations in the air.[11] Despite the visibly virile prowess exercised in the air, Barbette's performance when earthbound was sufficient to maintain the illusion of his feminine disguise. Thus, Cocteau refers to the sedentary part of the routine as "throwing dust in the audience's eyes," that is, dissuading the audience from processing the otherwise obvious discrepancies between feminine dress and masculine effort as Barbette clambered up to the high wire, swung upside down by one foot, or landed hopping on his feet: his most theatrically "vulnerable" moments.[12]

Cocteau locates the theatricality of Barbette's sexual enigma, however, in his behind-the-scenes preparation. His preliminary cross-dressing actually contains the fundamental paradox to be performed in public, though reversed as in a mirror image. That is, for Cocteau the protoscandal backstage occurs at

Figure 32. Barbette prepares for the unrepresentable transition.
Photo: Gaston Paris. (Courtesy of Roger-Viollet, Paris)

the moment when man becomes woman, whereas the public scandal of the
performance, which Barbette skillfully defuses, occurs in the final moments
of the act when he removes his wig and woman stands revealed as man.

Barbette's preperformance transformation into a woman, as observed and
reported by Cocteau alone, is subjected to a technical scrutiny: It is
"unintimidating" except to the neighboring "showgirls" backstage and yet
ultimately confounding.[13] It mystifies the essayist because, while Barbette
clearly plies his craft with care, his final metamorphosis cannot be tracked
with precision: The female appears on the site of the male as if magically
produced. In failing to account for anything but the gross mechanics of that
transformation, Cocteau also mimics the panic of being caught in a sexually
indeterminate middle stage. Thus, his rhetoric tends to reaffirm stereotypic
male-female dichotomies while denying all possible traces of the middle ground
to be traversed. Even as Barbette covers his face in makeup "like a box of new
crayons" and submerges his body in an "unreal" plaster, Cocteau reports that
the performer "remains a man, linked to his double by a thread."[14]

Once Barbette places the wig on his head, however, his gestural vocabulary abruptly shunts to "feminine," to "the most subtle postures of a woman doing her hair."[15] At this moment "the metamorphosis is accomplished" in a way portrayed as both profoundly disturbing to the male Cocteau and conversely reassuring to the neighboring female performers. They invade the dressing room "talking about fabrics," unconsciously gravitating toward Barbette as like to like. For Cocteau, who can no longer perceive the mechanism of simulacrum, the controlling male double generating feminine gesture from beneath the disguise, the metamorphosis is monstrous: "Jekyll is Hyde. Yes, Hyde! For I am afraid. I turn away. I rub out my cigarette. I take off my hat. It is my turn to be intimidated."[16] Cocteau studies Barbette's ability to inhabit both identities alternately but pretends to balk at their conflation. Throughout the dressing-room scene, and thus in the most improbable of circumstances, Cocteau deals with a rigid sexual stereotype as a cultural absolute.[17] Since there is no perception of a "neither/nor" in an unself-conscious middle ground, no sensible paradox develops. One does not see the man in the woman or vice versa. One only sees the man in the man, even though he is got up in feminine gear. And one is thoroughly convinced by the emergence of the woman who takes the man's place.[18]

Monstrosity—Jekyll become Hyde—is an effect of gender ambiguity historically associated with hermaphroditism.[19] Yet, what is monstrous in Barbette's first transformation is the invisible movement between sexual identities rather than the materialized woman herself newly in place. In other words, what Cocteau considers monstrous is precisely what escapes representation: The monstrous is represented, so to speak, by not being there. Barbette's changing sexual identity is accepted as a fait accompli but unexplored as a process because the crossing of sex barriers, the bridging of incompatibles, is traditionally monstrous. It is discursively elided. Movement between genders would, if represented, inevitably lay bare a natural interfacing instead of a polarization. Or, at least, this crossing movement would reveal the interstitial space as mediating. When he observes its effect on the audience, Cocteau later recognizes mediation as an effect of bisexual spectatorship constructing "the supernatural sex of beauty."[20]

> Barbette's success derives from his ability to address the instincts of several publics in one audience and to assemble these contradictory interests. He appeals to those who see the woman in him, to those who guess he is a man, and to others whose soul is moved by the supernatural sex of beauty.[21]

As the bisexual spectatorship emerges from the conventionally gendered public, the disavowal of ambiguity that was rigorously maintained in the dressing-room scene is transformed into a disavowal of sexual difference.[22] "Supernatural today, natural tomorrow."[23]

Nevertheless, Cocteau does not leave us with this epiphany. Just as his description of Barbette's backstage metamorphosis accentuates essentialist binarism, so the act's final moments allow the audience to "wake up." As

Barbette removes his wig, the audience, Cocteau reports, expresses consternation, disbelief, and profound discomfort, which Barbette appeases in performing a street urchin's dance and other stereotyped male gestures of denial. These gestures reassert the stong initial sexual polarity of the dressing-room scene and thus deemphasize the ambivalence that grounded the sexual crossover. In this epilogue, Barbette engenders a retrospective view of his performance as an elaborate prank and erases the act's ambiguity in the minds of his spectators. They are induced to replace Barbette's androgynous potential with a dichotomous screen memory: the either/or of male/female. The androgyne is bracketed by a collective amnesia.

The focus on conventional gender roles obviates the possibilities of camp in Barbette's act. "If camp has a politics," writes Andrew Ross, "then it is one that proposes working with and through existing definitions and representations, and in this respect, it is opposed to the search for alternative, utopian, or essentialist identities which lay behind many of the countercultural and sexual liberation movements."[24] Perhaps then, Barbette's act, insofar as it is "working with and through existing definitions," might qualify as a piece of protocamp. Yet, should that category be relevant, it must in all likelihood apply to the entirety of Cocteau's corpus, for in diverse ways, Barbette's performance is exemplary of Cocteau's poetic. "Barbette apes poetry, that is why he charms us."[25] On the contrary, though, Barbette's act seems to locate an alternative sexual space in the shadow of conventional difference, in the very ambivalence allowed that difference. Cocteau's amplification of that in-between is invariably a purgatory or semiconsciousness between an imagined male pole (life, activity, and creation) and a female pole (death, inspiration, and immortality): the dressing room versus the stage. Thus, Cocteau emphasizes Orpheus as a sleepwalker both in a 1926 play and a 1950 film of that name, and makes sleepwalking a frequent theme of his work.[26] He often represents sleep as an intermediate stage between life and death, an image of alarming inaccessibility for the living.[27] Yet from within the dream itself the sleeper is an active agent interacting with death, an Orpheus in the underworld.

Barbette's fundamental sexual ambiguity—his androgyny—is folded into the margins of the performance event. He is either a sleepwalker dreaming androgyny or a waking dream of androgyny for the audience, but the intersection of androgyny and full consciousness is excluded. Although the lie of his transvestism tells "the truth" of his audience's sexual indeterminacy, this spectatorship, like the androgynous moment it apprehends, is as fleeting and contingent as its own epiphanic perception of the androgyne:

> Barbette moves in silence. Despite the orchestra accompanying his evolutions, graces and perilous exercises, his number seems to be seen from very far, to be done in the streets of a dream, in a place from which no sound is heard, an image brought to us by a telescope or by sleep.[28]

This is the negative space and negative time of the androgyne. Instead of emerging alongside other options, the sexually enigmatic qualities of the Barbette figure come into focus only in utter isolation, at the expense of contextualization. Sound is bracketed out, and even vision is altered through estranging media. The disjunction of perceptual modes through which Barbette's performance is splintered, transmitted metonymically into new spaces, also opens a new space of sexual "presence." But that moment of thirdness is an imaginative leap away from theatrical realities. It does materialize but only as a prestigious effect of timing. Even as manifested in the wings, androgyny is "out of sight." Onstage, the androgyne appears by spanning the gender divide, by being suspended across and above it. The space on the ground is that of "female" domesticity; the space at the trapeze's summit is conquered by "masculine" prowess. This vision of suspension is also one of effective hiatus or potential disavowal. Sexual ambiguity appears not to be worked out through conventional gender roles—as in camp—but, rather, to emerge in a tenuous nether space that unchallenged and confident polarity permits.

Ultimately, Cocteau's fascination with Barbette resides neither in the impersonation nor in the stunts *per se* but in "this unclassifiable thing moving beneath the lights" and incurring mortal danger.[29] The theatrical lesson alluded to in the title of Cocteau's "Leçon," however, refers to the skillful maintenance of a lie as a sort of balancing act. Cocteau's rhetorical strategy is to blur for as long as possible the vertiginous, "life-threatening" ambiguity in the stereotypic extremes of male and female role-playing. The structure of Barbette's act illustrates a similar rhetoric of evasion, and thus in another sense Cocteau transcribes two performances. One involves cross-dressing, in which, paradoxically, conventional gender norms are rigorously respected. The other consists of the "act" itself, in which the ostensible female emits an androgynous charge, only to be abruptly negated as male. Just as the transitional moment between sexes is visually absent in the first part of Cocteau's essay, so the mystical moment of the androgyne is correspondingly occluded from the overt rhetoric of the act and, ultimately, from the audience's memory. Death, and the death of memory, is interstitial to the gender divide. Gender identity is figured as a binary opposition in which male and female are mutually exclusive and gender liminality is, by implication, a death-defying leap across those boundaries. Androgyny does not actually "take place": the leap is always conceived as a plunge into the nonplace of oblivion, the "*chute d'ange* fall" described by Janet Flanner as the high point of Barbette's act.[30]

Once Cocteau acknowledges the foundational yet invisible quality of sexual ambiguity, he also transmutes it into broader aesthetic preoccupations: Barbette's "solitude is that of Oedipus, of an egg by Chirico in the foreground of a city during an eclipse."[31] In this deathly calm, which Cocteau often alludes to in his 1928 study of De Chirico's painting *Le Mystère Laïc*, the androgyne, like Oedipus, is "an object, an object of horror—an egg, an apple, a T-square, in the foreground of the city."[32] In denying narrative and human agency, these scenes define Cocteau's avant-gardism as an avoidance of bi-nary oppositeness only through an affirmation of deathly agency: enigma as inanimate, visible allegory that has no narrative air to breathe. Barbette's body becomes androgynous the way other "objets trouvés" become poetry for Cocteau: They transform action into thing. Barbette becomes such a thing lost among the footlights, destined to suspend habitual categories of classifi-cation by replacing them with what Cocteau calls emblems of mystery, enigma, asphyxiating stillness: poetry.[33] Like the egg in the foreground of the cityscape, Barbette's androgyne is uncanny: Its fluid sexual profile is reminiscent of Cocteau's contemporary interest in "poésie plastique" as a kind of frozen theater. These objects thematize transformation and metamorphosis in a way that Cocteau would not handle discursively in their application to sexuality (except in the 1928 *Le Livre Blanc*, published anonymously); instead, he devel-oped them in multiple artistic forms.[34] By the mid-1940s, cinema afforded him an indirect means of figuring monstrosity in *La Belle et la Bête* through Jean Marais's triple role. Indeed, film was the medium that allowed Cocteau a needed freedom to move between the discursive and the figural.

In the oneiric voyage down the corridor of a tawdry hotel in Cocteau's first film, *Le Sang d'un Poète* (1930), the poet peers through the keyhole of a door before which have been left one man's shoe and one woman's. Through the keyhole, he sees, affixed to the slate backing of a divan, a chalk drawing of a woman. At the sound of drum rolls, cutouts of a masculine arm and leg are added. Finally a face covered in white makeup also appears.[35] The figure's live hand then lifts a small curtain from before its groin, only to reveal a sign that covers its sex: "Danger of death."[36] This message refers to the dangers of the high wire—the "stage" of Barbette's androgyny—underlined in the same film frame by a spiral to the figure's right. Revolving continuously, the spiral suggests a clichéd cinematic rendering of vertigo just prior to loss of con-sciousness and falling. As mentioned earlier, the high-wire segment of Barbette's act represented to Cocteau the danger of shattering the illusion of femininity, and the divan segments were interspersed to project feminine presence com-pellingly enough to sublimate audience skepticism. The supine figure of the androgyne in Cocteau's film is a visible allegory of the danger involved in equivocal appearances.[37] Like the society lady of Barbette's act, the film's androgyne figure reclines on a divan, suggesting thereby that for Barbette the divan and the impersonation with which it is associated are safety nets. The danger of death is the challenge of performance that explores sexual ambigu-ity before a society (that is, an audience) unwilling to recognize, let alone openly endorse, that ambiguity.[38]

OHNO'S WATER LILIES

Kazuo Ohno's *Suiren* (*Water Lilies*) takes active, if apparently eccentric, part in the representation of unconventional sexualities. The estrangement of Barbette's androgyne finds its counterpart and extension in Ohno's cultural

Figure 33. "The desperate rendez-vous of the Hermaphrodite,"
from *Le Sang d'un Poète*. Photo: Sacha Masour.
(Courtesy of the Museum of Modern Art/Film Stills Archive)

estrangement. Ohno works from across cultural and sexual divides by addressing issues of sexual identity through a positioning of Western art in the Japanese dance form of Butoh.[39]

In *Suiren*, Ohno addresses himself to displaced self-portraiture in Western art, with particular reference to Monet and Chopin, just as he had earlier addressed himself to Western dance through his solo work *Admiring La Argentina* (1977), his impression of the Spanish dancer La Argentina. As is well known, Monet's water-lily series, like much other postimpressionist painting in France, was inspired by Japanese art and culture.[40] Monet constructed his own water-lily pond, Japanese footbridge, and garden on his property at Giverny. This Orientalist landscape was Monet's life model from 1899 until his death in 1926.[41] Ohno's dance refracts Monet's water lilies from the simulacrum of their own representation by performing possible denizens of Monet's landscape.

In the first part of *Suiren*, Ohno's heavily made-up whiteface acts as a mask impersonating "woman" and recalls the stylized tradition of the No drama, in which men play the roles of women. Yet, he is in *fin-de-siècle* Western attire: His ankle-length dress is intricately adorned with lace and ribbon, and his accessories include pumps, parasol, and elbow-length gloves cut out to reveal his fingers. This segment is accompanied by the croaking of frogs, interspersed with a wind threatening the garden's calm. On an empty stage, Ohno follows imaginary paths with an uncertain gait, but his progress is resolved by the gestures he fashions with his hands, which often seem to catch up with him and overtake him. His gestures frequently serve as a form of self-cloaking or help express extreme elation or rejection. One hand sometimes rests on the other, both palms cupped and facing down. At other times, he holds his hands delicately before his chest with his little finger protruding both decoratively and demonstratively. The excessive fragility of a historicized social persona called "woman" emerges not from the figure's appearance *per se*, but from the suggestion of the feminine to itself as the relation of hand to face in a state of slow motion, awestruck *sensibilité*. Ohno walks with feet parallel, one foot tentatively replacing the other, and occasionally ends on his back with feet in the air and knees bent. Each successive movement phrase invokes the memory of some imagined interaction. In the course of this scene, the garden sounds modulate into an "Ave Maria."

Throughout *Suiren*, Ohno interprets the emotionalism of Western Romantic music (Chopin, Schubert, Liszt) and the femininity of a certain Western dress and gestural code, thereby underlining the historically Western equations among emotionalism, dance, and femininity. Reproducing the Western sublimation of emotional content in nature and its corresponding estrangement from the male, he seems to convey that only a sufficiently antiquated feminine figure could demonstrate and sustain such frail sensibility. He walks, languishes, and gestures furtively, hopefully, and then resignedly on a bare stage. His physical tentativeness, transmitted by the peculiar immobility of his neck and the small scale of his paces, reveals woman as a deconstructed man, while his actual frailties (Ohno is now over eighty) are transformed into signs of the morbidly dainty. Ohno appears to practice a form of reverse "japonisme" from within one of the Occident's own sublimating representations of Japan: the water-lily series. That is, a Japanese artist frames himself in a Western image of Japan to express his desublimated vision of Western emotionalism, an emotionalism that entails translating certain artistic values into sexual terms. Ohno's impressionism is a middle voice, one in which the female and the male necessarily frame each other, speak from within simulacra of each other.[42]

Toward the end of the first segment of *Suiren*, a younger man in a modern beige suit (Yoshito Ohno, the choreographer's son) appears behind the elder Ohno as a shadowy figure, perhaps an image in the "woman's" memory, whose arms are frequently aloft as though oppressing "her." Ohno seems not to see or respond to this male figure but nonetheless to experience him. Once Ohno leaves the stage, however, the younger "male," moving to the accompaniment of Japanese rock music, performs an impotent and frozen version of "her" earlier feminine gestures.

After this scene, Ohno appears as an old woman wearing a loose yellow kimono and carrying a staff. He makes slow progress across the back of the stage to the sound of thunder, which is followed by the high-pitched chanting of a falsetto "spirit" voice. A simple white feather is attached to his hair and

Figure 34. Kazuo Ohno in *Suiren*. © Linda Vartoogian, New York.
(Courtesy of the photographer)

to the end of the staff, which he polishes with the robe. During this scene, the staff becomes a weapon, a cane, and a phallus, while the robe changes from garment to cape to shawl or blanket. By partially disrobing during this segment, Ohno successfully presents his elderly male body as a female one, despite the obvious physical disparities. This uncanny effect is evidently dependent on Ohno's intention to present his body as a conceptual space of sexual splicing. Conflating nature, hackneyed femininity, and emotion, Ohno addresses the repression of the male in that Western system. The male character has no place in the triad except that we unmistakably perceive his physical body supporting this disguise and conveying these representations.

The structure of *Suiren* rests on a symmetrical alternation of its two male performers, who impersonate male and female roles in tandem, occasionally dividing the stage but never significantly interacting. They suggest the sexual polarities of Barbette's act, yet they do not exploit polar extremes as a foil for less defined positions.

A third scene features Yoshito Ohno in a long, filmy dress, with a large flower in his short hair. Though he sketches a series of *bourrées* and some hops reminiscent of Isadora Duncan's choreography, he does not attain the spatial or energetic scope of "dance." Later, Kazuo Ohno reappears in a feminine wig, whiteface, and a dark suit. Performing to Chopin, he both impersonates Chopin and dances in direct, interpretive rapport with the music: He "plays" the dance. In this scene, Ohno is doubly cross-dressed, since some remnants of the transparent feminine disguise (hair, makeup, gesture) form the armature of his Chopin figure. In fact, throughout *Suiren*, each new representation of sexual identity is founded on a deluded origin. When Yoshito Ohno first appears in drag, for example, no attempt has been made to transform his hair or makeup accordingly. During the final segment, the younger Ohno returns as a woman with a parasol and a long coat, his back to the audience—a shadowy muse giving focus to the older Ohno's enthusiastic Chopin.

Between the presupposition of a feminine inside and the evidence of a masculine outside, Ohno's performance compresses the odor of flowers and a hackneyed body language of feminine delicacy. This gestural delicacy becomes detached from dancer and role. Roland Barthes, describing the Bunraku puppets, notes that their "codes of expression are detached one from the other, unglued by the organic cement which maintains the occidental theater."[43] Ohno's performance is not concerned with the fixing and subverting of identities that usually occurs in Western theatrical cross-dressing. His cross-dressing does not play into or exploit the prestige of those illusions; rather, by playing "away" from them, Ohno abandons both illusion and delusion.[44] "Work," Barthes suggests, "is substituted for interiority," and work like Ohno's, which holds polarities at bay, is also a third term for theatrical theory: neither subjectivism nor alienation.[45]

Ohno's theatrical lesson, or at least its effect on us, consists in maintaining *dis*illusion. While Barbette ultimately reveals the source of his audience's delusion, Ohno has tipped his hand so that one observes him not as sexual

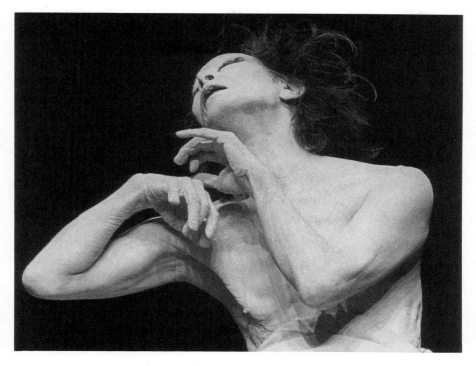

Figure 35. Kazuo Ohno disrobing in *Suiren*. © Jack Vartoogian, New York.
(Courtesy of the photographer)

uncertainty, but rather as a manipulator of sexuality's signs. In consequence, his ambiguity shifts from the question of sexual identity *per se* to the identities of genders as shapers of feeling from within experience. His transvestism is foreign to us because it speaks of disparate sexes in one body without invoking paradox or inviting us to delude ourselves about the "truth." Perhaps, in a Barthesian sense, Ohno moves "across the divide of sexual expenditure" by finding a third term "which is not . . . a synthesizing term but an eccentric, extraordinary term."[46] In attempting to transcend the double bind of *doxa* and *paradoxa* (whether male and female, heterosexuality and homosexuality, or dress and its crossing), Ohno may be in search of just such a third term, "which is not a synthesis but a *translation*: everything comes back, but it comes back as Fiction."[47] Since the third term does not pass through conventional binary gender distinctions, its cross-dressed manifestation "emulates" binarism without any parodic energy. It suggests that "sexual opposites coincide without fusion."[48] Barthes characterized Bunraku puppet theater in similar terms: "Bunraku mocks these opposites, this antinomy which rules all our ethic of discourse. In taking up a fundamental antilogy, that of *animate/inanimate* (present moreover in the very structure of the Japanese language) Bunraku obscures it, dissolves it, without promoting either of its terms."[49] So does, in

Ohno's performance, Butoh. Like the aged body of Ohno, a body virtually unsexed by age in this theatrical setting, the fictive body as third term assumes roles nonparasitically, through reminiscence rather than polemical masquerade. Ohno considers that his age endows him with a theatrical presence neither lifelike nor deathlike, although closer to death than to exuberance. He characterizes good Butoh performance as that in which "the dead begin to run."[50]

Thus Ohno's interpretive gestures vis-à-vis music also have deconstructive force. His moribund yet passionate figure expresses desire instead of soliciting it. Ohno's transvestism, a device that distances his audience from sexual polarities, makes polar extremes seem artificial and avoids theatricalizing their margins as transgressions (*paradoxa*). His aging male body is intentionally exposed as an improbable support for clichés of feminine distress conveyed with an outmoded sense of delicacy and loveliness. Ohno's performance has no place in the literature of hermaphroditism if we consider the hermaphrodite as a feminization of masculine traits and, consequently, as a figure of male-male desire.[51] Ohno questions gender polarities more philosophically, perhaps, by escaping the boundaries—thematic, cultural, but also libidinal—of that literature.

Ohno does not assert a redemptive, pastoral vision of sexuality. His position is neither "before the law" nor in a utopian beyond.[52] I am not arguing through Ohno for some ahistorical status that would also be disempowering but rather for newness. If the classification hetero/homo presupposes a hermeneutics of the self whose connection to sexuality has been called into question since Foucault, then why should gay theorists, in founding gay identity, seek a history that is internal to such a hermeneutics? Instead of producing that simulacrum of blending that we see as sexual ambiguity, Ohno simply opens the binaries to the possibility of mutual self-inclusion, folding their outer limits toward a center that is not conceptualized but purely performed. That performance suggests neither sexual blending nor a clinical doubling of the two sexes in one body but, rather, a range of differences that bodies lay claim to.

In an interview with Christie McDonald on feminism, Jacques Derrida has discussed the idea of a nonreactive choreography, which might also summarize the effect of Ohno's performance: "I believe in . . . this indeterminate number of blended voices, this mobile of non-identified sexual marks whose choreography can carry, divide, multiply the body of each 'individual' whether he be classified as 'man' or 'woman' according to the criteria of usage."[53] Similarly, Ohno's cross-dressing is fashioned from the death of both genders, their "blended voices," engendered through the meeting of physical age and anachronistic stereotype. Ohno appeals to a theoretical interfacing of sexual identities without engaging a "discourse" of desire. Barbette both negates and conserves gender polarities. His androgynous high-wire suspension is the phantasmic product of two active voices that remain apart from their projected actions: the male voice says, "I play woman"; the female voice says, "I am man." The androgyne is asserted in a "no man's land" by no one. Barbette's "truth" is the deathly indeterminacy between the two lies of gender polarity; his theatrical lesson is to embody Cocteau's "lie which always tells the truth."[54] Ohno's "truth" in *Suiren*, by contrast, is the death of gender as *the* theatrical polarity founding public space. Ohno asserts his "maleness" in middle voices whose mode is to reflect his action back on himself, and he traverses innumerable unmarked positions free of reactive parody. He performs a through- rather than a cross-dressing, abandoning the lateral model in which dressing "across" still confirms the old hermeneutics of the self at its terminal points. Ohno's dressing "through" suggests a voluminous or depth model in which any and all gender attributes—biological, dispositional, sexual, vestimentary, gestural—are subject to recombination at uneven intervals and to unequal degrees. He performs through transparent dress but does not "dress up" to perform. Through-dressing bypasses the lateral model of binariness because it avoids both parody and prestidigitation. It does not place a new configuration on the same axis of "truth as appearance" as the systems it would subvert. Rather, it suggests a nonontological model of gender performance not bereft of depth, not reliant on death and resuscitation.

Appendix

Left-Wing Dance Theory: Articles on Dance from *New Theatre*, *New Masses*, and *Daily Worker*

The following is a selection of articles treating American modern dance from a left-wing perspective. These writings appeared in *New Theatre*, *New Masses*, and the *Daily Worker* between 1929 and 1937. Although dance reviews also contained interesting theoretical insights, this appendix features writing with a theoretical approach to the problems of choreography, dance, and realism versus modernism.

THE LOVES OF ISADORA
Michael Gold
New Masses 4 (March 1929)

Isadora Duncan was a genius.

That word has been so cheapened by hacks it has no meaning left. But it can be applied to Isadora.

She destroyed the Ballet. She restored the Dance. Her work marks a new epoch. Her work is permanent.

She set humanity free in a new and important way.

2.

Among savages the dance was a sacred art. In "our" civilization it became a sex perversion, and a form of ostentatious waste.

The dance is probably older than speech. It is the poetry of materialism. Animals dance. It is their mating speech.

Among our hairy savage fathers, the dance was the speech of philosophy.

The dance was man's first comment on earth, fire, air, love, sun, plant—the world.

There are sacred dances thousands of years old. Their emotions are as exactly organized as science.

3.

Under "Christianity," the primitive dance split into two streams.

One was the folk dance, the mass joy of the people.

The other was the Ballet, fungus of the courts.

The ballet expressed the sterile formalism of the courtiers, their parasitism, their cheap, useless elegance.

The ballet ruled Europe for two centuries. It had no rivals, and seemed secure as the European thrones.

Generations of flunkey art critics chanted its praise. Its stupid acrobatic stunts were worshiped as if they meant something.

No one dared attack the ballet in the art world. This would have been Bolshevism.

No one had any alternative to suggest. The dance instinct had become atrophied.

4.

Isadora Duncan, a little Irish-American girl born of a poor musician's family in San Francisco, arose like David.

She toppled the giant fake to the ground. She was a new primitive. She discovered the motor of the savage dance. She created a new dance. She was a genius.

She did what Walt Whitman had done for poetry. She ripped off all the corsets. She let herself go. She denied the rights of private property in the dance. She made it free for everyone. She rushed into the sunlight. She laughed at the technical acrobats. She sneered at their mindless, soulless dancing.

Her dancing was not a stunt, but her philosophy of life.

She inspired others. Hundreds of new dancers have followed in her trail. Dancing has mystery in it again, and belief.

The court ballet now seems as futile and old-fashioned as a hoopskirt.

5.

This should have been enough for Isadora. Walt Whitman was satisfied with one career. But Isadora entered upon a second career.

Love!

In her book, "My Life," (Horace, Liveright, publisher) Isadora never spells Love without a capital letter.

O Love! Love again! Her book is one of the great autobiographies. Isadora was as direct as a man. She tells about her dozens of lovers, the famous and the infamous.

Among the famous ones were D'Annunzio, the operatic tenor, antique collector and world-known thesaurus.

Another was her last, Sergy Yessenin, a mad, gifted young Soviet poet who hung himself in exhaustion.

Isadora describes her men lovingly. She holds no grudges. This is not a book like the ones Casanova and Frank Harris used to write in idler days. Isadora does not crow and ask you to admire her prowess. She is not defiant or Luciferian.

She is like a mother who has had 22 children, and has loved each in turn.

Isadora is charming. She suffers through the 22nd accouchement as romantically as she did during the first. This is a gift.

6.

The old sex standard, based on private property, is breaking down in this revolutionary day.

The penalties have been lessened, and everyone has begun to practice Love.

Bernard MacFadden has made it popular in the tabloids, and Margaret Sanger now offers it as a cure for poverty and war.

V. F. Calverton, an authority, has made a statistical survey of the rubber goods counters in Baltimore drug stores. He declares almost the entire population of Baltimore has been converted to the philosophy of Life and Love.

Love is respectable now. Businessmen come to Greenwich Village on pilgrimage, and drink at the many fountains of Love. Congressmen mention it in speeches, and the President of a Bank recently admitted to a reporter he had read a book on Love.

There is no doubt of it: Ping-Pong and Love are the two most popular indoor occupations in America today.

The movement has triumphed! And Isadora Duncan was the Joan of Arc of this mighty movement! Her sacrifice was enormous! She suffered, and suffered, and suffered—Christ, how she suffered!

7.

She was a genius, and a wonderful woman. But it is difficult to accept her prayerful approach to sex. She sounds too much like the novels of Laura Jean Libbey. I wonder, does every woman feel that way about Love?

Sometimes I suspect Isadora is the first woman who has written down what every woman actually feels about Love.

If this is true, the future is a black one for males. The day will come when the human female will devour the male in the moment of Love, exactly like a female spider or locust.

8.

Sex will become free as air. This will be good. No one will have to think about it anymore. No one will pray to it, or feel noble or degraded over it.

Sex is the mechanical means by which life is continued. Lobsters and buzzards, equally with man, use this mechanism.

It is not intrinsically sacred, except in the sense that all life is sacred.

What has given it its mysticism, its poetry, its romantic beauty is the human mind.

When sex is free, friendship will assume its rightful importance.

And the social instinct will be found as fiercely romantic as the sex instinct seems today to repressed Americans.

The human mind can do all this.

It should. Sex has become a sort of bourgeois opium. It is a form of escape.

When sex is free, men and women may become friends. They are not friends at present, they are enemies and lovers.

9.

Poor Isadora! Her life held tragedies. But it was a crowded and glorious life, and one worth living.

All of us must suffer and die. This is not too tragic. What is tragic is that so many millions suffer and die in a gray fog [of] futility.

Isadora, with her splendid flamboyance, made speeches at her dance-concerts.

"Yes, I am a Red," she said once, "and I am proud to be one, because most people are Gray."

She was a Red, but not a real revolutionist. It was all emotion with her, glorious and erratic.

She was a genius of the transition period between two worlds, a forerunner like Walt Whitman.

She prophesied the future, when in a free society there will be neither money nor classes, and men will seem like gods, when the body and mind will form a radiant unity.

Her own mind and body approached that unity. But she was the product of an environment, and never shook it off.

She sensed the future, but she would have been unhappy if forced to live in that future.

With all her beautiful Platonic theories, in actual life she was spoiled like most stage prima donnas.

Some intimate followers and friends have written two books recently about Isadora.* The books are an anti-climax. They are like reports of a valet who reveals his master's secrets.

Irma Duncan whines and whines. She whines about Soviet Russia, and Isadora's hardships there.

She never lets one know for a second that 140 million people were suffering more extreme hardships during the time. Thousands of them even passed beyond the luxury of whining. They died.

Yes, little Irma complains that during the famine period Lenin and the Soviets had no time in which to provide Isadora with adulation, money and Parisian comforts.

Isadora Duncan's Russian Days, by Irma Duncan and Allan Ross Macdougall, Covici-Friede, N.Y. $3.50. *The Untold Story—Life of Isadora Duncan*, by Mari Desti, Horace Liveright, N.Y., $3.50.

This book should not have been written or published. It leaves a bad taste in the mouth.

Irma has not a word to say about workingclass Russia, and the great creation of a world. She is busy with gossip about crazy Bohemian artists, and the men who gave Isadora good things to eat, and sleek "cultured" Soviet bureaucrats, the ones that had not yet been caught.

Isadora gravitated to this kind of crowd all her life. It was not her fault, but the fault of her world.

She was a Californian, too, and at the end returned to the native blanket, and used a ouija board, Irma tells us.

Never mind. Hurrah, Isadora, you will never be forgotten! You had the courage and open-handedness of an old-time cowpuncher. You were a good sport. You were a genius.

You were a prima donna, too, but it was not your fault. You were born hundreds of years too soon, and in the wrong country.

THE TASKS OF THE REVOLUTIONARY DANCE
Nell Anyon*
New Theatre (September/October 1933)

To clarify the tasks of the revolutionary dance today it is necessary for us to understand the position of the modern bourgeois dance. Let us confine this discussion to the dance as we know it today in the studio and on the concert stage.

The well known dancers today are a direct product of the post-war period and the decline of capitalism. What is it their dances express? Are their themes in any way connected with the turmoil that is life today? Examine some of their dances: "La Valse", "Dytharambio", "Gymnopaedia", "Monotony Whirl", "Wood-block" and all the allegros, andantes and scherzos. Are these more than an empty presentation of some technical achievement? Dancers today are vying for prestige in creating striking and original dance patterns.

Take another category of modern dances, "Primitive Mysteries", "Shakers", and Mary Wigman's group dance "Der Weg" (The Way). Is it that we have exhausted all current material as a source of inspiration for the dance that we must go back to the primitive, mystic, and puritanical peoples for our theme? With capitalist society hanging by a thread surely we have a great deal to dance about that directly concerns us today.

The dance of today is on its way to perdition because it has made no contact with life, because it deals with trivial subjects, with abstract dance interpretations of rhythmic patterns or musical compositions. It has been swept into the private studios of individual dancers to express their intense personal moods. The dance of today is declining because it is steeped in commercial

---

*Nell Anyon was the pseudonym of dancer Nadia Chilkovsky.

careerism and opportunism. In this period of crisis, it is only another way for young dancers to earn a living. It has become the property of Broadway managers who care nothing for the real dance interest that has awakened in thousands of young people, but who will buy the "Best Seller." An owner of such a best seller has recently characterized the current Broadway attitude toward dancers in these bitter words: "Today I am famous because I can turn a somersault in the air. Tomorrow someone will show a double somersault and I will be thrown on the trash heap."

The dance has degenerated into a commercial enterprise to amuse the public, and the dancer must necessarily work on those things which big producers teach the public to like. Thus the gradual elimination of the art of the dance.

All history has shown that the dance reaches its peak simultaneously with the highest point in the development of the state. The decline of the art of the dance has also coincided with the decline of the state. Records show that the dance at its height was an instrument of education and culture and its source of inspiration and thematic material had its roots in the existing state.

Today the dance makes no conscious effort to express the conditions created by a disintegrating social system. American dancers consider their art as above their actual lives. Thus we have dances of "the life of the bee" and none of the lives of working men. Their dances are neither optimistic nor pessimistic; they do not express a conscious social view point. However, this conscious avoiding of the subject in itself indicates a passive adherence to bourgeois society.

There is one salvation for the dance today. Dancers must look to the future, to the eventual destruction of capitalism, to the building of a new society for their source of inspiration. Our way lies in the direction of collective mass activity, seeing the dance as a vital part of all revolutionary Theatre Arts. It is necessary, therefore, to consider the dance in a much broader sense. The essence of revolutionary drama is the expression of ideas and emotions arising from the struggle of the working class. It deals with the vital factor of life and activity among masses of workers in relation to their social existence. This demands an all embracing theatre technique. The content of our class struggle plays, with all the tension of class conflicts, with all the surging emotions of an awakened social consciousness, with the call for revolutionary action, is of necessity too overwhelming to stop at the spoken word. At such times when words become inadequate the proper conviction can be carried only through the medium of dance movement. It is a particular task of revolutionary dancers to reawaken the dance as a part of all dramatic expression. Dance movement must not be confined to carefully developed compositions, but must become an important part of every dramatic speech. The significance of all spoken words must be emphasized with gesture. Above all, in the revolutionary theatre it is important to develop dance movement in connection with rhythmic mass recitation of revolutionary slogans. This will result not only in making the revolutionary theatre a more potent educator, but it will also lead to the development of a dance that will be a true dramatic expression of the creative working class.

DIAGNOSIS OF THE DANCE
Emanuel Eisenberg
New Theatre (July-August 1934)

Revolutionary art is obviously not art which either announces, or depicts soberly in advance, the revolution; the completely automatic recording machine can do that just as well, and bourgeois artists are as slick at the game as any, if only because it is picturesque, dramatic and exciting. True revolutionary art demands an authentic and informed revolutionary point of view—and if I seem to labor a sheerly verbal truism, I plead as justification the occasion of their second annual Festival and Competition which the Workers' Dance League gave in Town Hall on Saturday night, June 2, before a large and distressingly (but understandably) unenthusiastic audience of comrades and sympathizers.

Since none of the dance groups is more than two years old and most of them of far more recent origin, one is constantly and reasonably cautioned not to "expect too much." The inevitable retort to that—at least from this highly concerned commentator—is that nobody expects anything from anybody: If a body of young workers is interested in preparing a theatrical presentation, either as dance or drama, and they need many months of rehearsal and experimentation and thinking through, it is doubtful if anyone would want them to perform before they feel ready. But once they reach the point of entering a public national competition and offering themselves as professional entertainers before large audiences, the natural and simple reaction is to evaluate them from the highest possible standards. And by these the evening of June 2 was a distinct and disheartening failure.

It would be manifestly unfair to maintain as a blanket indictment that the dances given were not *out of* or *towards* the revolution but *around* and *about* it; yet this is so close to the truth that the temptation to make a sweeping generalization is very strong. Out of twelve conceptions only the *Van der Lubbe's Head* of the New Dance Group, the *Comintern* of the Red Dancers, and the *Pioneer March* of the Junior Red Dancers did not follow the pattern of the evening.

This pattern, broadly speaking, was along the following lines: Six or ten young women, clothed in long and wholly unrepresentative black dresses, would be discovered lying around the stage in various states of collapse. Soon, to the rhythm of dreary and monotonous music they would begin to sway in attitudes of misery, despair and defeat. The wondering observer in every case was brought to the choiceless, if tired, realization that this must be the proletariat in the grip of oppression: not because that was one of the many decisions it was possible to come to, but because the program gave titles indicating both theme and contents—and the groups performing were known to have a revolutionary intent.

The swaying would continue for a couple of minutes in the rhythm of utter resignation . . . and then, a vision. Uprising. Revolt. Sometimes it came in the form of a light flooding suddenly from the wings of the balcony; sometimes in the form of sheer music intensity; sometimes as a dynamic figure in red, running passionately among the startled tragedians; once it was in the incredible person of a soap-box orator who moved both hands and mouth in an appallingly inept realistic parody. And always the group would respond with victory: hope had arisen, strength had come, freedom was won, the revolution had arrived. There was never any basis for the introduction of the new motif. Deadly swaying and intolerable oppression had gone on long enough, so a revivifier entered the scene and turned it from grave to gay. No problem of method. No transition. Break from your chains and go forth to the open world.

Now this theme, considered purely as a theme, is certainly not a contemptible one: so much the opposite, in fact, that indignation and outrage arise precisely because a shockingly inane treatment makes it seem something that should possibly never be attempted by anybody. Yet, even in the recital under discussion, two groups managed to make something of it. But the *Scottsboro* of the Red Dancers and the *Uprising* of the New Dance Group were so weighted down and overshadowed by the rest of the evening that their nearness to dramatic truth and contextual convincingness was as nothing to the audience.

To depict oppression and persecution it is not enough to have young women teetering jerkily as burden-bearers. The nature of the burden cries for clarification; the origin of the attack must be vividly implied; the physical and moral effect (and not the hollow postures of resignation) demand to be communicated. For what possible value can it have to those not yet class-conscious and those not yet stirred to significant action to be shown a pageant of blank mourners having a very sad and distinctly unanimated time? What should be shown seems so glaringly plain that I hesitate to venture into literalism for fear of blundering into absurdity. Still, here are some suggestions of the specific aspects created by oppression and persecution in the world of work: terrified cringing; hypocritical lip-service; tubercular sweat-shop deformity; exhausting and etiolating field-labor; the twisted emaciation of overwork and underpay and undernourishment; the sheer jitters of uncertainty, humiliation, unpredictability, unselfconfidence. On the basis of such physical features and their cognates the dancer can proceed to choreographic symbols as broad and abstract as he pleases. So long as there is no departure from something intrinsic in our daily lives; so long as a serious and appreciable recognition can take place in the audience; so long as the picture made is instructive and dynamic and exciting and not a cross-section of post-oppressional phenomena given for their own drab sake.

A parallel criterion applies to the depiction of the arrival of the revolution. The revolution is not a bright white light nor suddenly violent music nor a street-corner orator nor even an active girl in a red dress. These are poetic simplifications which can be useful, in spite of their acute banality, as references to a known thing, as stenographic reminders of an undergone experience or a well understood concept. But, while it is valuable to tell your audience that mass congregation, mass rebellion and mass usurpation of power should be the immediate steps consequent to oppression and persecution, this is a ridiculously and fantastically inadequate configuration of the mere outlines of the revolution. Far from touching the revolution itself, far from seizing it and fixing it and projecting its innermost meaning, it offers a wholly useless sentimentalization of freedom or liberation or any "idealistic" vision anyone wants to put into it.

Constructively, then: how shall the revolution be choreographically conveyed? There must be symbols richer, truer and fuller than music, a color or a light. And there are. The revolution should be presented as a whole way of life rather than as a liberating vision from almost anything; it should be seen as a struggle, an upheaval, a reconstruction, a tremendous project. And, clearly, it is imperative to define the fighters as the proletariat—because, again, anyone might seem to be struggling for anything, with no intimation of the worthiness of the cause. We have, then, dancers who are definitely workers straining under the specific burdens and oppressions which workers know and which the audience will recognize as conditions surrounding their own existences (always as dance, of course always as meaningful movement). The burden grows beyond bearing and they strain forward to protest—or one of them, more alert than the others, brings an awareness of the possibilities of rebellion. When they rise it must be unmistakably against someone, not merely out of the depths. When they mass together, it must be in a representative demanding body, not merely as an electrified group that is aspiring somewhere or other. And when they march into the revolution, it cannot be as a vaguely joyous aggregation surging toward the nondescript freedom of unrestricted territory, but as workers proceeding to a higher work, as builders, as executors of a large scheme, as informed and responsible sharers in the possession and the cultivation of the earth. Anything else is dreary bourgeois emotionalism and involves no more than an audacious superimposition of neo-revolutionary gestures on a decayed, juiceless and deceptively earnest body.

But all this lengthy talk is no more than preface to the full contents of the revolutionary dance. The theme of revolt against exploitation is a sound and important one; but surely it is only *one* and is far from meriting the misrepresentation of being almost the only idea which an evening of eight competitive workers' groups will offer a hungry dance audience. What are further themes? As initial answer I point to the three dances of the evening at Town Hall—and a half-good fourth dance—which ventured into other paths than the easy ideational road of abuse-awakening-amalgamation-revolution. *Pioneer March*, done by the Junior Red Dancers, children from about five to eight, was lame and "cute," but at least it had the quality of sheer community animation and cooperative joy. *Comintern*, one of the Red Dancers' offerings, lacked color and vibration, but it, too, gave a stirring sense of the strength of organization in numbers and the cleanness of willing coordinated action. *Van Der Lubbe's Head*, the New Dance Group's prize-winning dance, set its face in the highly laudable direction of current events and the blindingly vivid depiction not only of their literal actional values but of their political origin and their eventual significance. *Contempo*, the half-good dance, given by the Rebel Dancers of Newark, opened with a striking if completely naive and undeveloped motion picture of many different kinds of workers performing their various functions . . . and then went on to a tragedy-depression pattern. But its opening had at least revealed a fourth direction.

Group vitality, group power, dramatizations and analyses of political events, conversion of workers' movements into designs of dancing; here, surely, are tendencies worth studying and cultivating and elaborating to the highest degree. They are just as much qualities of the drama as they are of the dance, it is true, but this is scarcely anything that militates against the employment of them for choreographic values.

And then, where is comedy, the happy depiction of small absurdities in the struggle toward revolution? Where is folk-legend (the Negro, the Indian, and the European races from which so many of us are so recently derived)? Where is folk-dancing? And where is satire, the ruthless exposure of bureaucracy, hypocrisy, pretension, affectation, benevolent despotism, disguised fascism, impotent socialism, fake and opportunistic "workers'" parties? Where is the heightened realistic visualization of what we demand of life and what we would like our world to do? The coming to class-consciousness, the observation of the specific evils around us, evictions, strikes, demonstrations, the training and reconditioning of children, the changing of "human nature," the despair and futility of the church in the face of world crisis, the unabating pleasures of the rich, the mockery of legal procedure, the imprisonment of distributors of "insurrectional" literature, chauvinism, armaments, commercial ballyhoo, international relations, the mingled loathing and fear of Russia, the increase in naval and air fleets . . . all this could and should be authentic and exciting material for the revolutionary dance.

Any true projection of the countless motifs demands thorough familiarity with the life and demands of the worker, clear-headed grasp of the phenomena of the world directly around us, and an unwavering vision of the urgency of hastening—and the methods of producing—the revolution. Such a point of view can and must be developed by all of the groups that took part in the competition. For the most part they have a high degree of technique—with the exception of the appallingly ungifted, untrained and inert New Duncan Group. All seem able to think. When they come to understand the emotional bourgeois origin of most of their otherwise admirable training, when they acquire a new body style that is directly related to the literal physical functions and the general psychological background of the workers of the world, and when they become completely documented on the decay of capitalism and the necessity for communism, then the revolutionary dance movement will begin to take on meaning.

THE MASS DANCE
Jane Dudley
New Theatre (December 1934)

The mass dance, or choric dance, as well as the folk dance, can be put to revolutionary uses, the extent of which has not yet been tested. Large groups of lay dancers, even at times the most superficially trained people can, by careful direction, set simple but clear patterns of group movement into a form that presents our revolutionary ideas movingly and meaningfully. The dancer learns to move communally, to express with others a simple class-conscious idea. In this way, large numbers of people can be mobilized not only to dance but to observe, and through the discussion of the theme and the problems of movement brought forward by the leader and dancers, clarity of ideology can be given. Certainly the clarification that will come with the discussion of the theme at the end of the class, plus the experience of dancing in groups of twenty or thirty people such a theme as strike or anti-war, cannot fail to educate (propagandize) the members of such a mass class. The following is an outline of procedure and specific directions for the formation and teaching of a class in mass dancing.

Themes for a mass dance should be chosen as well for importance as for timeliness, e.g., current events, important days, historical events in the class struggle, anti-war issue, Negro rights, class war prisoners, Fascism. Care should be taken, however, that the approach to the theme is one that underlines the important issues and interprets them correctly, and that the approach to the theme is a *danceable* one. These classes should be called either at regular intervals, or during important events (such as the textile strike, San Francisco general strike), or before or on important days, i.e., May First, etc.

Twenty or thirty people are essential for this class, and as many as fifty can be used if space permits and the leader is skillful. Laymen interested in dancing can participate, and members for the class can be drawn from all groups, since no one technic is necessary. For accompaniment, such instruments as drums, cymbals, piano, gongs, even voice, chants, songs, are valuable, and should be used in order to provide rhythm, and so keep the unity of movement, and to help build intensity.

Finally there should be a chairman to lead discussion before class begins, and after class when questions are asked, and an actual dance leader for the class who can direct large groups of people, who understands the nature of a mass class, and who understands the theme as a revolutionary dance leader. A committee should be formed to decide on the theme and leader. The committee's responsibility would be to see that the leader thoroughly understands the theme. The committee can also handle the organizing of the class, the sending out of notices, selecting a studio, etc.

Before the class begins, discuss the theme decided upon. If an event, describe it, and interpret it. If a day, give history of day, its significance, etc.

In order to give the members of the class an understanding of what it means to move together as a group, a few simple exercises should be given, such as standing together and swaying from side to side, walking together backwards and forwards, sinking down and rising up. These are exercises purely on a movement basis. It is possible to color the exercise by adding meaning to the movement, e.g., the group should go towards a point as though asking for something or demanding something. What must be remembered is the goal—*achieving a group sense in the class.* The group is not a collection of solo dancers; the unity of everyone's movement should be worked for.

After these exercises, the leader begins on the theme. In the directing of this theme, several facts should be kept in mind. Choose movements that are simple, not limited to one technic, and movements which a dancer, no matter what her training, can do. Choose movements, the sequence of which must be suitable to group dancing. Remember that the more members in a group the more unwieldy it becomes, and the slower must be the changes in direction. For this reason, the simple, fundamental steps—the walk, the run—are the most useful and effective. Think of the possibilities in the walk—marching, creeping, hesitating, rushing forward, being thrown back, the group splitting apart, scattered in all directions, uniting, coming forward, backing away, being thrown down, rising up. For this one does not need "steps," *pas de basque, tour jeté,* etc. All that is important is the movement of the group in space. Keep in mind the technical level of the group. More difficult parts can be given to the better trained members.

The leader tells the group or groups how it begins, what the movement is, where the movement is directed, how many times the movement is done. She gives them a phrase, as much as they can easily remember. If the first phrase of movement has been correctly danced, the leader can go on to the next phrase or section. In this way piece by piece the dance is built up.

The process of building the entire dance may have taken an hour. Parts will have been repeated; it will have been danced through up to the place where a new part is to be added. By the end of the period, the dance should be done. It can be danced through three or four times by the group. It need not take more than three minutes to perform. It will of necessity be simple. It must be moving, especially to the participants. It must have significance. It is the leader's duty to emphasize this significance to them, explain it to them. Her description of the theme, of the movements, must be vivid, must mobilize the members in such a way that they throw themselves into the dancing of the theme.

As an example I will try to describe a mass dance suitable for a group consisting of any number of people. The theme is *Strike.* It is the conflict between pickets who call to the workers within the factory to put down their tools and come out on strike, and the militia which stands as a wall between the pickets and the workers. For the theme three groups are needed, the pickets, the militia, the workers. It is the leader's first job to divide the large group she has into three smaller groups, and to tell each of the three which part it takes. She explains how the dance starts. The rear of the floor space is for the workers. She puts them in a formation in groups of three or four depending on their number. To all of them she gives the same rhythmic work movement, a large swing perhaps so that it can be seen. She tries the movement out with them; sees if they can do it all together, exactly at the same time.

In front of the workers she places the militia. In this group no more are necessary than it takes to form a line across the width of the space, the members placed at least a step apart. They are facing the audience, on guard. The dance starts. The workers begin their movement. The militia stands on guard throughout the first section. After the rhythm of their movement has been established, a picket enters. He crosses the space—recrosses it; another picket enters; pickets come singly, in pairs, four at a time. It is a chaos of people passing back and forth in front of the militia. Slowly this chaos resolves itself into a unified group which turns, faces the workers, leans forward. With raised arms they call the workers out. The workers stop, turn. The militia shoulder their guns.

This is the first section of the dance. Those who are the pickets must enact the sequence of their entrances. The first section is a continuous crescendo climaxing in three sharp accents. One: the pickets turn to the workers with raised arms. Two: Workers stop. Three: Militia shoulder arms.

The first action should now be danced through two or three times so that the group grows more familiar with the sequence of movement. When this is done the leader outlines the next part—the conflict between pickets and militia. The militia on this part stands as a wall between the pickets and the workers. They do not move from their place until the end. The quality of their movement is brutal, explosive as the shot of a gun, sharp as the edge of a bayonet. In these qualities lies the approach to movement for the militia. If one merely copies (pantomimes) the action of shooting, brutality is lacking. But, by using the actual gesture of shooting only as a basis, and the qualities spoken of above as the means of amplification one adds the emotional impact. The quality of the movement of the pickets in contrast is dynamic, the crescendo and the decrescendo of swaying forward, being thrust back.

The first section ends with the militia shouldering their guns. The arms of each picket, which had been raised to call the workers, sinks and the pickets slowly back away from the guards. But this withdrawal is a preparation. The whole group of pickets surges forward. The militia strikes down. The group is thrust back unevenly. The group attacks again, but this time in sections. And in sections it retreats, preparing to strike again. One side charges forward on the diagonal to the center and is forced back on the diagonal to the other side. The center of the group rushes forward. Its front ranks are mowed down by the stroke of the militia, like tall grass under the stroke of a scythe. The whole group is now massed on one side.

During this there has been no movement on the part of the workers. Now from the group of pickets one breaks away, runs toward the workers. They lean towards him. The militia raise their arms, but as the picket backs away another from the group runs forward. This time the workers move to the side where the pickets stand. Now from the group of pickets single members break away, run towards the workers; they are thrown back by the militia and one is thrown down. Again the two forces face each other as at the beginning. Meanwhile the workers have shifted their group from the side to the center. As the pickets one after the other call them out, the workers, a few at a time, will shift positions into the center in back of the militia. The tension within the group of workers grows. As the pickets prepare to attack, the workers raise their arms to break through the militia. As the pickets move towards the militia the workers, their group wedge shaped, lunge forward. The line of the militia splits in the center. Through the opening surge the workers to join the pickets. From the center the workers and pickets together press the militia back to each side. Here the dance ends.

DANCE
WHICH TECHNIQUE?
Ezra Freedman
New Theatre (May 1934)

Despite frequent and prolonged discussion as to the technique revolutionary dancers should use, there is still some disagreement. The disputants fall into three main groups: (1) The advocates of one or another of the bourgeois schools who think that their particular technique is best suited for revolutionary themes; (2) Those who think we must develop a purely revolutionary technique; (3) The eclectics, who believe in choosing what is best for our purpose from what all the bourgeois schools have to offer and rejecting whatever is not useful to us.

Since progress will be most rapid under a unified program, let us attempt to achieve some sort of working unity. Each one of these three groups has something definite to contribute toward solving the technique problem.

The first, and perhaps most conservative, category would limit us to the point of stifling. We must remember that any particular bourgeois technique was invented as a means to project the intellectual concepts of its creator. It is doubtful whether even the total intellectual concepts of all the bourgeois dancers to date contain as much revolutionary energy as is latent in any one of our recognized revolutionary dancers. It is much less probable that any one of the aesthetes, mystics, escapists and what nots among the bourgeois dancers has devised an instrument capable of bearing the full weight of our message. Certainly no single bourgeois lens has sufficient scope and limpidity to pass the powerful light and images that we conceive without much blurring, loss and distortion.

The second contention, that of the "ultra-radicals," goes much too far. It would leave us with very little or nothing to work with. To discard even the valuable contributions to the dance of the bourgeois schools would be comparable to the folly of a Soviet automobile factory abolishing the belt method of mass production merely because Henry Ford, a member of the hated capitalist class, originated it. No one can deny the desirability of and eventual necessity for a characteristic revolutionary dance technique, but it hasn't arrived yet and we cannot knock away the old props until we have built new ones under us. Improvement of the ideological content of our dances comes first. Then we must fashion the technical instrument which will be the most accurate projector. Only as our ideology improves will the need for new technique spur creative work in this field.

The eclectics, who comprise the "center" or "liberal" party in the technique controversy, although possessing the most plausible policy, are nevertheless incomplete. Because their bag of tricks is bigger, they are apt to become too confident of its all-sufficiency and neglect the acquisition of new technique which will become more and more necessary as the class struggle and the building of socialism, our ideological basis, inevitably grows in volume and intensity.

The revolutionary dancer belongs to no one school, but belongs to all, yet stands out distinctly from all the rest, head and shoulders above them, by virtue of his contribution of vital ideology and the beginnings of a revolutionary technique. He realizes that the revolutionary dance was not miraculously conceived out of nothing at all; that it must, for a while at least, retain many of the characteristics of its forbears, the various bourgeois schools.

We must first enrich and vary the ideological content of our dances by drawing from the most fertile soil and environment of the class struggle. Then, in the interpretation, while applying the techniques we know, we must ever be on the alert and keep questioning: Is this technique the best for this particular passage? If we alter it somewhat, will it be more suitable? Can we perhaps invent something that will bring out our meaning more clearly than anything hitherto known? By this means the new technique will grow naturally out of our work. We will never arrive upon it, however, by merely arguing about the merits of this or that technique. Technique is nothing, does not exist for us, unless considered in conjunction with the idea-material to which it is to be applied.

We must ever be on our guard against dogmatism and the inertia of contentedness and not cling relentlessly to any particular technique, even if it be our own creation born out of hard work and sacrifice, when changing conditions call for change or alteration. We must rather be pliant, mobile and dialectical, with the enhancement of the class struggle as our measure of progress. If our art, of which technique is an essential factor, becomes intimately bound up with the class struggle, then it must advance as inevitably as the class struggle is advancing. (This article is published as discussion material in preparation for the Workers Dance Festival to be held in June.)

THE DANCE OF DEATH
From "Change the World!" column
Michael Gold
Daily Worker (Thursday, June 14, 1934)

I attended, recently, an evening devoted to the proletarian dance. Some ten different groups participated, and at the end of the evening, you forgot which had been which. The dances had many fine titles: Scottsboro Dance, Anti-Imperialist Dance, Dance of the Red Army, etc., but over them all hung the same gray twilight, the same incredible monotony of death.

If T. S. Eliot has influenced the proletarian poets, it is Martha Graham and Mary Wigman who have almost ruined the dancers.

Graham is a very gifted bourgeois dancer whose work expresses the despair and death of the present system. Her mood is that of the psychiatric ward and the graveyard. Sometimes, like T. S. Eliot she tries to escape from her torture chamber into a primitive mysticism, but even here she cannot shake off the disease that is destroying her.

Martha Graham may be a great artist. Morbid subject matter doesn't preclude that. But why should our proletarian dancers, who have something new and different to say, follow her technique so slavishly?

Where is the elan, the courage and passionate warmth of the revolution? Is this rattling dance of corpses on Walpurgis Night around the coffin of a corrupt world OUR revolution? Can you inspire the workers to struggle with such a dismal message?

Comrade Dancers, have you really nothing of your own to say? Has the revolution meant so little to you? Do you think you can keep this up forever—this labelling a gray standardized sterile dance by Martha Graham by a hundred different titles—Scottsboro, Anti-Fascism, etc., and make us accept the product as revolutionary?

THE REVOLUTIONARY DANCE MOVEMENT
Edna Ocko
New Theatre (June 1934)

The dance, because it immediately establishes rapport between audience and performer, is a remarkably flexible vehicle for the conveyance of revolutionary ideas. It concretizes a situation more graphically than music, with more mobility than painting, and at times, with more poetic beauty than the drama. Ideally, as the film, it is the projection of movement-forms into space and time; its focal point, however, instead of being the externalization of an idea or sequence of ideas (viz. drama, film), is the depiction of kinesthetically realized emotional states. In the revolutionary dance, these emotional crystallizations, apart from technical considerations, must be compounded with not only "sympathy" for the working-class movement, but a thorough intellectual grasp of Marxian dialectics as well. Our true revolutionary dancers cannot be those who from time to time include on their programs numbers possessing vague "revolutionary" titles or still vaguer "revolutionary" ideas; as yet they pay only body-service to the movement, and a perfunctory one at that. Working-class ideology, no matter how thinly sketched, cannot be a superficial integument slipped on to any skeleton of a dance technic, nor can it be an innovation in movement imposed on to an idea that becomes revolutionary by annotation.

The revolutionary dance can emerge only after the significant (revolutionary) emotion and the mode of expression have moved together for so long a time and have interpenetrated the composition to such an extent that the very movement of the dancers has revolutionary implications and the very idea arises not from casual inspiration, but from a living with and a thinking for the proletariat. It must be so subtle a welding together of manner and matter, of emotional content and dynamic ideational form, that it can, at its best and greatest agitational heights, commandeer revolutionary mass feelings of the profoundest and most stirring sort, and project proletarian ideas of vast implications on the one hand, or specific everyday class issues on the other. And it is beginning to do so. More and more is it becoming part of the daily cultural education of the working-class, more and more is it entering the theatre as vaudeville ally of the drama (vide: *Newsboy,* prize-winner at Theatre Competition), more and more is it assuming through performance on the concert stage an independence and vitality never before enjoyed by this type of art in the bourgeois world.

Yet it remains one of the most shabbily treated of all the revolutionary arts, with its progress being unquestionably retarded by the total disregard it receives from professional workers in other fields. Artists in the vanguard of the revolutionary movement from whom the dance groups are so eager to receive criticism and aid, neglect to a reprehensible extent the work of these people. Either they retain unpleasant associations of bourgeois dancers of the past whom they once observed, or else they receive erroneous reports of the actual work of these groups; at any rate, they have remained, out of misguided preference, totally detached from activities in this field. They have failed to realize the potential drawing power of the dance for the masses, and the importance that a movement of such dimensions should not only be adequately publicized, but painstakingly analyzed and directed.

At present, our revolutionary dancers and dance groups are part of the *Workers' Dance League.* This coordinating body has 800 dues-paying members. In addition to its performing units, it has twelve amateur groups and over 50 classes. It has an Eastern section comprising groups in New York, New Jersey, Pennsylvania, Massachusetts, and has formed groups in Chicago,

Detroit and Los Angeles. It has received information of a revolutionary dance group in Paris, and one in Berlin.

One of its aims at this time is the building up of performing troupes so that they can reach ever-increasing masses of people through dancing at strike halls, union meetings, affairs, benefits, concerts, etc. and activize more of their audience into sympathy and cooperation with the working-class movement of which they are a definite part.

They have contacted a tremendous audience already. On January 7th for the benefit of the *Daily Worker*, these performing groups presented a program of dances at City College Auditorium. Not only was the hall full (seating capacity 1,500), standing room sold out, but hundreds were turned away at the doors. On April 20th these same groups performed, again a benefit, this time for the *Labor Defender*, at the Brooklyn Academy of Music to a capacity crowd of 2,000. Between October and April, the W.D.L. had requests for 240 paid performances, of which only 140 were accepted, due to limited forces. Assuming that only 200 people attended each of these 140 affairs, which number is ridiculously small, considering the fact that among the performances are numbered those at the U.S. Congress Against War and Fascism, when 6,000 packed the St. Nicholas Arena, the *Daily Worker* Bazaar at Madison Square Garden and the 10th Anniversary of the *Daily Worker* at the Bronx Coliseum, the League performed in one season before about 34,000 workers.

Nor do workers alone attend these performances; the faces of the most important bourgeois dance critics, dancers, pedagogues, and students appear time and again, watching with an admixture of admiration and envy; the one for the indubitable talent the groups possess, the other for the cheers the audience gives a performance that is not solely an exhibition of physical virtuosity, but in addition, a presentation of revolutionary working-class ideology and rich emotional content. John Martin, dance critic of the *New York Times*, in an article appearing there, refers to the W.D.L. as one of the most important trends in the American dance. "E.E." of the *World-Telegram*, who seems constantly at variance with Martin on other issues, in his review of the April recital, not only substantiates this praise, but commends the groups more specifically.

Who are these groups? At the time of the April 20th recital, they were the Red Dancers, the New Dance Group, the Theatre Union Dance Group, the New Duncan Group, and the Modern Negro Dance Group. These groups in toto represent all technical trends in the American dance today. The Red Dancers and the Theatre Union Dance Group stem from the Martha Graham School, the New Dance Group from the Mary Wigman School, The New Duncan Group from its namesake, while the Negro group is a product of the now deceased Hemsley Winfield, the witch-doctor in *Emperor Jones* at the Metropolitan Opera House. On June 2nd, these groups again performed at the Second Annual Dance Festival, which was held at Town Hall with both amateur and professional groups competing. A new group had been added at that time to the list of performing units, the American Revolutionary Dancers, and a

Children's Dance Group was presented for the first time. *Van der Lubbe's Head*, performed by the New Dance Group to a poem by Alfred Hayes, was awarded first place at the competition, with the *Anti-War Cycle* of the Theatre Union Group and the *Kinder, Kuche und Kirche* of the Nature Friends Dance Group receiving second and third places respectively.

There is no doubt that these groups as a whole have among their numbers some of the best of our young American dancers today, giving up the fame they could undoubtedly achieve in bourgeois circles on the basis of their talent, to be active in the revolutionary movement. Soloists, however, have not as yet been encouraged, and it is the groups in combination who offer a full evening of outstanding revolutionary art.

Yet the Workers Dance League, with these groups as a nucleus, has unending promise. Its future is assured it by the generous masses who support each concert with unwavering enthusiasm. Besides a completer artistic and ideological development in its own ranks, it looks forward to a more friendly acceptance of its activities from co-workers in other fields on the cultural front, whose traditions are more firmly entrenched in the movement and whose assistance could be of great benefit. One cannot be too urgent in requesting that support be given to this popular ally of the worker's movement in the United States.

PERSPECTIVES OF THE DANCE (excerpt)
Harry Elion
New Theatre (September 1934)

During the past few years I have watched with keen interest the development of the Workers' Dance movement. One cannot deny that much has been done toward the development of this field of proletarian culture. However, while I was watching the dances presented at the Dance Festival it became clear to me that a thorough examination of the aims and methods of the workers' dancers is necessary if the dance movement is to make immediate progress. The weaknesses so glaring in almost all the dances result mainly from a lack of understanding of the relations between content, form and style. Although one could notice a general improvement in the mastery of the technique of dance form, the content, though selected from class struggle events, did not get across the footlights clearly. It was as though content and form were not integrated but paralleled. At times content overshadowed form and at other times form completely obscured the content. This seeming contradiction between improved technique and lack of clarity in expression is the very basic difficulty of dancers. It arises from the rigid adherence to formal technique when the question of a new content is involved.

It is a generally accepted principle that revolutionary art form is dependent upon its content. This principle was reiterated at the last Dance Convention and was accepted as a basis for work. When we examine the content of the various dances presented at the Festival we find that most of it was abstract. In *Bruno Tesch Memorial* dancer after dancer walks to death of his own free will. Intuitively they are drawn to the butcher's axe. These dancers may have reason for doing it, but the audience was never let in on the secret.

In the same manner were the dancers in *Dirge* attracted by the light. In *Uprising* they were drawn, just as intuitively, upward, forward, as a moth is drawn to the light. Certainly terror, upsurge and uprising are manifestations of a very bitter class struggle. In this struggle every gain, every defeat is a result of terrific class conflicts. If the subject matter of workers' dances is to be class struggle, these conflicts must become more apparent in the content of the dances.

If the workers' dancers honestly and truly make it their task to use the manifestations of class conflicts in life as content for their dances, the form of the dance will of necessity have to undergo some development in the direction of becoming more dramatic. I stated in my introductory paragraph that most of the dances failed to develop their subject matter. This failure was due to the fact that the dance embodied no conflict. Development without conflict is impossible because such conception is undialectical. Every dynamic art form must base its conception upon conflict. Eisenstein formulated this principle in the following manner: "In the realm of art, as the fundamental basic principle (this dialectic principle of dynamics incarnates itself in conflict) of the substance of every art-work and every art form. For art is always conflict."

The static influence in the dance conception comes from the bourgeois dance. There is only one way to overcome this influence and that is to make dramatic development, or conflict, part of the dance form.

The problem of style and its relation to the content of the dance requires a thorough analysis; for it is in the field of style that the workers' dances show most the influence of the bourgeois dance. The dance images with few exceptions are not derived from the content of the dances but from some preconceived styles. As a result it would probably be necessary to equip every member of the audience with a dictionary, defining the meaning of every movement in order to make the dance understood. If the content of the dance is a specific incident in the class struggle the basic image, in order to be communicable to the audience, must be derived from the incident and not from any abstract movements. The content of a dance, if it is specific and not abstract, will provide a basis for a communicable image. From the particular the general is derived. Lenin formulated this truth in the following passage quoted by V. Adoratsky in *Dialectical Materialism*:

> The approach of the mind (of man) to a particular thing, the taking of a cast of it (in other words, an impression) is not a simple direct act; a lifeless mirror reflection, but a complex, twofold and zig-zag act, which harbors the possibility that the phantasy may entirely fly away from reality; what is more, it harbors the possibility that the abstract conception, the idea, may be transformed (imperceptibly and unwittingly on the part of man) into phantasy (and in the long run into God). For even the simplest generalization and the most elementary general idea is a fragment of phantasy.

How much more are we subject to flying away into the realm of phantasy when we begin with the most abstract ideas, such as *Uprising* and *Upsurge?*

The researches into the art creations of the aborigines can teach us much in this regard. Harrison writes in *Themis,* p. 44, that

> . . . when the men return from the war, the hunt, the journey, and re-enact their doings, they are at first undoubtedly representing a particular action that actually has taken place. Their drama is history, or at least narrative; they say, in effect, that such and such a thing did happen in the past. Everything with the savage begins in this particular way. But it is easy to see that if the dramatic commemoration be often repeated, the action tends to cut itself loose from the particular in which it arose and becomes generalized, abstracted, as it were. The particular hunt, journey, battle is in the lapse of time forgotten or supplanted by a succession of similar hunts, journeys, battles, and the dance comes to commemorate and embody hunting, journeying, fighting.

This is not only confined to the savage but is the life history of every idea or concept. The dancers can learn from this that if they proceed in the same manner to dance out the specific incidents of the class struggle they will in due time acquire a dance language which will enable them to represent struggle in general. This does not mean that they will remove the "possibility" of getting into the field of phantasy.

The contradictions between the facts that the dancers have reached a higher level of technical development while the content of the dances remains obscure, results from the fact that while the dancers generally accept the proposition that form is derived from the content, their preoccupation with the existing technique in the dance makes it impossible for them to carry this truth into practice. The dancers cannot find the solution to their difficulties in the study of the contemporary dance alone; they must acquire a historical perspective of the dance in its relation to other cultural forms and to society as a whole. When they do this they will of necessity come to the conclusion that while dance throughout its history had its internal development, it had to undergo changes in accordance with the demands placed upon it by every change in society as a whole.

LADIES OF THE REVOLUTIONARY DANCE
Emanuel Eisenberg
New Theatre (February 1935)

In a remarkably short period it has become a convention of rebuke against the revolutionary dance that it suffers from obvious enslavements to the forms and patterns of bourgeois technique. The complaint has been exceedingly mystifying to many; they are earnestly convinced that there is an absolute abstract foundation of sheer training and skill and that this can be exercised toward any chosen end. Does not content determine form, they want to know, and must not an authentic revolutionary concept automatically produce its sound objective and architectural counterpart?

As one of the more persistent of the complainants I should like to attempt a justification of the stand that there is such a thing as bourgeois technique which is distinguishable from other potential techniques and which is harmfully and preposterously irrelevant as the basis of a revolutionary approach to the dance.

The majority of revolutionary dancers are extremely recent converts to the cause—and there is nothing the matter with this, except as a partial explanation of their inevitable and unyielding methods. They present themselves as *ladies*; they have the aspect and psychology of ladies; their behavior is always that of ladies.

Many studied at the Wigman school; more with Martha Graham; some with Irma Duncan; a few with Humphrey-Weidman, Tamiris, and Fe Alf. In each instance of break and departure the dancer believed that her days of estheticism, preciosity and self-expression were happily past. Having a trained body capable of moving with any agility or delicacy or intensity, she could proceed to adapt this infinitely useful instrument to choreographic depictions of hunger, oppression, charity, hypocrisy, uprising, strike, collectivism, racial fraternity. The transition of a dance called "Mater Dolorosa—Quo Vadis, Anacreon?" to a dance called "Song of the Worker" had been accomplished with shining facility through a sudden intensification of energetic movements, a glow of red in costume, a brief but hearty session of practice at clenching the fists.

Now this is no attack on the titles of revolutionary dances, although they are artless enough in their gigantic scope and frequently do the embarrassing job of expressing more of the dancer's ideas than her actual movements. Nor is it a dissatisfaction with costume and theme, two sore points on which I have expanded before in the pages of NEW THEATRE and which deserve further extended treatment of their own. The point is that the revolutionary dancer has made no pictorial—theatrical or political—cultural progress whatever, although internally the new locale and horizon may have affected her immeasurably. As a performer on the stage, she looks exactly like her avowedly bourgeois sister, with the simple and negligible difference that she appears to have gone off on a labor-slumming holiday and is showing her liberal-sympathetic audiences what those interesting working people think about and go through. She is essentially presenting a character dance; she is someone pretending to be somebody else through mood assumption and soul-state, for, by the cultural conditioning of a training and a style, she is still and unmistakably the Lady of bourgeois ideals.

Technique is fundamentally a formalization of the cultivated instincts and impulses of any given period. And in such anatomical-representational arts as the dance, an ideal standard figure has corresponded with uncanny precision to the social philosophy of each era. The soulless manikin of the ballet, with utterly inhuman ethereality on the one hand, and fantastically overdeveloped gymnastic dexterity on the other, served wonderfully as a symbol of isolated diversion for the aristocracy during the seventeenth, eighteenth and nineteenth centuries. And the romantic dream-obsessed Lady, with a "free" (though sometimes muscularly disciplined) body, and a Mind unfettered enough to explore the profoundest recesses of her Soul, is surely the ideal standard figure which the predominantly middle-class culture of the last forty or fifty years has produced and has handed over with necessary intactness to the revolutionary dance movement.

Observe this dancer as she moves about the stage. (I refer to the performer in the feminine for the simple reason that soul-expression has a particular fascination for the unoccupied *bourgeoisie*. The epicene male, revealingly enough, has been almost the only kind attracted to the dance during its middle-class reign.) Her hair hangs free to her shoulders, her garments flow in unbroken line from hip to ankle, her feet are bare to show you that she is unbound in any way. Carriage is the truest index to psychological state—and the mock-elegant erectness of her spine, the firm gentleness and delicacy of her head on a taughtly arrogant neck, the gracious serenity with which she sways or merely occupies space, all bespeak the dignity and secure community position of the spiritual-intellectual Lady. Observe the play of her wrists, the lift and slump of her shoulders, the recessive agitation of her torso, the linear tensity of hips, buttocks and thighs, the calculated purities of geometry in the pedal movements, the sheer indulgence of her presence on the platform.

If I seem to have given arbitrarily qualifying phrases to actions which are understood as normal physiological functions in the dance, it is not with the intention of disparaging any of the accomplishments in pictorial form but of underscoring the ideational foundation on which all technical development rests. For it is nonsensical and valueless to deplore that a dancer's spine is erect, that she can exercise her wrists with exceptional suppleness, or that she can lift herself wholly in the air while resting on her elbows,—and then expect indignation. These are good things within a good framework. They are befuddling and exacerbating hangovers of symbolic bourgeois idealism when the performer is clearly not one who has been trained to strive toward any identification with her audience, whose whole presentation has been a kind of personal neurotic confidence into a curtained confessional, whose approach and behavior have been that of a cultured, superior and withdrawn lady, momentarily and graciously on display.

Generalizations, always dangerous, are particularly to be avoided here, and I hasten to anticipate some of the sure exceptions that will be offered in protest. Suppose the statement of the ideal standard figure really applied to the bourgeois dance, how would this explain the highly abandoned maënad, the impish gamin, the grotesque clown or the disembodied fantasy-creature who are often the subjects of their compositions? None of these would seem to be indicative of the Lady. But they are. On the one hand she is exposing her "human" and subliminal Freudian preoccupations, always a "respectable" compulsion; on the other hand, she is offering a small group of "different" and vagrant portrait-fancies for the comprehension and delectation of a restricted and precious audience. The test of the *haute bourgeoisie* is her loathing of popular appreciation. She may be saint, clinical case and pagan—just as it is the classic privilege of aristocracy to be vulgar—but she begins and ends by being a Lady.

Now where, the revolutionary dancer will impatiently break in, have you ever seen this Lady in action in any of our programs? For one, we are invariably a group, thus destroying the individual soul-dance; then, we are always to be found in a state of electric vitality; further, we enact themes we can prove the audience to be concerned with; finally, an unshakable vision conditions all of our characterizations and redirects all of our movements into a new set of patterns.

The contention remains. Training and technique have molded the dancer to the point where her whole picture of suffering—for an example—is founded on bourgeois neuroses. The symbols of discontent, misery and unrest are still derived from psychoanalysis and iconography, two definitely related forms of world-escaping opiate. The movements of rebellion and protest are absolute parallels to those romantically circular and inspirationally upward-straining gestures of "release" which characterize bourgeois nonconformity and individualism. The satiric body style in revolutionary dancing not only lacks distinguishability from the precise equivalent in the bourgeois dance (vide Martha Graham, Angna Enters, Agnes de Mille, Charles Weidman) but even fails to achieve as sharp a social edge as theirs. And the new-found vitality and militancy are additionally reminiscent of the ideal standard Lady because their wide-eyed stepping Toward The Light is psychological-aspirational and so unspecific as to be interpretable by any vision one selects.

I am aware that the sheer pointing out of origins in style and similarities in movement proves nothing in itself. My effort is to account for what I feel is the grave and almost unrelieved failure of revolutionary dancers to win over any true new audience. Their agitational titles and infrequent story-telling interludes avail them very little indeed, since the opening and closing movements present the entrance and departure of distant, selfconscious Ladies—and all body manipulation has been based on obscure foreign symbols from a romantic-individualist world.

Any diagnosis of this kind seems to demand the suggestion of a cure: and here I am at a real loss. The counteragent to bourgeois training in the dance is scarcely a hurling of oneself groundward on all fours and an extravagant series of simian faces in the name of the revolution or the proletariat; yet this would appear the alternative to so dreary, juiceless and outmoded a figure as the Lady. But no one has yet dared to be so cocksure a prophet as to predict the form the novel, painting, music and drama will or should take after revolution, and I am relieved to be equally unoppressed by the urges of vaticination. What the other arts have succeeded in doing, however, is in finding a partial language of communication with people which promises eventually to speak to all the workers of the world. Let revolutionary dancers ponder their failure to create genuinely receptive and responsive audiences. Let them grow aware of the extent to which their physical artistic functioning has been infected by sickly bourgeois concepts, let them strive to rediscover the essential and universal instincts and impulses of the body which are not related to class labels and class ideals—and let them then create the technique and methodology for a dance which we can all have the natural empathic urgency to join, even if we are without training and sitting spectatorially in an auditorium.

A REVOLUTIONARY GENTLEMAN
New Theatre (March 1935)

To *New Theatre*:

Emanuel Eisenberg's piece, *Ladies of the Revolutionary Dance*, printed in your February issue, may be useful to the revolutionary dance movement only as an example of the kind of extreme "leftism" that has long been discredited and discarded by most active workers and critics in all fields of revolutionary art. Stripped of its high-sounding vocabulary, this article amounts, in substance, to a complete denial of the very existence of the revolutionary dance. For one thing, Eisenberg maintains that "the revolutionary dancer has made no pictorial—theatrical or political—cultural progress whatever" (!) since "on the stage she looks exactly like her avowedly bourgeois sister, with the simple and negligible difference that she appears to have gone off on a labor-slumming holiday and is showing her liberal-sympathetic audiences what those interesting working people think about and go through." For another, he speaks of "their failure to create genuinely receptive and responsive audiences" as of something taken for granted. Every type of style and technique presented by the various revolutionary dancers and their groups, the more-revolutionary-than-thou critic condemns as "of the devil," of bourgeois origin, as "befuddling and exacerbating hangovers of symbolic bourgeois idealism." What, then, is left of the revolutionary dance movement? Nothing, indeed, but a misnomer—if we are to accept Eisenberg's appraisal.

Fortunately for that movement, Emanuel Eisenberg is talking through his hat. The revolutionary dance has scored a sensational success precisely in the manner of creating "genuinely receptive and responsive audiences"; and if there is any one thing that distinguishes a revolutionary from a bourgeois dance program, it is precisely the compelling sincerity of the performers, their revolutionary and militant verve, *their oneness with the mood and political ideology of the proletarian and revolutionary audiences*. Instead of the revolutionary dancers' pondering their "failure" to create responsive audiences, would it not be advisable for Eisenberg to ponder his own failure to take cognizance of facts? And instead of denouncing these dancers as insincere and out of contact with their audiences, perhaps he should make a canvass of both the dancers and their audiences? To build a "theory" on such an obvious denial of facts is to build on something less substantial than nothing.

But what of the "theory" that all revolutionary technique, as now current, is of the devil, of the "haute bourgeoisie"? Well, I think our ultra-"revolutionary" critic fell in love with his own cussword—calling the revolutionary dancers "ladies"—and simply cannot part with it. So much so that he ingeniously invents a whole "theory" to match his "clever" epithet. As a matter of common sense (not to speak of the Marxist view on the cultural heritage of the past, which may not be binding for Emanuel Eisenberg), revolutionary art must and should borrow from the accumulated experience of the past, even if stored up by the bourgeoisie. No responsible revolutionary artist or critic will maintain today that we must start with a clean slate, wiping off all that the bourgeoisie has created in the course of centuries. Perhaps *flaneurs* in the field of revolutionary art and gentlemen of "revolutionary" criticism to whom the whole thing is a mere diversion or escapade, can afford such an attitude; the makers and followers of proletarian culture cannot. I remember when similar strident leftisms were heard in our young revolutionary theatre movement—one of its exponents stated with high disdain that "we have nothing to learn from the bourgeois theatre." In the international circles of the revolutionary theatre this phrase is still used as a perfect example of "pure" leftism, characteristic of certain elements among bourgeois intellectuals who went left emotionally, as a violent reaction against the evils of capitalism. Some of these new converts would turn their backs to the old world and start everything anew. To such people we must say: "We admire your ardor, but not your misinterpretation of revolutionary culture." We must make it clear to them that in developing a given field of revolutionary art we start not from technique, not from a revolt against bourgeois forms, but from content, from a revolt against bourgeois ideology. True, certain formalizations of bourgeois art are inextricably bound up with their class-content. But we may use bourgeois forms, nevertheless, making them our own by virtue of the new content we infuse into them. It goes without saying that we select and modify and develop to a higher level the borrowed bourgeois forms. Essentially our preoccupation is not with form and technique as a criterion but as a means.

Nor would I grant Eisenberg's premise that all dance forms now used are bourgeois in their origin. Without being a student of the dance, I take it for granted that work-processes as formalized in what we call folk dancing have also contributed their share to the development of dance technique. It strikes me that "we, the people" also have a large stake in the dance technique and that much of what we borrow from the bourgeoisie is rightfully our own.

Perhaps Emanuel Eisenberg's slate-wiping criticism would have some validity, if he proposed something else and something definite instead. Then we could, at worst, regard his "theory" as special pleading. But what does he propose instead of the "lady" technique? Nothing more concrete than to "rediscover the essential universal instincts and impulses of the body which are not related to class labels and class ideas." O-la-la!—the revolutionary dance must avoid a technique which is related to "class labels" (working class included, of course) and "class ideas" (proletarian ideas included, I supposed?).

You see, that's what you get for being a *flaneur* and gentleman of revolutionary criticism.

Sincerely yours,
NATHANIEL BUCHWALD

A REPLY BY E. EISENBERG

The charge of extreme leftism is always a sure arrow of devastation, even if it errs a little on the side of glibness, facility and gleeful pedantry. To Nathaniel Buchwald's certain disgust and eventual fatigue, I suppose I am incurring it all over again by a stubborn repetition of my insistence that the bourgeois dance has absolutely nothing to give to the revolutionary form of this art.

To assume that this is a brief for the same truth in all the arts is where Buchwald's own ardor sadly misleads him. It is my conviction that the vitality and validity of revolutionary fiction, drama, music and architecture would have been and will be helpless without an intense and elaborate employment of bourgeois forms. For these have already engrossed and affected very large masses usefully and soundly. But the dance must start absolutely fresh—or it must return to folk-patterns and the periods preceding the decades of what we understand as bourgeois culture. The last fifty years have seen this art degenerate into such nauseating onanism, self-indulgent idiot babblings and pure playing-with-form that it has had meaning almost only to the inner circle. I generalize, of course, but I think it will be easily admitted that the first four mentioned arts have made infinitely greater revolutionary progress than the dance.

Buchwald's relish of large audiences is so naive that I hesitate to break the news to him that revolutionary dance recitals are attended in the greatest part by other dancers and intellectuals and that these are the only ones who pretend to understand them. My article was written after a growing realization of the dancers' own acute discontent with their work and the confession of complete befuddlement and incomprehension by the few worker-laymen who happened in. As for concentrating on form instead of content, may one not write a piece wholly on form? For a piece on content I recommend Buchwald to an article I contributed to the July-August, 1934, issue of NEW THEATRE.

EMANUEL EISENBERG

THE LAY DANCE
Ruth Allerhand
New Theatre (April 1935)

The dance in America today is undeniably more important, more constructive, than it ever was. But in spite of the fact that audiences are growing, that soloists and groups are increasing in number and ability, there is a potentiality in the dance that has not been touched.

It is not enough for ten soloists to spring up, for a few groups to do outstanding work. If we look back on the short history of this contemporary dance, we find the roots in a *mass movement*, in a feeling of the people to create for themselves a new outlet, healthier and nearer to their problems. It is for us today to redeem *that* side of the dance, which need not be put on a stage to reach the people. Although dance audiences are larger they are still specialized. The masses are yet to be reached. So long as the dance remains a visual experience, it is separate from the people, whereas it should be part of everyday life. Large groups of people can be taught to dance, to take part in vast, mass dance spectacles. Then there would be no audience in the sense of onlookers at a performance, because this enthusiastic group of people would also be participating. And through a vital lay dance the professional dance would gain.

For the dance to be of the people we must form dance choruses as we have formed singing and speaking choruses. Adults, stiff and inarticulate in their bodies, can be taught to broaden their entire communal and social outlook through the development of the individual within the group. Children, misled in schools, ground either through the weary one-two one-two of physical training, or led through a maze of folk-dancing, tap routines, and so-called aesthetic outlets, must be rescued. They can be rightly directed in their motor impulses, their bodies functioning naturally, their reactions stimulated, their minds developed.

To accomplish the really educational goal in the dance, a new approach to the problem, by both lay student and teacher, is necessary. The student must no longer come with set aims or ideas of accomplishment. So must the teacher, as a teacher, no longer exist, but only as a friend, an experienced leader. The student must begin with the simple sincerity of a child, finding out about his body, what it can do, and what he can say with it. The leader will never correct but suggest, he will solve problems and bring up new ones with the group. His only aim is sincerity, directness and vitality to further the essentially creative quality of the dance. A great pleasure and satisfaction will be discovered as the workings of the body are pointed out and revealed.

A profound development on the basis of anatomy alone can take place. For instance, the worker student will be impressed with the parallels to be drawn between himself and the machine. His joints, his circulation, his breathing, his entire functioning self will be discussed, shown to him more clearly than ever before. From the first simple movements, which grow out of a naturally working physical being, he will find a co-ordinating mental stimulus and development. Relaxation will bring him much more than a momentary physical pause. It means to him going down to the very depths of his being and starting fresh, throwing off the layers of false control. Following complete relaxation, complete tension will be so much more sincere, the dynamic realization of oppositional movement and all its possibilities will be explored. The simplicity, directness and elemental quality of all movement will come to him more and more. Now, well balanced and eager, his horizon broadened, he turns from his introspective gropings toward a relationship with the world around him. He is drawn into moving forward. He actively cuts into space, using his body impulsively, he runs, leaps, turns, he creates and composes within space.

From all directions, others approach, galvanized by the same forces within themselves, the result of the same development through which he has just come. They appear to him myriad reflections of himself. Spontaneously reaching toward them he is absorbed into the group.

The group experience is a practical school which teaches something that can never be forgotten, nor taught as eloquently through any other medium. Through union with others, in adjusting himself to the group, he comes to an active discovery of a real solidarity. From the individual to the mass! The individual no longer feels that he is the whole, he now sees that he represents the substance. He is not so much a link in the chain, a cog in the machine, as a very alive, very productive cell within a body.

The possibilities of group expression are unlimited. Movement is the most elementary form of reaction in life. Motion and rhythm are basic means of communication. The groups, fundamentally lay-dance groups, will use the present, the world around them, their own acquaintance with life, for their expression. Their world will not only be absorbed by them, but projected stirringly in many new implications.

In the mass dance, the people will find a twofold gain of tremendous significance. The first, the educational development, through which they found themselves and each other, and which has awakened in them a strong feeling of respect and responsibility for others. The second, a group ability to express, to articulate, and formulate what was before only half clear in their own minds—to rise in great dance choruses and shout aloud, in real sincerity now, what they feel, no longer sitting silent and uncomprehending as others attempt to speak for them.

MODERN DANCE FORMS
Paul Douglas
New Theatre (November 1935)

[It is hoped that the following article will stimulate further discussions on the relative values of our modern dance forms. By no means is this stand that of *New Theatre*. It presents the personal opinion of Mr. Douglas whose article, by the way, has been considerably shortened because of space limitations. Those who differ with those evaluations expressed by the writer are urged to send in their comment and discussion.]

No one has yet written an analysis of the relationship between content and form in the modern dance. As a result, many dancers have merely adopted existing techniques and used them to express material for which those techniques were never intended. Some dance critics have limited themselves to a discussion of whether or not thematic material has been significant and then in an unrelated manner have gone on to an "aesthetic" appreciation of composition, choreography, movement, etc., as though they were two different entities. This approach is completely undialectical because it overlooks the fundamental truism that content and form in any art medium are inseparable. It is my purpose to help clarify and perhaps provoke discussion upon this most vital problem which has been given much thought in the other arts, but seems to have escaped the attention of the modern dance world.

With the exception of the Martha Graham group, there is neither a creative force nor a substantial audience except in the New Dance League. Where else is it possible to see such interest and activity? Like other new movements, the New Dance League has attracted many elements who are using the opportunities presented to them to exhibit their work without understanding the medium in which they desire to express themselves and therefore seizing upon what has already been created without first stopping to analyze whether it could be used. The dance is perhaps one of the most difficult mediums of expression, and to trifle with it is to weaken and ruin its potentialities as a revolutionary weapon.

It is important to trace briefly the evolution of modern dance forms and their relationship to the content or subject matter for which they were used. The modern dance flourished mainly in Germany and in the beginning evidenced itself chiefly in the mechanistic form of the Rudolph von Laban School.

The post-war disillusionment manifested itself in Middle Europe where the modern school, which reached its criterion in Mary Wigman, refused entirely to draw from the world of reality. It assumed a defeatist attitude and found inspiration for its work in mysticism. There was a tendency toward a preoccupation with fate, a "back to the earth" symbolism, and an appeal for beauty to an objective world completely unrelated to the dancer herself. The social forces which caused this escape were neither understood nor was there an attempt made to cope with them. This resulted in an ego-cult, which rhapsodized "art for art's sake."

The space through which Wigman projects herself is always filled with imaginative spirits of a metaphysical world. Even her affirmations are concerned with chasing away bad spirits of an outer cosmos. Thus her technique is solely adaptable for the formulation of mystic ideas and has logically become a useful "art" for fascist Germany where Wigman continues to function.

That Wigman's form is of no use to the dancer struggling with contemporary problems is evident when we consider the work of some of her students. Abramovich and Groke were featured recently as Europe's greatest dancers and appeared in New York this winter. Their thematic material was devoid of importance and their movement was confined to hand exhibition. Kreutzberg, who years ago flashed across the horizon because of his superb technical facility, has contented himself with a continued repetition of his old dances in which he leaps beautifully but says nothing. Consider too, the promising solo work of Jane Dudley and Miriam Blecher. Originally students of the Wigman School, they have found it necessary to discard the fundamental features of that technique in their modern dances (*Time is Money, Cause I'm a Nigger*).

The Democratic traditions expressed in the Declaration of Independence were the greatest creative force in American art. It produced a Whitman in poetry and an Isadora Duncan in the Dance. These great artists believed in the equality of all men and fought for the preservation of those rights attained through revolution. Duncan was the highest development in the bourgeois dance. She had unbounded faith in the values of bourgeois democracy and believed that they could be used for the good of all classes. The technique and forms through which she projected her faith were progressive, in that they were related to the thought content and ideals which she stood for. She rejoiced in the accomplishment of the common man, in the freedom from the yoke of oppression which the Declaration of Independence had supposedly accomplished and which American bourgeois democracy was supposed to foster and develop. To aid her dance she used music most expressive of that ideal which she worshipped (Beethoven, songs of the French Revolution, etc.). She was consistent too in her constant struggle to glorify the dance as a healthy, normal, beautiful and natural function of the human body and did more to rid that art of the inhibitions placed upon it by outmoded convention than any of her predecessors. Her chief contribution in the realm of movement was her understanding of the worthlessness of the ballet technique as a truthful expression of her contemporary life.

Her technique was characterized by an erect affirmative stance and a free use of every part of her body, arms extended upward as though accepting and rejoicing in the universality of mankind. The movement was distinguished by a freedom of action and a flowing rhythm and she moved through a large expanse of space. *These fundamental characteristics of her technique are more closely related to our modern dance than the dance forms of any other modern dancer.*

Duncan's limitations lay in the fact that her free flowing gracious technique and her love for humanity were based ideologically on an acceptance of the indestructibility of society as it was then known to her. She was creative just so long as the culture of which she was the highest dance expression was progressive. She broke down when that culture broke down, but her value and importance cannot be underestimated. She showed more truthfully than anyone before her that creation can be beautiful only when it is wholly related to the objective world in which it lives and of whose problems it is an expression.

Not understanding the richness and importance of the material which existed in our own country, dancers such as Ruth St. Denis and Michio Ito, etc., went to the far flung corners of the earth (the Orient, India) for their subject matter. They were able for a while to satisfy the needs of an audience who believed that all the pageantry which they were witnessing was a faithful artistic reproduction of life as it existed outside of America. That the basic problems which existed all over the world were fundamentally alike was unknown to the politically backward and temporarily apathetic enthusiasts of these schools. Ruth St. Denis and her followers were symptomatic of the beginning of a decadent culture unable and unwilling to utilize the life force of their time. Their mystic pictures were untrue because the far flung corners of the earth where they obtained their sources were as much affected by the class struggle as the more advanced countries. There too, the battle between the old and the new was raging and any art that did not express this struggle was unreal and could not survive. The St. Denis School was not rooted in America and it was totally unrelated to anything contemporary. This is obvious to us now, particularly when we remember that her dancing became so lifeless that instead of projecting dance forms, she had to resort to spectacular pageantry. It is difficult to associate any contributions of hers in terms of movement.

The social isolation of the dance continued even into the years after the crisis had set in, but there were changes in form. The Wigman School because it seemed to represent at least outwardly our machine age greatly influenced the dance in America. Some of the disciples of St. Denis were quick to seize upon the German School as a base from which to develop their own ideas.

The most important figure who emerged from this development was Martha Graham. No longer satisfied with the oriental pageantry of her teacher and yet unaware of the forces within society which were revolting against the destruction of the best traditions in our culture, she became the most developed bourgeois dancer since Isadora Duncan. The very important difference between the two is that Duncan functioned for a rising bourgeoisie and Graham still functions for a declining class, desperately attempting to find values where they no longer exist. Duncan expressed values related to the social forces which were most vital at the time she lived, because to her there was still the possibility of fulfilling the hopes which seemed to be the aims of democracy. Now those hopes and aspirations exist only in the aims of the revolutionary proletariat. Martha Graham being a bourgeois dancer seems to be seeking *external* values wholly unrelated to the dynamic struggle of existing social forces as a source for her material.

Her influence has been so great that those engaged in the development of the modern dance have accepted her success and used her forms without appraising from a dialectical standpoint whether or not her technique can be used in the expression of newer and more vital ideas. They have assumed that because she possesses a great deal of technical skill and perfection in her execution that it is important for them to use at least part of that technique for the expression of their content. Thus, the inseparability of form and content is forgotten by those who in their eagerness to use the dance as a revolutionary weapon seize upon forms which have been perfected for the projection of ideas totally different and sometimes completely at odds with progressive thought and material.

The perfection of Martha Graham's dancing is limited to her own ideology. She will be remembered as the greatest dance exponent of the last stages of capitalism struggling in its final agonies to salvage something out of its chaotic and decaying torment. Her contribution is analogous to that of Proust in literature. Such a contribution cannot be underestimated for it gives a clear picture of that world we no longer want and a better and greater incentive for building a better world.

A recent attempt by Graham to apply herself to vital subject matter should be studied. This was in *Panic*, the play in verse by Archibald MacLeish for which she devised the movement. It was a failure because the dance was unrelated to the thought content and idea of the play. Thus instead of there being a synthesis of verse and movement, the dancing seemed superimposed upon the play often distracting from the beauty of the poetry. This was no accident and the result will be similar in all instances where there is no understanding on the part of the creator of the relationship between form and content.

There is discernible in Graham's recent group dances, however, a noticeable change. In *Celebration*, for instance, a greater use of space and more elevation is attained than ever before. This, I believe, indicates the influence of some of her students, who from an ideological viewpoint are more advanced than Graham herself. The change is encouraging. The group has superb technical ability. But it will be wasted unless they continue to depart even more radically from the fundamental features of the Graham dance forms.

It is clear that we must look somewhere else for the beginnings of that fusion of form and content which will make the modern dance a real weapon for the emancipation of culture. I think that the only dancer who has gone a long way in this organic development is Tamiris. She alone has refused to bow to that eclecticism to which most of our younger modern minded dancers are still guilty. She has not sought the assistance of others simply to borrow from them an easy way to synthesize a new technique. Her arrival into the modern dance has been the result of many years of intellectual development and a constant evolution into new forms based upon concepts which were always growing in relation to a greater understanding and intimacy with her objective world. In struggling with these forces she clarified her own position and needs.

Her refusal to adopt bourgeois dance forms is a dialectic negation and in this sense she is the only dancer who is carrying forward the positive tradition of Isadora Duncan. What are the features of her technique?

The space through which she moves seems limitless. There is a full use of her entire body in flowing rhythm and it is equally as strong in its mellifluous movement as in its contractions. Candidly aware of the beauty of her body, she is unafraid to use it as a valuable asset. Tamiris has seldom sought escape into subjectivism or abstraction. Always conscious of the social forces which were determining her relationship to society, her forms have never remained static but are in a constant process of change. Her early work (*Negro Spirituals*, etc., and later Walt Whitman cycle) was firmly rooted in contemporary America. It was always realistic and although she had not yet attained a Marxian understanding of our social problems, she never sought escape from them. Through this natural development she became a modern dancer. Her latest solo compositions (*Flight* and *Escape*) are the most convincing dances she has ever created and they indicate a clarity of perception which promises much for the future. She understands fully that the form of a composition is always determined by the subject matter. And that fundamental truism is the guide to the future of the modern dance.

REMEMBERING ISADORA DUNCAN
Michael Gold
New Masses 25, no. 1 (Sept. 28, 1937)

Her stormy and generous career is seen as having been part of the democratic tradition in our art.

Dancing is an art that dies with the artist. In America, there is a double death, since art, as an expression of the national spirit, is still rated far below the aluminum business.

There is a statue in New York to Samuel S. Cox, a minor congressman. But where are the monuments to Isadora Duncan? Does the younger generation of revolutionary dancers ever speak of her or remember the great pioneer?

It was ten years, this September 14, that the first creator of an American dance, Isadora Duncan, completed her generous and stormy life. Even before her death, she had begun to be "out of fashion" in America. The postwar generation in Europe was passing through its decade of shell-shock. Bourgeois war-makers had betrayed all the human values; and bourgeois artists, ignorant of the social forces that contained a heaven as well as a hell, found refuge and protest in a new ivory tower that resembled, at times, nothing less than a padded cell.

Here phantoms were mistaken for reality, and humanity was locked out as though it were an assassin. This was the period that substituted geometry and technique for emotion and the spirit; that celebrated ugliness and death, using sneers, angularities, perversions, contortions, and mystifications for its medium.

Some called the period a waste land; others spoke of themselves as the lost generation. But whatever the forms, over all the chaos snickered the bawdy, crackpot face of Dada, father of confusion and lies.

Europe had earned the right to such profound despair; in France alone a million young men had been slaughtered in the imperialist war. But what place had it in America, which had suffered little?

What right had any artist, American or European, to lose his faith in the people?

We witnessed, however, in our country, the rise of an art, talented enough, but sterile because it had no roots except in Montparnasse. It was a negation of democracy, it was a complete secession from the American folk-life. Is it any wonder that during this time Isadora became a stranger in her own house, a naive old devotee surrounded by the young philistines of a new sophistication?

Today some young revolutionary dancers continue the geometrical contortions of the post-war German Dadaists. They attempt to put the spirit of
the native democracy into these strange and alien molds, and never know
why they fail.

But Isadora Duncan did not fail; she had discovered a way of dancing
democracy.

It was the old transcendental democracy of Emerson and Walt Whitman
that inspired her. It is difficult today to realize what an effect she had on her
time. The formal ballet of the czar's court ruled the dance world then; there
was nothing else. Like feudalism, the ballet had frozen into a static pattern
that put an end to expanding life. At its worst it was a matter of wigs, corsets,
and acrobats; at its best, it had the soulless beauty of a machine.

Isadora stripped off the corsets and the wigs and all the feudal artificiality.
She rediscovered the flowing line of the Greeks, a line that was not imposed on
the human body, but was its most natural expression. She brought spontaneous
joy back to the dance, the sunlight, the serenity of Mother Nature.

Hers was, I believe, a complete vision of life and revolution. Let us admit
that the prewar democratic artists of her generation were utopian; the Carl
Sandburgs, the Frank Lloyd Wrights, the Edward Carpenters. Perhaps it was
because they had never faced the enormous and incredible brutality of this
new period of war and fascism.

Their sin was generosity and a too easy faith in man. But it was a lesser
sin against reality than some of the deliberate ugliness and despair of today,
which allows itself to be crushed by the horrors of the struggle, and offers us
no hope.

Marx said of the Proudhonists: "While they are still seeking science in
their heads and drawing up systems, while they are only at the beginning of
their struggle, they see only misery in the people's misery, and fail to realize
the revolutionary side of misery which will overthrow the old society."

Isadora, in the darkest days of the Russian revolution, came out for it
with all her ardent soul. But she saw more than misery. She knew that here at
last was being born the shining world-democracy of the future. Her dancing
was an attempt to create images of what this future would mean for humanity; a time when each human body would take on the splendor and freedom
of the Greek gods.

Do our young revolutionary dancers and poets create such images of a
new human beauty toward which the race may strive in socialism? To my old-
fashioned mind, some of them need to go back to such American democratic
sources as Walt Whitman and Isadora Duncan, not to imitate, but to learn an
ultimate faith in the body and spirit of man. Emerson had it, but T. S. Eliot
does not have it, and it has led him as all such fear and hatred of the masses
must lead, to the last negation called fascism.

We are Communists, because we believe in man. We are Communists,
because the world was made for human joy. We are Communists, because

within each member of the human race are contained all the seeds of perfect moral and physical beauty.

This is what Isadora Duncan said in her dancing. I am glad the *New Masses* is remembering her—she belongs to us forever. And I am glad that Walkowitz, the artist who spent happy and devoted years recording the dancer and her dance, is represented in this memorial.* All that I could wish now would be a dance festival by the young dancers in honor of Isadora to testify that struggle is not enough, there must also be a vision and goal.

---

* This article was accompanied by Walkowitz drawings to signal a Tenth Memorial Exhibition of his Isadora Duncan drawings at the Park Art Galleries in New York City, Sept. 27-Oct. 29, 1937.

Notes

THE POLITICS OF EXPRESSION

1. For an exception to this status quo, see Susan Manning, *Ecstasy and the Demon: Feminism and Nationalism in the Dances of Mary Wigman* (Berkeley: University of California Press, 1993). It should be noted that "modern dance" is little more than a name whereas the term modernism covers a complex of aesthetic procedures currently under intense critical scrutiny. Although all modern dance is not modernist, a significant portion of it, I maintain, needs to be reevaluated in this light.

2. Francis Sparshott, *Off the Ground: First Steps toward a Philosophical Consideration of Dance* (Princeton: Princeton University Press, 1988), pp. 76–77. Sparshott's own work is not founded on any subscription to the modernist credo.

3. See, in particular, Andreas Huyssen, *After the Great Divide: Modernism, Mass Culture, Postmodernism* (Bloomington: Indiana University Press, 1986).

4. See Agnes Heller, *A Theory of Feelings* (Assen, The Netherlands: Van Gorcum, 1979), p. 77.

5. M. H. Abrahms, *The Mirror and the Lamp: Romantic Theory and the Critical Tradition* (New York: Oxford University Press, 1971), p. 48.

6. See Modris Eksteins, *Rites of Spring: The Great War and the Birth of the Modern Age* (New York: Anchor, 1990). For an account of "transcendentalizing versions of subjectivity" as a modernist solution to subject-object dualities, see Andrew Ross, *The Failure of Modernism: Symptoms of American Poetry* (New York: Columbia University Press, 1986).

7. Jacques Rivière, "Le Sacre du Printemps," in *What Is Dance?*, ed. Roger Copeland and Marshall Cohen (Oxford: Oxford University Press, 1983), p. 116.

8. Ibid., pp. 119–20.

9. Siegfried Giedion, *Mechanization Takes Command: A Contribution to Anonymous History* (New York: Norton, 1948), p. 104.

10. The issue of emotion in historical modern dance has frequently been associated with an unstable self-expressive process. By invoking expression theory, I do not intend to rehabilitate self-expression. Rather, I employ expression as an analytical schema but also as an unavoidable artistic given. Analogous to what Ronald Brogue calls "the stability of the sign" after structuralism, expression is "something that involuntarily asserts itself whether we wish it to or not." See Ronald Brogue, "Introduction," in *Mimesis in Contemporary Theory: An Interdisciplinary Approach. Vol. 2: Mimesis, Semiosis and Power*, ed. Ronald Brogue (Philadelphia: John Benjamins, 1991), p. 4.

11. I wish to reconsider the following view: "It is notable that the decade of 'red' dance produced no enduring body of Left dance criticism—a failure all the more striking in view of the pioneering role of socialists in this field." See Franklin Rosemont, "Modern Dance," in *Encyclopedia of the American Left*, ed. Mari Jo Buhle, Paul Buhle, Dan Georgakas (New York: Garland, 1990), p. 480. Whether or not one wishes to dignify this writing as an "enduring body of dance criticism," its theoretical import and historical value appear undeniable.

12. Remo Guidieri and Francesco Pellizzi, "Shadows: Nineteen Tableaux on the Cult of the Dead in Malekula, Eastern Melanesia," in *Res 2* (autumn 1981): 67.

13. See *Aesthetics and Politics*, trans. Ronald Taylor (London: Verso, 1980), p. 40.

14. I am emboldened by Helen Krich Chinoy's perception that the most politically oriented decade of American theater produced a particular theatricality and styliza-

tion. It is the connection of the personal to the political through the aesthetic that is here at issue. See Helen Krich Chinoy, "The Poetics of Politics: Some Notes on Style and Craft in the Theatre of the Thirties," in *Theatre Journal* 35, no. 4 (December 1983): 476–98.

15. See Michael Gold, "The Loves of Isadora," in *New Masses* (March 4, 1929): 20–21. This article is reproduced in the appendix.

16. "The central and innovative figures of modern dance have been women, exemplifying an important aspect of feminist culture that not only persisted but flourished after the eclipse of organized feminism following the passage of the Nineteenth Amendment in 1920" (*Encyclopedia of the American Left*, p. 426). As Nancy F. Cott has determined: "In any recent history of women in the United States, you are likely to find comment on the demise of feminism in the 1920s rather than recognition that the name and the phenomenon had just recently cropped up." See her *The Grounding of Modern Feminism* (New Haven: Yale University Press, 1987), p. 4. I understand the performance of feminist culture in historical modern dance as complicated by simultaneous performances of modernism or Marxism in the same works.

17. See Ramsay Burt, "Dance, Masculinity and Postmodernism," in *Postmodernism and Dance: Discussion Papers* (West Sussex: Institute of Higher Education, 1991), pp. 23–32.

18. This is, of course, not to claim that Merce Cunningham looks like, or in any way dances like, Isadora Duncan. Such absurdities can hardly be the point.

19. Siegfried Kracauer, "The Mass Ornament (1927)," trans. Barbara Correll and Jack Zipes, in *New German Critique* 5 (spring 1975): 72–73.

20. Norman Bryson, *Word and Image: French Painting of the Ancien Regime* (Cambridge: Cambridge University Press, 1981), p. 7.

21. What I describe here as a performance phenomenon resembles Norbert Elias's concept of "figuration": "the network of interdependencies formed by individuals." See his "Introduction to the 1968 Edition," in *The Civilizing Process: The History of Manners*, trans. Edmund Jephcott (New York: Urizen, 1978), pp. 261–63. Figuration turns on Elias's critique of "inside" and "outside" as criteria for the understanding of social change. My notion of *manipulations* of expression theory as an alternative explanation of aesthetic change corresponds to that critique. The "internality" of those manipulations to the entire artistic practice under discussion owes much to Louis Marin, *La critique du discours: sur la "logique de port-royal" et les "pensées" de Pascal* (Paris: Minuit, 1975).

22. Michel de Certeau, *The Writing of History*, trans. Tom Conley (New York: Columbia University Press, 1988), pp. 85–86.

1. THE INVENTION OF MODERN DANCE

1. Isadora Duncan, *My Life* (New York: Liveright, 1927), p. 75.

2. Ibid., p. 341.

3. Paul Valéry, "Philosophy of the Dance," in *Aesthetics*, trans. Ralph Manheim (New York: Pantheon, 1964), p. 207.

4. William Pietz, "The Problem of the Fetish, 1," in *Res* 9 (spring 1985): 7.

5. Allegory, in this view, is generally compromising for the sensuousness, and therefore for the political agency of performance, whose meaning is then consigned to a transcendent elsewhere. See Hazard Adams, *Philosophy of the Literary Symbolic* (Tallahassee: University of Florida Press, 1983).

6. Duncan, *My Life*, p. 76.

7. "Iconostasis is loss of body, *ekstasis*, and, as such, a state in which the tension between the spiritual and the corporeal is resolved completely to the benefit of the first through the elision of the second." Remo Guidieri and Francesco Pellizzi, "Editorial," trans. John Johnston, in *Res* 1 (spring 1981): 6.

8. Louis Untermeyer, "The Dance," in *The Seven Arts* (November 1916): 81.

9. The term has been reintroduced by Raymond Williams: "An *organic* society was one that has 'grown' rather than been 'made.'. . . It later acquired relevance to contrasts between primarily agricultural and primarily *industrial* societies." See *Keywords: A Vocabulary of Culture and Society* (Guildford, Surrey: Fontana, 1976), p. 191. As an antitechnological, utopian socialist perspective, "organic" society is marked by the return to a conservative past from which to construct a radical future. Within this perspective, technology is unredeemable because unnatural. As Williams shows, the term organic is associated historically with Edmund Burke, "the first modern conservative." See Raymond Williams, *Culture and Society: 1780-1950* (1958; reprinted New York: Columbia University Press, 1983), pp. 11–12.

10. Anne L. Ardis, *New Women, New Novels: Feminism and Early Modernism* (New Brunswick: Rutgers University Press, 1990), p. 121.

11. The issue of subjectivity is, of course, the catalyst of feminist critique: "Despite the variety of ways in which man has construed her essential characteristics, she is always the Object, a conglomeration of attributes to be predicted and controlled along with other natural phenomena. The place of the free-willed subject who can transcend nature's mandates is reserved exclusively for men." Linda Alcoff, "Cultural Feminism Versus Post-Structuralism: The Identity Crisis in Feminist Theory," in *Signs* 13 (spring 1988): 406.

12. See Amy Swanson, "Isadora Duncan: à propos de son enseignement et de sa filiation," in *La Recherche en Danse* 2 (1983): 63–74, and Norma Adler, "Reconstructing the Dances of Isadora Duncan," in *The Drama Review (Reconstruction)* 28, no. 3 (T103) (fall 1984): 59–66.

13. "The problematic character of any interpretation of Duncan," notes Randy Martin, "lies in an opposition of nature and science, conceived of as an obligation of analysis that divides dance's essential sources from the activity of dancing." See Randy Martin, "Dance Ethnography and the Limits of Representation," in *Social Text* 33 (winter 1992): 107.

14. On the relationship of bodies to relics in performance, see Remo Guidieri and Francesco Pellizzi, "Shadows," pp. 5-69. "As remains, it [the relic] can only affirm that the annihilation of the body is never absolute (we could say that matter is the residue of spent energy)" (p. 45).

15. A statement made to the audience by Julia Levien prior to a performance of "The Art of Isadora Duncan" by Lori Belilove and Company, June 5–8, 1991, at Good Shepherd-Faith Presbyterian Church, New York City.

16. Eugène Carrière cited in Duncan, *My Life*, p. 82.

17. Duncan, *Ecrits sur la Danse* (Paris: Grenier, 1927), n.p. All translations from this collection are my own.

18. *My Life*, p. 75.

19. See Duncan, *The Art of the Dance*, ed. Sheldon Cheney (New York: Theatre Arts, 1928), pp. 55–56.

20. Ibid., p. 77.

21. Constantin Stanislavski, *An Actor Prepares*, trans. Elizabeth Reynolds Hapgood (New York: Theater Arts, 1948), p. 160.

22. Stanislavski believed in the sensory basis for emotion retrieval and therefore imagined the unconscious as part of a larger Nature, a storehouse of emotions to be unlocked by physical sensations. His method was philosophically in accord with Duncan's natural process. "I watched her," he wrote, "during her performances and her rehearsals, when her developing emotion would first change the expression of her face, and with shining eyes she would pass to the display of what was born in her soul." Stanislavski quoted in Duncan, *My Life*, p. 168.

23. Their thinking is tied to Romantic concepts of culture, the development of which can be traced back through Ruskin to Coleridge. See Raymond Williams, "The Romantic Artist," in *Culture and Society*, pp. 30–48.

24. This amounts to seeking, in Paul de Man's terms, the grammatization of rhetoric. If grammar is syntactical because it obeys a linear logic and rhetoric is paradigmatic because it introduces figures and tropes that can disrupt grammatical flow, then we must see grammar as analogous to dancing, whereas rhetoric is fundamentally choreographic. When de Man quotes Yeats's famous line, "How can we tell the dancer from the dance?" to suggest that the literal reading of this verse is to ask how meaning and sign can rightly be distinguished and kept apart, he points to the sort of confusion I am dealing with here between expression and fetish or legacy and reconstruction. See Paul de Man, "Semiology and Rhetoric," in *Allegories of Reading* (New Haven: Yale University Press, 1971), pp. 3–19.

25. See Hillel Schwartz, "Torque: The New Kinaesthetic of the Twentieth Century," in *Zone* 6 (*Incorporations*), ed. Jonathan Crary and Sanford Kwinter (Cambridge: MIT Press, 1992), pp. 79–80.

26. Ibid., p. 95.

27. Michael Gold, "The Loves of Isadora," p. 20.

28. Duncan, *My Life*, p. 3.

29. Duncan, *Der Tanz der Zukunft (The Dance of the Future): Eine Vorlesung* (Leipzig: Eugen Diederichs, 1903), p. 25.

30. "America Makes Me Sick: Nauseates Me," in the *San Francisco Examiner* (March 4, 1923), from a typescript in the Isadora Duncan Collection, San Francisco Performing Arts Library and Museum, folder 23. Duncan continues:

> There are, in the world, persons of three colors. There are the whites. Their color typifies a purity which is useless; a starved quality of the body and mind and emotions from which no young may spring; a sterility which is praised only by its own barrenness. That's your ultra pure, all over the country. The next color is gray. . . . That's Boston. Dead, politely, positively dead, so far as any thought or any feeling, or any quickened intelligence are concerned. The last color of all is red. That's the color of the people who do the real work of the world. That's the color of the people who have enough guimpe in their upper story to ask "why—why—Why?" That's the color of the blessed folk who won't lie down under the old tyrannies, but who rise in honest revolution. That's the color of the artists and the creators, the great soldiers and fighters and poets. And that's my color, praise the Lord! For, you see, the color of my blood I am glad, glad to say is still red, even after my American tour. (Ibid., pp. 6–7)

Duncan's class politics were unmistakable to Gold:

> But I will predict. I have seen the Russian revolutionists in Moscow standing in the street, some so poor that their feet are done up in newspapers, for lack of shoes. I have seen the freedom in their faces, as they sang the Internationale, waving the red flag. I have seen your workers parade, also, down Fifth avenue. I have watched the poor, starved bodies, their weak backs and shrunken limbs. Yet I see, in those downtrodden exploited ones, the promise of America. Wake up on time! Or else those crushed will start thinking, from over burdened necessity. And on Fifth avenue, they will start up the Internationale, while the Red Flag is waving all about. After all, since red is the color of youth and promise and vigor and initiative and all virile creation, that may be the only cure possible for these dreary, routinized United States. (Ibid., p. 8)

In regard to precursors of thirties radicalism, see James Burkhart Gilbert, *Writers and Partisans: A History of Literary Radicalism in America* (New York: Wiley, 1968), especially the "New Paganism," pp. 8–47.

31. Rather than chart Duncan's changing relationship with her homeland, I point to the doctrine of the two Americas that would also be central, although in a different way, to Martha Graham. Ann Daly writes: "[Duncan's] American tours can be separated into three distinct groups: her initial tours (twice in 1908, 1909, 1911), during which spectators learned to 'read' this new art form; the second group of tours (1914–15, 1916–18) during World War I and after the much-publicized deaths of her children, during which she came to symbolize motherhood and nationalistic pride; and the third group (1922–23), when she returned from Soviet Russia with a young poet husband to a suspicious and increasingly hostile audience." See Ann Daly, "Dance History and Feminist Theory: Reconsidering Isadora Duncan and the Male Gaze," in *Gender in Performance: The Presentation of Difference in the Performing Arts*, ed. Laurence Senelick (Hanover, N.H.: University Press of New England, 1992), p. 242.

32. Ralph Taylor, "Isadora and the Dance of the Future," in *Dance Observer* 1, no. 2 (March 1934): 16.

33. Or ideologically conflicted notions of production within one society. See William Pietz, "The Problem of the Fetish, 1," note 24, p. 11.

34. T. S. Eliot, "Tradition and the Individual Talent (1917)," in *Selected Essays* (London: Faber and Faber, 1934), p. 17. Duncan did work from tradition, as she said herself: "I didn't invent my Dance, it existed before me; but it was sleeping and I awoke it." See Duncan, *Ecrits*, p. 80.

35. Duncan, *Ecrits*, p. 26.

36. This phenomenon may go a long way toward explaining the perceived sexuality of Duncan's dance for some viewers. Rayner Heppenstall, for example, sees "unprojected ecstasy" as demanding "erotic empathy." See his "The Sexual Idiom," in *What Is Dance?*, p. 288.

37. See Sherry B. Ortner, "Is Female to Male as Nature Is to Culture?," in *Woman, Culture, and Society*, ed. Michelle Zimbalist Rosaldo and Louise Lamphere (Stanford: Stanford University Press, 1974), pp. 67–87.

38. Richard Sennett has determined that in eighteenth-century Europe, culture was considered the public sphere, nature the private. The "natural realm of the self" was in the privacy of the home and family. The self had no publicly expressive identity and, by the same token, public expression had less resonance for the self, being more strictly of the order of convention. This dichotomy assured the existence of the public domain itself. See Sennett, "Public and Private," in *The Fall of Public Man* (New York: Knopf, 1977), pp. 89–106.

39. It is not yet, of course, fully modernist since it operates as "applied aesthetics" or decoration rather than "object." As Jack J. Spector shows, the move from decoration to autonomy occurs in the collage works of Picasso and Braque around 1911. See his "The Avant-Garde Object: Form and Fetish between World War I and World War II," in *Res* 12 (autumn 1986): 128. The power of the decorative as opposed to the illustrative or the narrative resides in the nonsymbolic space provided, for example, by architecture to sculpture or by choric dance to drama. Within these subordinating contexts, the decorative arts of sculpture and dance are freed to accommodate self-expression, impulse, and emotional life. These impulses maintain autonomy from the "host" art but are not autonomous, not objectified and distanced from social life. In fact, as Anny Mali Hicks explains in "Vital Art," an article published in *Mother Earth* 1, no. 3 (May 1906), "The value of applied esthetics is as a medicine to stir up social unrest and discontent." See *Radical Periodicals in the United States, 1890-1960: Mother Earth Bulletin*, series 1, vol. 1 (1906-1907) (New York: Greenwood, 1968), p. 48. For a different view of the relationship between the "New Woman" and the craft movement in France, see Debora Silverman, "The 'New Woman,' Feminism, and the Deco-

rative Arts in Fin-de-Siècle France," in *Eroticism and the Body Politic*, ed. Lynn Hunt (Baltimore: Johns Hopkins University Press, 1991): 144–63.

40. In particular, the notion of color vibration in the genesis of abstract form corresponds in interesting ways to Duncan's aesthetic of light. See Sixten Ringbom, "Art in 'the Epoch of the Great Spiritual': Occult Elements in the Early Theory of Abstract Painting," in *Journal of the Warburg and Courtauld Institutes* 29 (1966): 386–418; Steven A. Mansback, "The Universal Language," in his *Visions of Totality: Laszlo Moholy-Nagy, Theo Van Doesburg, and El Lissitzky* (Ann Arbor, Michigan: UMI Research Press, 1980), pp. 87–103; and Mark A. Cheetham, *The Rhetoric of Purity: Essentialist Theory and the Advent of Abstract Painting* (Cambridge: Cambridge University Press, 1991). Duncan's definition of the solar plexus as movement's central spring involves a form of light vibration: "[I] sought the source of the spiritual expression to flow into the channels of the body filling it with vibrating light—the centrifugal force reflecting the spirit's vision. . . . When I listened to music the rays and vibrations of the music streamed to this one fount of light within me . . ." Duncan, *My Life*, p. 75.

41. Duncan, *The Dance of the Future*, p. 25.

42. Floyd Dell, *Women as World Builders: Studies in Modern Feminism* (1913; rpt. Westport, Conn.: Hyperion, 1976), p. 49.

43. See Bram Dijkstra, *Idols of Perversity: Fantasies of Feminine Evil in Fin-de-Siècle Culture* (New York: Oxford University Press, 1986), pp. 3–63.

44. See Dijkstra, *Idols of Perversity*, p. 18. Edward Gordon Craig remarked: "To see her shepherding her little flock, keeping them together and specially looking after one very small one of four years old, was a sight no one there had ever seen before and, I suppose, will never see again." "Memories of Isadora Duncan (1952)," in Edward Gordon Craig, *Gordon Craig on Movement and Dance*, edited by Arnold Rood (London: Dance Books, 1978), p. 250.

45. Evan Alderson, "Utopies Actuelles," in *La Danse au Défi* (Montreal: Parachute, 1987), p. 68.

46. See Thierry de Duve, *Pictorial Nominalism: On Marcel Duchamp's Passage from Painting to the Readymade*, trans. Dana Polan (Minneapolis: University of Minnesota Press, 1991), p. 134.

47. Elaine Scarry, "Three Paths from Bodies to Artifacts," paper written for the conference "Choreographing History" held at the University of California, Riverside, February 16–17, 1992.

48. Anne L. Ardis, *New Women, New Novels*, p. 152.

49. Teresa de Lauretis, *Technologies of Gender: Essays on Theory, Film, and Fiction* (Bloomington: Indiana University Press, 1987), p. 114. De Lauretis's contradiction is realized by Duncan in the "subverted support" of movement lexicon and choreographic syntax just discussed.

50. Genevieve Stebbins, "Artistic Stature Posing," in *Delsarte System of Expression* (1902; rpt. New York: Dance Horizons, 1977), p. 144. See also Katherine M. Adelman, "Statue Posing in the Late Nineteenth Century Physical Culture Movement," in *Proceedings of the Fifth Canadian Symposium on the History of Sport and Physical Education* (University of Toronto: 1982), pp. 308–17. I thank Selma Odom for bringing my attention to this article. Genevieve Stebbins was the foremost exponent of American Delsartism from the 1880s until approximately 1915. See Nancy Lee Chalfa Ruyter, *Reformers and Visionaries: The Americanization of the Art of Dance* (New York: Dance Horizons, 1979), pp. 20–27, and Ruyter, "The Intellectual World of Genevieve Stebbins," in *Dance Chronicle* 11, no. 3 (1988): 381–97. Nancy Ruyter has pointed out to me that much believed original with Duncan actually stems from American Delsartism. I look forward to Ruyter's forthcoming study, which will help place Duncan in her cultural context.

51. François Delsarte (1811–71) was the French theoretician of gesture whose work passed to America through Genevieve Stebbins via Steele McKaye.

52. See Stebbins, p. 448.

53. Ibid., p. 450.

54. Eugenio Barba, "The Female Role as Represented on the Stage in Various Cultures," quoted by Peggy Phelan in "Feminist Theory, Poststructuralism, and Performance," in *TDR* 32, no. 1 (T117) (spring 1988): 108–109. Barba explains that the actor's purest presence consists in this very minimal activity of "representing his own absence." See Eugenio Barba, *Beyond the Floating Islands* (New York: PAJ, 1986), p. 139. Peggy Phelan has noted that the pre-expressive level instances a pre-Oedipal imagination because it eludes, by appearing to pre-date, the symbolic imperative of given language, or, in theatrical terms, particular expressive forms. Phelan nuances the concept of the pre-Oedipal put forward by Melanie Klein and Julia Kristeva as, following Laura Mulvey, "in *transition* to articulated language: its gestures, signs, and symbols have meaning but do not transcend into the full sense of language" (Mulvey cited in Phelan, p. 109).

55. Duncan, *Ecrits*, p. 25.

56. Duncan's admiring descriptions of the actress Duse yield an analogous interpretation. Duncan values magical moments of expanding interiority in Duse's presence on stage, moments of great intensity by definition but whose intensity is in no way determined by their expressive service to the text. Instead, they become a second, private text suggesting a magical transcendence of the body's literal powers and plastic limitations.

57. Duncan, *My Life*, p. 224.

58. Ibid., p. 144.

59. See Robert Greer Cohn, *Mallarmé's "Un Coup de Dés": An Exegesis* (New York: AMS, 1949), p. 20, note 38.

60. Duncan's goal of "visional movement created from music" should be understood in this quasi-invisible sense (*My Life*, p. 2). She conceived of sensation as a physical soul, a "motor": "Before I go out on the stage, I must place a motor in my soul. When that begins to work my legs and arms and my whole body will move independently of my will. But if I do not get time to put that motor in my soul, I cannot dance" (ibid., p. 168). That motor is the recycling apparatus of impressions into sensations: It is in the soul because impressions are impalpable, but it is a motor because feelings must gain physical form without becoming set expressions.

61. See Charles Taylor, "Theories of Meaning," in *Human Agency and Language: Philosophical Papers* (Cambridge: Cambridge University Press, 1985), vol. 1, especially pp. 259-92. I thank Evan Alderson for calling my attention to Taylor's work. Alderson discusses Taylor's theory in "Dance and Postmodern Communities," a paper delivered at "The Shadow of Spirit" Conference, King's College, Cambridge, July 1990.

62. Ibid., p. 264.

63. Richard Sennett, *The Fall of Public Man*, p. 313. See also Randy Martin's theory of dance as the social body's production of desire, and of desire as "the motion of social interaction, the physical agency of activity." *Performance as Political Act*, p. 73, and in general the chapter "Locating the Body" (pp. 51–80).

64. In her discussion of Isadora Duncan as subvertor of the male gaze, Susan Manning maintains that "early modern dancers had to fashion representational strategies that addressed the female spectator's identification with their performance." See her *Ecstasy and the Demon*, p. 34. I describe Duncan's spectatorship as male because throughout her autobiography she positions herself vis-à-vis illustrious male spectators whose receptiveness she welcomes.

65. D. W. Winnicott, "The Location of Cultural Experience," in *Playing and Reality* (New York: Basic, 1971), pp. 95–103.

66. Ibid., p. 100.

67. Gaston Bachelard, *The Poetics of Space*, trans. Maria Jolas (Boston: Beacon, 1969), pp. 217–18.

68. Joseph Libertson, *Proximity: Levinas, Blanchot, Bataille and Communication* (The Hague: Martinus Nijhoff, 1982), p. 17.

69. Georges Bataille's theory of proximity paraphrased here avoids what Ann Daly has called "the no-win situation" forced on the feminist dance historian when she uses male gaze theory. Daly notes: "The outcome of analysis—whether the dancer or choreographer in question is a 'success' or 'failure' from a feminist point of view—is decided before the analysis is even begun." See Daly, "Isadora Duncan and the Male Gaze," p. 243.

70. Ibid., p. 10.

71. "La danseuse," wrote Mallarmé as an axiom of ballet, "*n'est pas une femme qui danse*, pour ces motifs juxtaposés qu'elle *n'est pas une femme*, mais une métaphore." Stéphane Mallarmé, "Ballets" in *Crayonné au Théâtre* in *Oeuvres Complètes de Stéphane Mallarmé*, ed. Henri Mondor and G. Jean-Aubry (Paris: Gallimard, 1945), p. 304. The translation is by Mary Lewis Shaw in "Ephemeral Signs: Apprehending the Idea through Poetry and Dance," in *Dance Research Journal* 20, no. 1 (summer 1988): 3.

72. See Mary Lewis Shaw, "Ephemeral Signs," p. 3.

73. Paul Valéry, *Aesthetics*, p. 205.

74. See Frank Kermode, "Poet and Dancer before Diaghilev," in *Puzzles and Epiphanies: Essays and Reviews, 1958-1961* (London: Routledge and Kegan Paul, 1962), pp. 1-28. Duncan thought of Fuller as "a sudden ebullition of nature which could never be repeated", terms that are usually applied to Duncan herself (Duncan, *My Life*, p. 95). She also calls Fuller "one of the first original inspirations of light and changing color" (ibid.).

75. Frank Kermode, "Poet and Dancer," p. 27.

76. See Duncan in *Touchstone*, p. 14.

77. When Duncan opposed the puppet-like articulation of ballet, the counterexample she chose was that of light: "I on the contrary sought the source of the spiritual expression to flow into the channels of the body filling it with vibrating light—the centrifugal force reflecting the spirit's vision" (Duncan, *My Life*, p. 75).

78. Dierdre Pridden, "L'Acte Pur des Métamorphoses," in *The Art of Dance in French Literature* (London: Adam and Charles Black, 1952), p. 135.

79. Teresa de Lauretis, *Technologies of Gender*, p. 10.

80. Ibid.

81. Ibid., p. 114.

82. Duncan, *My Life*, p. 152.

83. Ibid., p. 213.

84. Duncan, *Ecrits*, p. 45.

85. Ibid., p. 136.

86. Ibid. This experience was ultimately distilled in Duncan's solo *Dance of the Furies*.

87. Duncan, *My Life*, p. 140.

88. Duncan, "The Dance: Chorus of Tragedy," in *Ecrits*, p. 49.

89. Duncan, "What the Dance Should Be," in *Ecrits*, p. 42.

90. Ibid., p. 43.

91. Ibid., p. 45.

92. Duncan, *Ecrits*, p. 85.

93. "We need a new world of symbols," wrote Nietzsche in *The Birth of Tragedy*, "and the entire symbolism of the body is called into play, not the mere symbolism of the lips, face, and speech but the whole pantomime of dancing, forcing every member into rhythmic movement." Friedrich Nietzsche, *The Basic Writings of Nietzsche*, trans. and ed. Walter Kaufmann (New York: Modern Library, 1968), p. 40.

94. "By dissolving the boundaries between self and other, the theory of imitation-suggestion embodied a highly plastic notion of the human subject that radically called into question the unity and identity of the self." Ruth Leys, "Mead's Voices: Imita-

tion as Foundation, or, the Struggle against Mimesis," in *Critical Inquiry* 19 (winter 1993): 281.

95. Isadora Duncan, "Dancing in Relation to Religion and Love," in *Theatre Arts Monthly* (August 1927): 592.

96. Duncan, "The Dance," in *Touchstone* 2, no. 1 (October 1917): 14.

97. Duncan, *Ecrits*, p. 27.

98. Note the unease with which classicists and dance critics alike approach Duncan's professed intention to reconstruct Greek dance. Lilian Lawler, for example, writes,

> In our own time, certain dance forms which owe some of their inspiration to ancient Greece have attracted wide attention. Many of these were in the nature of a reaction from the rigorous discipline of the formal ballet, the futility and sterility of the dances of ballroom and theatre, and, incidentally, from the restraints of clothing and manners of the dancers of our day. Few of them have represented serious attempts to study and reproduce exactly any specific dance of the Greeks. Isadora Duncan, for example, one of the leaders of the modern movement, often said, "We are not Greeks, and therefore cannot dance Greek dances."

See Lawler, *The Dance in Ancient Greece* (Middletown: Wesleyan University Press, 1964), p. 24. From the perspective of dance criticism, Deborah Jowitt has written: "That so many writers saw in her their favorite museum figures vivified or an imagined antiquity brought to life reveals their own slant of mind." It seems to me, however, that this is precisely what Duncan was doing: The project of reconstruction/reinvention is an eminently modernist project. Jowitt continues: "When Duncan began to develop her art, European cultural life had been tinged with Hellenism for more than a century; she fitted herself, most satisfyingly, into a trend. To link something with Greece automatically dignified it." "Images of Isadora: The Search for Motion," in *Dance Research Journal* 17, nos. 2 and 18 (1985–86): 26.

99. "Nous serions, du Rêve et de l'Action / Le sublime Androgyne" is the final line of Valentine de Saint-Point's poem "l'Etre" ("Being"). See Claudia Salaris, *Le Futuriste: Donne et Letteratura d'Avanguardia in Italia (1909/1944)* (Milan: Edizioni delle donne, 1982), p. 42.

100. See Lucia Re, "Futurism and Feminism," in *Annali d'Italianistica* 7 (1989): 253–72. For more information on the relationship of Italian futurism to dance, see Leonetta Bentivoglio, "Danza e Futurismo in Italia: 1913-1933," in *La Danza Italiana* 1 (autumn 1984): 61–82.

101. The masculinist ideal of machine dances, biomechanical exercises, and theories of the body as puppet was that of an outside within an outside, or an "inside-out" without an inside.

102. Filippo Marinetti, "Manifesto of the Futurist Dance," in *Marinetti: Selected Writings*, trans. R. W. Flint and Arthur A. Coppotelli (New York: Farrar, Straus and Giroux, 1972), p. 138.

103. Valentine de Saint-Point, "Manifesto della Donna futurista," in Salaris, *Le futuriste*, p. 31. All translations of Saint-Point are my own.

104. Valentine de Saint-Point quoted in Salaris, *Le Futuriste*, p. 34.

105. Filippo Marinetti, "Futurist Dance," p. 138.

106. Valentine de Saint-Point, "La Métachorie (1914)," in Giovanni Lista, *Futurisme. Manifestes-Proclamations, Documents* (Lausanne: L'Age d'Homme, 1973), p. 255.

107. Valentine de Saint-Point, "La Métachorie," in *Montjoie! Organe de l'Impérialisme Artistique Français* 2 (1914), n.p.

108. Ibid.

109. Ibid.

2. BODIES OF RADICAL WILL

1. James Burkhart Gilbert, *Writers and Partisans: A History of Literary Radicalism in America* (New York: John Wiley, 1968), p. 4.

2. Revolutionary modern dance bears comparison with left avant-gardes in Germany and Russia. See David Bathrick, "Affirmative and Negative Culture: Technology and the Left Avant-Garde," in *The Technological Imagination: Theories and Fictions*, ed. Teresa de Lauretis, Andreas Huyssen, and Kathleen Woodward (Madison, Wisc.: Coda, 1980), pp. 107–22.

3. A review of this concert notes that it was the first undertaking of the W.D.L. but actually the third "joint activity of the [dance] groups: First was the mass dance which several groups (before the Workers Dance League was formed) gave at the Bronx Coliseum on May 1, 1932; second was the competitive Spartakiad held at the New School for Social Research on January 4, 1933." Oakley Johnson, "The Dance," in *New Theatre* (February 1934): 18.

4. Edna Ocko, "The Revolutionary Dance Movement," in *New Masses* 11, no. 11 (June 12, 1934): 27. Ocko also notes that the Workers Dance League has "an Eastern section comprising groups in New York, New Jersey, Pennsylvania, Massachusetts, and [it] has formed groups in Chicago, Detroit and Los Angeles." Malcolm Goldstein calls the Workers Dance League "one of the most seminal developments in radical art during the decade." See his *The Political Stage: American Drama and Theater of the Great Depression* (New York: Oxford University Press, 1974), p. 41.

5. *New Theatre* was "an organ of the worker's theaters of the U.S.A. (section of the International Union of Revolutionary Theatre) and Workers Dance League" according to its first issue in September/October 1933. Actually, however, it continued *Worker's Theatre*, a publication that first appeared in April 1931, published by the Workers Laboratory Theatre, a section of the Workers International Relief Cultural Activities Department. The last issue of *Worker's Theatre* appeared in May/June 1933. In 1937, *New Theatre* changed its title to *New Theatre and Film* and ceased publication in that year. The Workers Dance League itself was founded in December 1932. Exceptions to silence in the critical literature are recent: Stacey Prickett, "From Workers' Dance to New Dance," in *Dance Research* 7, no. 1 (spring 1989): 47-64; Prickett, "Dance and the Workers' Struggle," in *Dance Research* 7, no. 1 (spring 1990): 47–61; and Mark Wheeler, "New Dance in a New Deal Era," in *Dance: Current Selected Research* 2, ed. Lynnette Y. Overby and James H. Humphrey (New York: AMS, 1990), pp. 33–45. For a rare example of scholarship on this subject prior to the late eighties, see Jeanne Lunin Heymann, "Dance in the Depression: The WPA Project," in *Dance Scope* 9, no. 2 (1975): 28–40. In 1985, Giora Manor read a paper titled "Red, Pink and Naive Dances: Dance in the Social Scene in America in the Thirties" to the Society of Dance History Scholars. This paper focuses on the themes of revolutionary dance and the details of specific works of Sokolow and Dudley. He does not, however, explore the debate over modern dance in contemporary little magazines and he confuses "progressive" with "radical," calling everyone involved with the movement "progressive." An abstract of this paper was published in the 1985 *Proceedings*, but a copy of the manuscript is available in the Dance Collection at the Lincoln Center Library for the Performing Arts, New York City. The most impressive research to date on this subject is Ellen Graff's dissertation "Stepping Left: Radical Dance in New York City, 1928–1942" (New York University, 1993). See also Lynne Conner, "'Bristling with Revolutionary Protest': Socialist Agendas in the Modern Dance, 1931–1938," in *Crucibles of Crisis: Performing Social Change*, ed. Janelle Reinelt (Ann Arbor: University of Michigan Press, forthcoming). See also *Studies in Dance History (Of, By, and For the People: Dancing on the Left in the 1930s)*, ed. Lynn Garafola, vol. 5, no. 1 (Spring 1994) which includes selected reviews by Edna Ocko.

6. Emanuel Eisenberg, "Diagnosis of the Dance," in *New Theatre* (July/August 1934): 25.

7. Edna Ocko, "The Revolutionary Dance Movement," in *New Masses* 11, no. 11 (June 12, 1934): 27 (my emphasis).

8. Oakley Johnson, "The Dance," p. 17.

9. James Burkhart Gilbert, *Writers and Partisans*, p. 123.

10. A letter to the editors by Maryn Myers titled "The Dance in Moscow" asserts that the Soviets "know nothing of modern dancing and cling passionately to ballet," but adds: "If we are ahead of them in dance form, they are ahead of us in dance spirit." See "The Voice of the Audience," in *New Theatre* (October 1934): 25. Other articles claim that the Soviets were developing a form of mass dance. See "Mass Dance in Soviet Union," in *New Theatre* (February 1934): 4–5; Chen I-Wan, "The Soviet Dance: The Basis for a Mass Dance Culture," in *New Theatre* (January 1935): 17–19.

11. In his article "Revolutionary Ballet Forms," in *New Theatre* ([October 1934]: 14), Kirstein conflated absolute and mass dance in classical ballet by arguing that "mass" refers to the potential size of the audience for ballet: "The dance audience in New York and in America is potentially enormous." Kirstein's rhetorical sleights of hand identify mass dance with entertainment, thus eliding the more radical sense in which mass dance incites the mass to replace the individual in its claims for class recognition. Kirstein reached the height of glibness in a second *New Theatre* article, "The Dance as Theater" (May 1935), by conflating mass and absolute dance: "A healthy revival in interest towards the more absolute forms of theatrical dancing has recently been precipitated in this country. . . . Theatre in the service of the great mass public" (p. 20).

12. This raises interesting complications in the "realist-modernist" debates of German Marxism. See *Aesthetics and Politics*. Annette T. Rubenstein has written of left-wing theater in America: "There wasn't the kind of theoretical debate that one had in the Soviet Union; there was not the material for it." Although the left-wing dance movement was smaller than the theater movement, clearly there was a theoretical debate in dance. See Rubenstein, "The Cultural World of the Communist Party: An Historical Overview," in *New Studies in the Politics and Culture of U.S. Communism*, ed. Michael E. Brown, Randy Martin, Frank Rosengarten, and George Snedeker (New York: Monthly Review Press, 1993), p. 256.

13. James Burkhart Gilbert, *Writers and Partisans*, p. 112.

14. Edna Ocko, "The Revolutionary Dance Movement," p. 27.

15. Emanuel Eisenberg, "Ladies of the Revolutionary Dance," in *New Theatre* (February 1935): 10.

16. Ibid.

17. Irving Ignatin, "'Revolutionary' Dance Forms," in *New Theatre* (December 1935): 28.

18. Paul Douglas, "Modern Dance Forms," in *New Theatre* (November 1935): 26.

19. Ezra Freedman, "Dance: Which Technique?," in *New Theatre* (May 1934): 17.

20. Eisenberg, "Diagnosis of the Dance," p. 25.

21. Jane Dudley, "The Mass Dance," in *New Theatre* (December 1934): 17.

22. Ibid.

23. Ruth Allerhand, "The Lay Dance," in *New Theatre* (April 1935): 26.

24. Edith Segal, "Directing the New Dance," in *New Theatre* (May 1935): 23. For Dudley, too, the very choreographic process of mass dance had political benefits: "In this way, large numbers of people can be mobilized not only to dance but to observe, and through the discussion of the theme and the problems of movement brought forward by the leader and dancers, clarity of ideology can be given" (Dudley, "The Mass Dance," p. 17). Moreover, Dudley's plan for the mass dance class is highly hierarchized:

> Finally there should be a chairman to lead discussion before class begins, and after class when questions are asked, and an actual dance leader for the class who can direct large groups of people, who understands the theme as a revolutionary dance leader. A committee

should be formed to decide on the theme and the leader. The committee's responsibility would be to see that the leader thoroughly understands the theme. The committee can also handle the organizing of the class, the sending out of notices, selecting the studio, etc. (Ibid.)

It is interesting to note that despite the organizational structure with its checks and balances, each time it is a question of the dance leader or of dance movement, the practice of dance and of revolution become exactly equivalent.

25. Steve Foster, "The Revolutionary Solo Dance," in *New Theatre* (January 1935): 23. Soloists who would subsequently join this movement included Lilian Shapero, Sophia Delza, Letitia Ide, Merle Hirsh, William Matons, Marie Marchowsky, Jose Limon, and Rose Crystal.

26. See Edna Ocko, "The Dance," in *New Masses* 13, no. 10 (December 4, 1934): 30.

27. Emanuel Eisenberg, "Ladies of the Revolutionary Dance," p. 10.

28. Ibid.

29. Ibid., p. 11.

30. Nathaniel Buchwald, "A Revolutionary Gentleman," in *New Theatre* (March 1935): 24.

31. Eisenberg, "A Reply by E. Eisenberg," in *New Theatre* (March 1935): 24.

32. Buchwald, "A Revolutionary Gentleman," p. 24.

33. Paul Douglas, "Modern Dance Forms," p. 26.

34. Ibid.

35. Ibid., p. 27.

36. Ibid.

37. Irving Ignatin, "Revolutionary Dance Forms," p. 29.

38. Paul Douglas, "Modern Dance Forms," p. 27.

39. Edna Ocko, "The Revolutionary Dance Movement," p. 27.

40. Harry Elion, "Perspectives of the Dance," in *New Theatre* (September 1934): 18.

41. Blanche Evan, "The Dance: An Open Letter to Workers' Dance Group," in *New Theatre* (April 1934): 20.

42. Edna Ocko, "The Revolutionary Dance Movement," p. 27.

43. These remarks should be read alongside Jane Dudley's: "The New Dance Group used to go to parties, trade union parties. It would do some Russian folk dances and then it would do something called 'On the Barricades,' for example. And they were very popular, people adored them. . . . What was exciting was that all of these young people were just welcomed with open arms, because alot of these trade union groups— International Ladies Garment Workers—came with strong cultural traditions, strong. They had their own chorus. There were many small theater groups, language groups, you know the Ukrainians and the Yiddish group, and they'd use their own language in their productions. They would have good theater directors who came from Germany, who were influenced by Piscator or Brecht, and so forth. And so the quality and the inventiveness was absolutely fascinating." "Jane Dudley talking to Tobi Tobias (June 28, 1976)," Oral History Archive, Dance Collection, New York Public Library for the Performing Arts, p. 40.

3. EMOTIVIST MOVEMENT AND HISTORIES OF MODERNISM

1. Bette Davis, *The Lonely Life* (New York: G. P. Putnam's Sons, 1962), p. 67. An earlier version of this essay appeared in *Discourse* 13.1 (fall/winter 1990–91) several months before Graham's death. I wanted to start writing about Graham before her

departure clouded my personal history of spectatorship with a sense of closure and a strain to synthesis. Having already, in a sense, outlived herself, Graham became a subject of intense curiosity overnight. I wish to thank Evan Alderson, Maher Benham, Selma-Jeanne Cohen, and Kathleen Woodward for their help in defining my own discourse on Graham. I am endebted to Kathleen Woodward in particular for the title, to Evan Alderson for many formulations, and to Maher Benham and Selma-Jeanne Cohen for their critical expertise, connoisseurship, and willingness to share.

2. "Every time I climbed a flight of stairs in films—and I spent half my life on them—it was Graham step by step" (ibid.)

3. Ibid. Davis also remarks: "She was all tension—lightning! . . . Miss Graham was the true modern" (ibid.). Davis may have thought of Graham as "the modern woman," rather than as an aggressive modernist artist. Certainly, much of Graham's own emphasis from the start of her choreographic career was on the "virile" character of dance, which in her time could stamp her as a particularly self-reliant woman.

4. This was in reaction, of course, to the exotica of the Denishawn tradition with its presentation of dancers in Egyptian, Hindu, and other scenes of a quasi-spiritual, quasi-sensual nature. Margaret Lloyd writes that Graham's experimentation with dance autonomy began with her teaching at the Eastman School two years after leaving the Denishawn company. She cites Graham as saying of this period: "I was through with character dancing. I wanted to begin, not with characters, or ideas, but with movement. So I started with the simplest—walking, skipping, leaping—and went on from there." See Margaret Lloyd, *The Borzoi Book of Modern Dance* (New York: Dance Horizons, 1974), pp. 49–50. My point in resisting Davis's interpretation of Graham's expressivity is not to argue that Graham was wholly abstract. Instead, I argue that the emotional import of Graham's aesthetic was heavily ambiguated by the formal concerns associated with visual abstraction current in the 1920s.

5. Martha Graham, "Dancer's Focus," in Barbara Morgan, *Martha Graham: Sixteen Dances in Photographs* (Dobbs Ferry, N.Y.: Morgan and Morgan, 1941; rpt. 1980), p. 11.

6. Martin goes on to note: "All theory which is more than hypothetical must be by deduction from the practice of the best artists." See Martin, *The Modern Dance* (1933; rpt. New York: Dance Horizons, 1965), p. 1.

7. "Letters from Sally Banes and Susan Manning," in *Drama Review* 33/1 (spring 1989): 14. The Greenbergian gallery aesthetic is the doctrine of minimalism as expounded by art critic Clement Greenberg in his 1949 essay "The New Sculpture." See Greenberg, *The Collected Essays and Criticism: Arrogant Purpose, 1945–1949*, ed. John O'Brian (Chicago: University of Chicago Press, 1988), pp. 313–19. Earlier expressions of this doctrine date back to 1939–40. Minimalism is interpreted by Greenberg to be the process by which "painting, sculpture, music, poetry become more concrete by confining themselves strictly to that which is most palpable in them, namely their mediums, and by refraining from treating or imitating what lies outside the province of their exclusive effects" (ibid., p. 314).

8. According to art historian Timothy J. Clark, Greenberg reiterated his theory of the absolute in support of Jackson Pollack. See Timothy J. Clark, "Jackson Pollack's Abstraction," in *Reconstructing Modernism: Art in New York, Paris, and Montreal, 1945–1964*, ed. Serge Guilbaut (Cambridge: MIT Press, 1990), p. 207. In this article, Clark demonstrated that Pollack's interest in abstraction between 1947 and 1950 was "in abstract painting's literal, physical 'relation to the world.'" Analogously, Graham replaced the representation of emotions with a concept of absolute physical relation. This is the very rationale that underpins Merce Cunningham's use of chance procedure, as well as much subsequent minimalism in modern dance. Because dance is an art of living bodies, it already has presence on its side; that is, dance has an unorthodox perspective on representation as presentation built into it. Modern dance works its way further out of mediacy and toward immediacy by jettisoning specified emotional con-

tent, its clearest anchor to representation. Nevertheless, transposing painterly definitions of abstract expressionism to dance is difficult because the body itself maintains a
literal relation to the world regardless of any particular choreographic program imposed on it.

9. "'Modern' in dance did not mean modernist." See Sally Banes, *Terpsichore in
Sneakers* (Middletown: Wesleyan University Press, 1987), p. xv.

10. In 1973, David Michael Levin applied Greenberg's theory of sculpture to dance,
in precisely the same manner as does Banes, to argue that George Balanchine is the
true modernist choreographer. See Levin, "Balanchine's Formalism," in *What Is Dance?*,
pp. 123–45. Greenberg's theory of modernism is aesthetically *and* historically determined. He proposes four historical stages in Western art which lead from simple mimesis in the Renaissance to reflexivity in the twentieth century. This theory does not
apply to dance history because the origin of ballet in European court entertainment,
the dance equivalent of Levin's "merely theatrical event" (p. 129), does not correspond to "simplicity of mimesis" in painting (p. 126). Late Renaissance and early
baroque dance are not about the imitation of reality. Once again, history is serving an
aesthetic ripe for critical promotion. On the ends of early dance, see Franko, *The
Dancing Body in Renaissance Choreography* (Birmingham: Summa, 1986); Rudolf
Zur Lippe, *Naturbeherrschung am Menschen* (Frankfurt-am-Main: Syndikat, 1979);
and Franko, *Dance as Text*. The problem concerns the historical interpretation of
minimalism and its applicability to conceptual art of the 1960s. To pursue it here
would take us far from our focus on Graham's evolving aesthetic. See Victor Burgin,
"The Absence of Presence: Conceptualism and Postmodernisms," in *The End of Art
Theory: Criticism and Postmodernity* (Atlantic Highlands, N.J.: Humanities Press,
1986), pp. 29–50, and Mark Franko, "Some Notes on Yvonne Rainer, Modernism,
Politics, Emotion, Performance, and Its Aftermath," in *Meaning in Motion: New Cultural Studies of Dance*, ed. Jane Desmond (Durham: Duke University Press, 1995).

11. See Susan Manning, "Modernist Dogma and Post-Modern Rhetoric," in *Drama
Review* 32:4 (winter 1988): 32-39, as well as her *Ecstasy and the Demon: Feminism
and Nationalism in the Dances of Mary Wigman* (Berkeley: University of California
Press, 1993). In a similar manner, Randy Martin has pointed out that the aesthetic
goals of Judsonites—the rejection of psychological emphasis and the foregrounding of
a performance's materials—were also typical of early modernist innovators such as
Duchamp and Meyerhold. See Randy Martin, *Performance as Political Act: The Embodied Self* (New York: Bergin and Garvey, 1990), p. 87. Manning locates Banes's
reappropriation of modernism in "postmodern rhetoric." Banes's sense of historical
modern dance is, indeed, postmodern in that it operates through cultural stereotypes
of historical modern dance. It is a form of history as pastiche.

12. This thesis is further developed with reference to Martin's relationship to Graham in Franko, "History/Theory—Criticism/Practice," in *Corporealites*, ed. Susan Foster (New York: Routledge, 1995).

13. Even Lincoln Kirstein, no loyal admirer of Graham, recognized her claim on
ambiguity: "Her long pale mask, her deep eyes, her expression half between pain
and foetal blindness, has the ambiguous, frightened humor of an idiot's games. This
ambiguity is chronic." Lincoln Kirstein, *Ballet: Bias and Belief: Three Pamphlets
Collected and Other Dance Writings of Lincoln Kirstein* (New York: Dance Horizons, 1983), p. 39.

14. Donald B. Kuspit, *Clement Greenberg: Art Critic* (Madison: University of Wisconsin Press, 1979), p. 92. My aim, however, is not to redeem Greenberg's theory of
modernism.

15. In 1939, John Martin thought subjective abstraction was at work only in
Graham's earliest works, that is, only in the famous first concert of 1926. But to think
of Graham's dance as "essentially dramatic" is to read those early works from the
perspective of the late 1930s. See "Martha Graham," in his *Introduction to the Dance*
(New York: Dance Horizons, 1939; rpt. 1965), pp. 251–56.

16. This is the term Banes applies to "analytic post-modern dance." See *Terpsichore in Sneakers*, pp. xx-xxii.

17. See Nancy Ruyter, *Reformers and Visionaries*, p. 125. Ruyter calls the New York concert dance of the late twenties and early thirties "the next stage in the development of an anti-formalist tradition in American dance."

18. Banes, *Terpsichore in Sneakers*, p. xv.

19. Yvonne Rainer, "The Mind Is a Muscle," in *Work, 1961–73* (New York: New York University Press, 1974), p. 64. This is one of the key essays in the literature of postmodern dance to connect dance to Greenberg's theory.

20. On the roots of that ideology, see Joseph R. Roach, "Darwin's Passion: The Language of Expression on Nature's Stage," in *Discourse* 13:1 (fall/winter 1990–91): 40-58.

21. Paul Goodman, *The Empire City* (Indianapolis: Bobbs-Merrill, 1942), p. 19.

22. Martin, "Expressional Dance," in *Introduction to the Dance*, p. 253.

23. Its use-value becomes substituted by its exchange-value. "Where the classical decadence was a machine that manufactured nothing, and the romantic revolution [Duncan] was an attempt to manufacture something without a machine—to express something outside and above oneself, the modern dance has arisen to manufacture something with a highly perfected machine" (John Martin, *The Modern Dance*, p. 30).

24. Ibid.

25. Ibid.

26. Paul Strand cited in Barbara Buhler Lynes, *O'Keeffe, Stieglitz and the Critics, 1916–1929* (Chicago: University of Chicago Press, 1991), p. 87. Lynes republishes the entire article pp. 216-20. I thank Norman Bryson for calling my attention to the connections between O'Keeffe and Graham.

27. The strategy that O'Keeffe applied only with great difficulty once she became recognized as a painter was more successfully implemented by Virginia Woolf.

28. See Lynes, pp. 120–23. It is within this critical context that the artist as an embodiment of America arises with regard to O'Keeffe, as it would also for Graham.

29. Louis Horst, "Immediacies in Modern Life: (I) Introspection," in *Manuscripts: Horst, Louis* (folder 69), unpaginated. Dance collection, New York Public Library for the Performing Arts at Lincoln Center. Citations from Horst's teaching notes will be referred to hereafter as *Horst Manuscripts*.

30. Ibid.

31. Horst, "Archaic," in *Horst Manuscripts*.

32. Ibid.

33. Horst, "Immediacies," in *Horst Manuscripts*.

34. Horst, "Archaic," in *Horst Manuscripts*.

35. Through the famous series of photographs taken of her by Alfred Stieglitz. See *Alfred Stieglitz, Georgia O'Keeffe, a Portrait* (New York: Metropolitan Museum of Art, 1978).

36. Graham cited in Armitage, *Martha Graham*, pp. 105, 97.

37. Martha Graham, *Blood Memory* (New York: Doubleday, 1991).

38. Graham, *The Notebooks of Martha Graham* (New York: Harcourt Brace Jovanovich, 1973). This work will be referred to hereafter in notes as *Notebooks*.

39. Martin, *Introduction*, pp. 251–52. Martin elaborated a communication theory, called "metakinesis," to account for the communication of subjectivity.

40. Dane Rudhyar, "Modern Dance Group at the Cross-Road," in *Dance Observer* 2, no. 8 (November 1935): 92–93.

41. Ibid.

42. See "*Terpsichore* Combat Continued," letter from Sally Banes, *Drama Review* 33/4 (1989): 17. The theoretical model behind her methodology realigns the terms "modern," "modernist," "postmodern," and "postmodernist" in a way that Banes herself admits is unwieldy. Levin, however, still argues the Greenbergian model for dance history. See his "Postmodernism in Dance: Dance Discourse, Democracy," in

Postmodernism: Philosophy and the Arts, ed. Hugh J. Silverman (New York: Routledge, 1990), pp. 207–33. I remain suspicious of the "nomenclatural schematism" (p. 221) purveyed by Levin's terminology. Once history is so neatly schematized, critical historiography can practically "do itself," that is, become "immanent" to a sort of effortless, "cool" writing. Such dance history is itself influenced by the reduction of minimalism: Its theory is self-disclosing. As Victor Burgin has pointed out, "Greenberg collapses the project of art into that of art criticism" (*The End of Art Theory*, p. 15).

43. Yve-Alain Bois, "Kahnweiler's Lesson," in *Representations* 18 (spring 1987): 39.

44. See Stark Young on early Graham: "There was . . . too great an absence of movement: the dancer's technique involved steps and positions, but the transition, which is the living element, was close to nil." Young, "Martha Graham," in *Immortal Shadows: A Book of Dramatic Criticism* (New York: Hill and Wang, 1948), p. 255.

45. Lloyd, *Modern Dance*, p. 57.

46. "Martha Remembered, Interviews by Joseph H. Mazo," in *Dance Magazine* (July 1991): 41. According to H. T. Parker in 1932, "Her presence is remote rather than sympathetic, less ingratiating than impressive." Parker, *Movement Arrested: Dance Reviews of H. T. Parker*, ed. Olive Holmes (Middletown: Wesleyan University Press, 1982), p. 180.

47. Edwin Denby, *Dance Writings*, ed. Robert Cornfield and William Mackay (New York: Knopf, 1986), p. 42.

48. Ibid., p. 229.

49. Ibid., p. 234. "In Graham dance, postural bound flow has aesthetic value. It serves as a salient quality that visualizes tenseness, a holding back, restriction, and uneasiness." See Billie Lepczyk, "Martha Graham's Movement Invention Viewed through Laban Analysis," in *Dance: Current Selected Research* 1, ed. Lynnette Y. Overby and James H. Humphrey (New York: AMS, 1989), p. 48.

50. Martha Graham, "A Modern Dancer's Primer for Action," in *Dance as a Theatre Art*, ed. Selma-Jeanne Cohen (New York: Dodd, Mead, 1975), p. 138. This 1941 article was originally published in *Dance: A Basic Educational Technique*, ed. Frederick R. Rogers (New York: Macmillan, 1941). It will be referred to hereafter in notes as "Primer."

51. Bois sees this refusal even in "the expressionist deformation of the mask" ("Kahnweiler's Lesson," p. 61). Marianna Torgovnick describes how Roger Fry's *Vision and Design*, published in 1920, established primitive and modern art as "twin phenomena." See *Gone Primitive: Savage Intellects, Modern Lives* (Chicago: University of Chicago Press, 1990), p. 86.

52. The following remarks are based on viewings of Dwight Godwin's cinematic study of the work (1941), as well as on later reconstructions live and on film.

53. Graham's style is blatantly contradicted in the reconstructed version of *Lamentation* as danced by Peggy Lyman for a "Dance in America" broadcast (1974).

54. Stanley Burnshaw, "The Dance," in *New Masses* 22, no. 8 (November 30, 1934): 27.

55. Horst, "Archaic," in *Horst Manuscripts*.

56. Ibid.

57. Ibid.

58. Ibid. Horst goes on to explain that "Cezanne and Matisse are 'archaic' in their feeling for planes and their absorption in the Materials of their art."

59. Elizabeth Kendall, *Where She Danced*, p. 41.

60. Thus, Roger Copeland's dictum that "primitivists confuse theatrical and ritualistic dance" does not apply to this work, nor probably to any of Graham's works, even though it was framed with them in mind. This is a pitfall of an intellectual approach to dance deprived of an aesthetic. In other terms, the visual nature of dance can induce a mistaken intellectual reductionism. See Copeland's "Postmodern Dance and the Repu-

diation of Primitivism," in *Partisan Review* 1 (1983): 114. My comments are based on a performance of *Primitive Mysteries* as reconstructed by the Graham Company in 1965 and, more recently, on viewing the film of that same reconstruction produced in the previous year by Dwight Godwin (Connecticut College, 1964).

61. Horst, "Archaic," in *Horst Manuscripts*.

62. Francesco Pellizzi, "Adventures of the Symbol: Magic for the Sake of Art," in *Lectures on Constructed Thought* (New York: School of Architecture of Cooper Union, 1988).

63. I would add that this choreographic intent was also independent of any expressive direction given to the dancers. For example, in *Modern Dance Forms in Relation to Other Modern Arts* (San Francisco: Impulse, 1961; rpt. New York: Dance Horizons, 1975) Louis Horst and Carroll Russell describe what could easily be some elements of the processional entrances and exits of *Primitive Mysteries* as a classroom study: "The primitive walk (feet straight or turned in) might be the primal discovery that a human being can walk—every step an adventure, an exploration. 'Come down into the earth with your heels!' Martha Graham tells her pupils. 'Walk as if for the first time'" (p. 61). Even if Graham actually used such a directorial approach, the effect of these sections in her work was, in Edwin Denby's words, to "exaggerate the pseudo-naive stylization." See Denby, *Dance Writings*, p. 230.

64. Subtitles given the three scenes— "Hymn to the Virgin," "Crucifixus," and "Hosanna"—do not point to an exhaustive interpretation.

65. Bois, "Kahnweiler's Lesson," p. 44.

66. Julia Kristeva's theory of the semiotic and the symbolic would be a useful tool to describe Graham's early aesthetic were it not for the panlogism making any adaptation of Kristeva's semiotics to dance tautological.

67. Susan Manning, "Modernist Dogma," pp. 32–39.

68. Dance performances frequently appear to elude the weight of their own history, probably because they are subject to the imperative of newness and its attendant mythology of vitality in action, a mythology that Graham also made ample use of. Thus, history is rarely evoked in the performance fabric outside of historical reconstructions that allow for an acceptably reduced energy level.

69. Richard Kostelanetz, "Profile of Merce Cunningham," in *Michigan Quarterly Review* 14 (fall 1975): 366. Kostelanetz also says that their work uniformly "evoked a plot and/or depended upon a familiar literary allusion."

70. Susan Sontag, "For 'Available Light': A Brief Lexicon," in *Art in America* 71 (December 1983): 102.

71. Friedrich Nietzsche, "The Birth of Tragedy," in *Basic Writings of Nietzsche*, section 19, pp. 114–21.

72. There are marked similarities between Graham's choreographic preoccupations in the 1920s and Antonin Artaud's theatrical theory. Artaud wrote *The Theater and Its Double* in the early thirties, although it was only published in 1938. Both Graham and Artaud were drawn by the body's potential for direct communication. Modernist experiments with directness are formalist in the way they limit the scope of their subject matter to the body and its power to communicate as signifier and referent. All connotations (the signified) are swallowed up in "the thing itself." However, there are also marked differences between Artaud and Graham. Artaud rejected myth whereas Graham ultimately embraced it.

73. Graham, "Primer," p. 136.

74. John Martin sees this as a tension in her work between impersonation, which is never "pure," and identification, which is more subjective than observation but never falls into subjective abstraction, except in her earliest works. His use of this terminology is inconsistent because "external identification" becomes in one instance a synonym for impersonation. See *Introduction*, p. 255.

75. As with the beginnings of abstraction in cubism (also firmly anchored, as

Graham's work would be, in the primitive), formal experimentation was superimposed on a figural ground. The body in space could be considered both the figural ground and the material for formal experimentation. Graham did not exemplify Greenberg's theory of minimalism, but she did illustrate Ortega's account of dehumanization in modern art. See Jose Ortega y Gasset, *The Dehumanization of Art and Other Essays on Art, Culture, and Literature* (Princeton: Princeton University Press, 1968). Ortega's reflections on modernism were first published in 1925, one year before Graham's choreographic debut.

76. Martha Graham, "Seeking an American Art of the Dance," in *Revolt in the Arts: A Survey of the Creation, Distribution and Appreciation of Art in America*, ed. Oliver M. Sayler (New York: Brentano, 1930), p. 253. This article will be referred to hereafter in notes as "Seeking."

77. Graham quoted in Armitage, *Martha Graham* (New York: Dance Horizons, 1966), p. 100 (my emphasis).

78. Horst and Russell, *Modern Dance Forms*, p. 52.

79. Martha Graham, *Notebooks*, p. 205.

80. Graham cited in Armitage, *Martha Graham*, p. 105.

81. "Two Guggenheim Fellowships," writes Selma-Jeanne Cohen, "awarded to her in the Thirties, enabled her to study the primitive rituals of the American southwest and of Mexico." See "The Achievement of Martha Graham," in *Chrysalis* vol. XI, nos. 5–6 (1958): 6.

82. See the section "Mass Dance" in the present chapter.

83. Graham, "Seeking," p. 255.

84. Perhaps this is why Eric Bentley, following Havelock Ellis, thought of Graham as ecstatic rather than pantomimic. Bentley distinguishes between the pantomimic and the ecstatic in the following way: "The pantomimic theater depicts life, holds the mirror up to nature. The ecstatic theater affirms life and celebrates nature. The one shows life as it has become—what we call psychology and sociology. The other is concerned with life still unlived, unindividuated . . . she [Graham] is the fullest realization we know of that magical theater which Craig and Yeats and so many others have dreamed." See Eric Bentley, "Martha Graham's Journey," in *What Is Dance?*, pp. 197–98.

85. Graham, "Primer," p. 140. Compare with James Agee writing in 1939: "Each of you is a creature which has never in all time existed before and which shall never in all time exist again and which is not quite like any other." James Agee and Walker Evans, *Let Us Now Praise Famous Men* (Boston: Houghton Mifflin, 1988). p. 100.

86. Graham quoted in Karl Leabo, ed., *Martha Graham* (New York: Theatre Arts, 1961).

87. Graham quoted in Armitage, *Martha Graham*, p. 101.

88. Ibid., pp. 101, 103.

89. Ibid., p. 102.

90. Ibid., pp. 100, 103.

91. This phrase originated with Serge Guilbaut in *How New York Stole the Idea of Modern Art: Abstract Expressionism, Freedom, and the Cold War*, trans. Arthur Goldhammer (Chicago: University of Chicago Press, 1983), p. 2.

92. The set designer Isamu Noguchi wrote:

> It was for me the genesis of an idea—to wed the total void of theater space to form and action. A rope, running from the two top corners of the proscenium to the floor rear center of the stage, bisected the three-dimensional void of stage space. This seemed to throw the entire volume of air straight over the heads of the audience.

See Noguchi, *A Sculptor's World* (New York: Harper and Row, 1968), p. 125.

93. *Frontier* was an allegory of the manifest destiny of modern dance and, in this

sense, reflexive. Graham's Americana cycle surely led to the term "pioneers" being applied to modern dance innovators of her generation. It was as if she had taken up Duncan's phrase, "I see America dancing," and transformed it into "I am America dancing."

94. "It did show a sincere and genuine nature," Young wrote, "but a nature not yet flowered in culture and freedom." See Stark Young, *Immortal Shadows*, p. 255.

95. Denby, *Dance Writings*, p. 56.

96. Martin even suggested "the complete abandonment of any intellectual effort to understand" as the proper approach to Graham's work. See *Introduction*, p. 252.

97. Graham quoted in Horst, *Horst Manuscripts*.

98. Martin cited in Armitage, *Martha Graham*, p. 8.

99. Graham quoted in Armitage, *Martha Graham*, p. 101.

100. "Why should a hand try to be rain?" Graham wrote in 1936. "Think of what a wonderful thing the hand is, and what vast potentialities of movement it has as a hand and not as a poor imitation of something else" (quoted in Armitage, *Martha Graham*, p. 107). That is, Graham originally thought of the body not as a vehicle for metaphors but as a mode of presence close to the experience of being.

101. Graham, "Seeking," p. 249 (my emphasis). She also wrote that "virile gestures are evocative of the only true beauty." Graham quoted in Armitage, *Martha Graham*, p. 97.

102. See Torgovnick, *Gone Primitive*, especially the chapter on Conrad, pp. 141–58.

103. For remarks from this period on women's art as imitative rather than inventive, see Lynes, *O'Keeffe*, pp. 15, 19.

104. Graham quoted in Armitage, *Martha Graham*, p. 97. For Graham, the "foreign element" was both classical ballet and any impulse to employ dance in the service of imitation that might recall an aristocratic and therefore un-American, "representational" aesthetic.

105. See John J. Winkler, "Double Consciousness in Sappho's Lyrics," in *The Constraints of Desire* (New York: Routledge, 1990), pp. 162–87.

106. Graham quoted in Armitage, *Martha Graham*, p. 103.

107. Richard Sennett defines holism as "being really alive to the present moment." See Sennett, *The Fall of Public Man* (New York: Knopf, 1974), p. 263. For a different discussion of holism, see Betty Jean Craige, "Literature in a Global Society," in *PMLA* 106, no. 3 (May 1991): 395–401.

108. Kendall, *Where She Danced*, p. 19.

109. Cunningham's use of chance was meant to restore dance to a praxis of life. On Hawkins, see *Erick Hawkins: Theory and Training* (New York: American Dance Guild, 1979).

110. See Rosalind E. Krauss, *The Originality of the Avant-Garde and Other Modernist Myths* (Cambridge: MIT Press, 1985), p. 229. Stephen Polcari explores correspondences between Graham's work of the forties and fifties and abstract expressionism in "Martha Graham and Abstract Expressionism," *Smithsonian Studies in American Art* (winter 1990): 2-27.

111. Graham cited in Armitage, *Martha Graham*, p. 102. Graham also referred to our land's "monstrous vital rhythms, crude glowing colors, dynamic economy of gesture, and that divine awkwardness which is ever a part of what is vital, fresh and masculine in the arts." See Graham, "Seeking," p. 250.

112. Hal Foster, "The 'Primitive' Unconscious of Modern Art," in *October* 34 (fall 1985). See also Ann L. Ardis, "Turning the Century, Writing New Histories," in *New Women, New Novels: Feminism and Early Modernism* (New Brunswick: Rutgers University Press, 1990), pp. 167-76.

113. Michael Gold used this phrase to characterize Ring Lardner, William Carlos Williams, and Edgar Lee Masters. See James F. Murphy, *The Proletarian Moment: The*

Controversy over Leftism in Literature (Urbana: University of Illinois Press, 1991), p. 133. See also Michael Gold's "Go Left, Young Writers!" in which he says, "The America of the working class is undiscovered. It is a lost continent" (*The Mike Gold Reader* [New York: International, 1954], p. 51).

114. Murphy, op. cit., pp. 132, 134.

115. Graham, "Seeking," p. 250.

116. Don McDonagh, *Martha Graham: A Biography* (New York: Praeger, 1973), p. 113.

117. This quote is transcribed in recent programs of the Graham company as a note to "Steps in the Street."

118. Jane Dudley talking to Tobi Tobias, Oral History Archive, Dance Collection of the New York Public Library (June 28, 1976), transcript, p. 16.

119. Edna Ocko, "Martha Graham—Dances in Two Worlds," in *New Theatre* (July 1935): 26. "Meaningless" here means socially insignificant.

120. For the background and essential texts of this debate, see *Aesthetics and Politics*, trans. and ed. Ronald Taylor (London: Verso, 1977).

121. Alan M. Wald has attempted "to rectify the social amnesia that has caused us to forget the radical and Marxist heritage of American letters in our century." See Wald, *The Revolutionary Imagination: The Poetry and Politics of John Wheelwright and Sherry Mangan* (Chapel Hill: University of North Carolina Press, 1983), p. xiii.

122. Emanuel Eisenberg, "Ladies of the Revolutionary Dance," in *New Theatre* (February 1935): 10.

123. Ibid., p. 11.

124. Richard Sennett, *The Fall of Public Man*, p. 184. Sennett goes on to explain that "In a culture of personalities . . . freedom becomes idiosyncratic expression rather than an image of how humanity can live" (p. 190).

125. Paul Douglas, "Modern Dance Forms," in *New Theatre* (November 1935): 27.

126. Ibid.

127. See chapter 2 of this book.

128. Edna Ocko, "The Dance," in *New Masses* 13, no. 70 (December 4, 1934): 30.

129. In the same column, Gold also wrote: "If T. S. Eliot has influenced the proletarian poets, it is Martha Graham and Mary Wigman who have almost ruined the dancers. Graham is a very gifted bourgeois dancer whose work expresses the despair and death of the present system. Her mood is that of the psychiatric ward and the graveyard. Sometimes, like T. S. Eliot she tries to escape from her torture chamber into a primitive mysticism, but even here she cannot shake off the disease that is destroying her" (*Daily Worker* [Thursday, June 14, 1934]: 5). Edna Ocko responded to Gold:

> Technics do not pop out of a Jack-in-the-box. They are the product of years of training, and it requires many more years of training to destroy what one has lived by and to build anew. The young revolutionary dancer has neither time nor inclination at present to sit down and consciously plan an uncharted technical course to pursue for herself merely because an artist who has already evolved a complete system of body training happens to be bourgeois. She uses what time and talent she has to compose dances based on those issues she deems revolutionary. . . . As our dancers develop, as their contact with the struggles of the working class becomes increasingly involved and all-encompassing, as their political education intensifies their point of view to include vaster implications and broader themes— in short, the more revolutionary they become, and I reiterate mildly, that takes time, the more they will find the bourgeois technic they employ inadequate and sterile, and out of the pressure of new, ex-

citing, courageous, revolutionary ideas will come the urgency to discard old technics and create a revolutionary one peculiar to their
needs. At any rate, they will have used Graham and Wigman and
Duncan and have found it wanting; they will not have regretfully
chucked it overboard willy-nilly because Michael Gold thought it
stultified. Give them a chance.

See Edna Ocko, "Reply to Michael Gold," in *New Theatre* (July-August 1934): 28.
   130. Blanche Evan, "From a Dancer's Notebook," in *New Theatre* (April 1936): 45.
   131. Stanley Burnshaw, "The Dance," in *New Masses* 22, no. 8 (November 20, 1934): 27.
   132. Ibid.
   133. Paul Love, "Martha Graham," in *Dance Observer* 1, no. 2 (March 1934): 16.
   134. "Martha Graham and Her Dance Group," in *Dance Observer* 9 (December 1935): 100.
   135. Ibid. Yet, although Love heralds Graham's growing accessibility in physical-emotional terms, he cannot but regret the loss of technical definition that would ensue: "Movements taken in isolation are superb, but their performance is so much a joy to Miss Graham herself, in addition to her audience, that the form is very often lost."
   136. Paul Douglas, "Modern Dance Forms," in *New Theatre* (Nov. 1935): 27.
   137. Evan, "From a Dancer's Notebook," p. 44.
   138. Edna Ocko, "Martha Graham—Dances in Two Worlds," p. 27. The question of Graham's "verbal sympathies" will be addressed shortly.
   139. Evan, "From a Dancer's Notebook," p. 31.
   140. Eisenberg, "Ladies of the Revolutionary Dance," p. 11.
   141. Marjorie Church, "The Dance in the Social Scene," in *Dance Observer* 4, no. 3 (March 1937): 27, 30.
   142. Irving Ignatin, "Revolutionary Dance Forms," in *New Theatre* (December 1935): 28-29. In this article, Ignatin argues, "At the present time we can see the main seeds of the future growth in the technic of Martha Graham and her school" (p. 29).
   143. Edna Ocko, "Whither Martha Graham?," in *New Theatre* (April 1934): 7. A year later, Ocko added:

> Miss Graham still makes her affirmation of the future in such ab-
> stract terms that the average audience must create, out of good faith
> in the artist, the ideational background for this future. If she will
> make of her dance, as she describes it, "a social document," Martha
> Graham must decide for whom, for which society she speaks. Is it
> for a nation? Is it for a class of people? If so, when will she reach out
> to that class of people and dance for them?

See Ocko, "Martha Graham—Dances in Two Worlds," p. 27.
   144. Edna Ocko, "Artist and Audience," in *New Theatre* (March 1937): 64.
   145. Ibid. Ocko wrote, too:

> Martha Graham is concerned with the wide recognition of her art
> as a powerful and meaningful social force. She seems conscious of
> present-day America, an America of strikes and picket lines, of bit-
> ter poverty and unproductive wealth. She is also aware that a large
> public demands that her dancing reflect this life. She writes "the
> dance reveals the spirit of the country in which it takes root. . . .
> Our work is to create subject matter, significant and contemporary,

for the American dance. . . . As we increasingly find something significant to dance, we shall find more and more persons to dance for." These statements were published several months ago. Her new work, *Horizons,* reaffirms certain American traditions. We take exception not to her choice of material but to her failure to interpret her theme from a "significant and contemporary" viewpoint. By isolating her theme from contemporary references, and then stripping it of human, emotional qualities, Miss Graham makes unsuccessful her efforts to communicate with the very people for whom she is creating. The audience, as critic, becomes unwilling to justify the form in which the ideas are presented (in this case an experimentation with moving decors) when it is unmoved and indifferent to content.

See Ocko, "Dance Reviews," in *New Theatre* (April 1936): 37. Similarly, Owen Burke wrote of the "Masque" section of Graham's *Chronicle*:

> What is the meaning of a central figure that alternately controls and is controlled by unpredictable group movements? Symbolically following the ideological development of the choreography, the solo figure is evidently the masque (title of the movement) of an order— social, economic, or political—which alternately controls or is controlled according to the necessities of imperialist dictates. The question is—just how much of this does the mass audience get? And if it cannot comprehend this particular movement, how much can it pick up of the ensuing movements, and how can it possibly understand the climactic *Prelude to Action* which sums up the dancer's ideological approach?

See Burke, "A Note on the Modern Dance," in *New Masses* 22, no. 4 (January 11, 1937): 18. By 1936–37, it is difficult to gauge to what extent the same historical events that had undone radicalism had also modified critical expectations and to what extent an accommodation to radical critical expectations in artistic production had reorganized critical response.

146. Graham quoted in Armitage, *Martha Graham,* p. 104.

147. In a strange and unexpected light, one can see within this view the profile of Cunningham's "laissez-faire" attitude toward his dancers in everything that did not concern the exact performance of the work in its technical sense.

148. Graham quoted in Leabo, ed., *Martha Graham,* unpaginated.

149. Evan Alderson, "Metaphor in Dance: The Example of Graham," in *Dance History Scholars Proceedings* (Riverside: Dance History Scholars, 1983), p. 114.

150. Evan, "From a Dancer's Notebook," p. 44.

151. Oliver M. Saylor, "The Fact of Revolt," in *Revolt in the Arts,* p. 16.

152. Ibid., p. 133. On the bankruptcy of progressivism, see Amos Pinchot, "The Failure of the Progressive Party," in *New Masses* 6, no. 3, issue no. 43 (December 1914): 9–10.

153. Agnes De Mille, *Martha: The Life and Work of Martha Graham* (New York: Random House, 1991), p. 193.

154. The Dance Repertory Theater with which she presented her early work advertised one concert in *New Masses.* The ad appeared in vol. 6 (February 1931): 20. The Dance Repertory Theater included Tamiris, Doris Humphrey, Charles Weidman, and Agnes De Mille.

155. Michael Gold, "The Loves of Isadora," in *New Masses* 4 (March 1929): 20.

156. Ibid. This article is reproduced in its entirety in the appendix.

157. Ibid., p. 21.

158. Ann L. Ardis, *New Women, New Novels*, p. 65.

159. Graham, "Seeking," p. 254.

160. Graham quoted in Armitage, *Martha Graham*, p. 99.

161. The film that Graham had done of that work emphasizes this approach cinematically by focusing on details, rarely on the entire figure. The body becomes a textured and extendable surface that expands and contracts as a material, accompanied by the feet, face, and one uncovered hand.

162. Graham, "Seeking," p. 254.

163. Graham quoted in Armitage, *Martha Graham*, p. 98.

164. Graham, "Seeking," p. 254.

165. Stanley Burnshaw, "The Dance," in *New Masses* 16, no. 9 (February 26, 1935): 27.

166. Blanche Evan, "The Star Spangled Dance," in *New Theatre* (October 1934): 24.

167. Michael Gold, "Remembering Isadora Duncan, " in *New Masses* 25, no. 1 (September 28, 1937): 17.

168. See "Olympic Protest," in *Dance Observer* 3, no. 4 (April 1936): 38. Graham's "official" anti-Nazi statement, "A Dancer Speaks," was transcribed from an "extemporaneous talk" given at the Professional's Conference against Nazi Persecution, published in *TAC* (January 1939): 23.

169. Owen Burke, "The Dance," in *New Masses* 22, no. 3 (January 12, 1937): 28.

170. Owen Burke, "The Dance," in *New Masses* 22, no. 13 (March 23, 1937): 29.

171. Owen Burke, "Martha Graham: Revolutionary Dancer," in *New Masses* 26, no. 9 (February 22, 1938): 26.

172. Blanche Evan, "Her Chosen Theme: A Modern Dancer's Credo," in *New Masses* 26, no. 5 (July 26, 1938): 17.

173. *Dance Observer* 5, no. 1 (January 1938): 8.

174. Ibid.

175. Owen Burke, "Music Lovers and Martha Graham," in *New Masses* 27, no. 10 (May 31, 1938): 30.

176. That dancer was Erick Hawkins. *American Document* was prepared by five earlier studies: *American Provincials* (1935), *Frontier* (1935), *Panorama* (1935), *Horizons* (1936), and *Chronicle* (1936).

177. In 1937, *New Masses* had sponsored the Broadway debut of Anna Sokolow's company, Dance Unit, at the Guild Theater. See Margery Dana, "Anna Sokolow and Dance Unit in Prominent Debut," in *Daily Worker* (Saturday, November 20, 1937): 7. Sokolow was the most artistically successful of the revolutionary dancers, and had "definite reactions against all the ignorances, incongruities, and injustices by which the underprivileged are made to suffer," and was able to analyze through dance "the uncertainties and platitudes which are the fetishes of the privileged." See Margery Dana, "Dancing to the Tune of the Times: Young Anna Sokolow among the Leading Modern Dancers of America," in *Daily Worker* (November 10, 1937), clipping file, San Francisco Museum of Performing Arts.

178. Of the titles already mentioned from Graham's early concert career, De Mille singles out *Fragilité* for the way Graham's "wonderful breasts showed through" her costume in the half light. See *Martha*, p. 88.

179. I am endebted here to Susan Manning's "The Mythologization of the Female: Mary Wigman and Martha Graham—A Comparison," in *Ballett International* 14, no. 1 (September 1991): 10–15.

180. In the same year as *American Document*, Lincoln Kirstein argued that the least democratic of forms, classical ballet, was to become the indigenous American dance. Like Graham in search of the American primitive, Kirstein was in search of the

American prototype. "Our style," he wrote, "springs from the personal atmosphere of recognizable American types as exemplified by the behavior of movie stars like Ginger Rogers, Carole Lombard, or the late Jean Harlow. It is frank, open, fresh and friendly." See Lincoln Kirstein, *Blast at Ballet: A Corrective for the American Audience*, pamphlet reprinted in *Ballet: Bias and Belief* (New York: Dance Horizons, 1983), p. 201.

181. Denby, *Dance Writings*, p. 231.

182. Lloyd, *Modern Dance*, pp. 61–62.

183. "Dance," in *New Masses* 28, no. 10 (August 30, 1938): 29.

184. Lincoln Kirstein, "Martha Graham at Bennington," in *Ballet: Bias and Belief*, p. 70.

185. Diana Snyder describes Graham's rapport with the theater world through the commentary of critic Stark Young in "The Most Important Lesson for Our Theater," in *Ballet Review* 10, 4 (winter 1983): 6–20. In preparation for this infusion of theatricality in her work, Graham staged two plays for Katharine Cornell and collaborated in other theatrical productions, notably with Blanche Yurka, during the 1930s.

186. In his biography of Graham, Don McDonagh writes that "the years 1936 and 1937 were to be transitional for Graham. Basically, she was turning away from the abstract starkness of great works like 'Heretic,' 'Lamentation,' 'Primitive Mysteries,' and 'Celebration' and moving toward a new theatricality. In effect, she was trying to bring together the resources of the theater and the vocabulary of movement she had hammered out." See Don McDonagh, *Martha Graham*, p. 113.

187. Graham quoted in Armitage, *Martha Graham*, p. 109.

188. Owen Burke, "Dance Holiday," in *New Masses* 34, no. 4 (January 16, 1940): 30.

189. Graham quoted in Armitage, *Martha Graham*, pp. 102, 110.

190. Graham, "Seeking," p. 250.

191. Yet we need to develop a less reductive idea of how indifference actually functioned in Cunningham's work. See chapter 4, and also Moira Roth, "The Aesthetic of Indifference," in *Artforum* (November 1977): 46–53. Despite its intriguing thesis, Roth's article does not pursue Cunningham's case at any length.

192. Cunningham quoted in Calvin Tomkins, *The Bride and the Bachelors* (New York: Penguin, 1976), pp. 246–47.

4. EXPRESSIVISM AND CHANCE PROCEDURE

1. Part of this essay was first presented as part of the panel Philosophy, Dance, and Ordinary Bodies, at the conference "Bodies: Image, Writing, Technology," sponsored by the International Association for Philosophy and Literature at the University of California, Irvine, 1990. Thanks are extended to the dancers, choreographers, and scholars whose different thoughts and contributions helped shape this essay: Evan Alderson, Richard Bull, Ann Daly, Douglas Dunn, Susan Foster, Susan Manning, Juliet Neidish, Cynthia Novack, George Russell, and Valerie Wise.

2. "The dilemma of modern dance," Siegel writes, "and to some extent all contemporary Western dance, has been how to honor physical expressiveness without descending to trivial levels of thought." See Siegel, "The Truth about Apples and Oranges," in *Drama Review* 32/4 (winter 1988): 24–31. On post-Cunningham work, see Sally Banes, *Terpsichore in Sneakers: Post-Modern Dance*.

3. Francis Sparshott, *Off the Ground*, p. 156. While eminently applicable to dance, expressivity is not limited to an ideology of spontaneous effusion. Clearly, there can be an *art* of the expressive gesture just as there can be an art of imitation. That is, expressive movement can be metaphorically as well as spontaneously emotive in dance. It imitates inwardness. Thus, by referring to the expressivity of dancing in what follows, I do not mean to suggest that expressive properties of a dancer's performance *must*, in

the words of Alan Tormey, "be linked noncontingently to some particular inner state of the performer." On that question, see Tormey, *The Concept of Expression: A Study in Philosophical Psychology and Aesthetics* (Princeton: Princeton University Press, 1971), p. 111.

4. I am concerned here with expressivity in its narrow sense, the expression of emotion, rather than in its broader sense, the expression of ideas. For an interesting treatment of these two topics, see Noël Carroll, "Post-Modern Dance and Expression," in Gordon Fancher and Gerald Myers, *Philosophical Essays on Dance* (Brooklyn: Dance Horizons, 1981), pp. 95–104. In this chapter, however, I wish to modify the view expressed by Carroll and Sally Banes that the Cunningham dancer was neither a personal nor a social agent. See their "Cunningham and Duchamp," in *Ballet Review* 11:2 (summer 1983): 74.

5. Loie Fuller, *Fifteen Years of a Dancer's Life* (New York: Dance Horizons, 1978), p. 70.

6. Sparshott, *Off the Ground*, p. 156. Both Constantin Stanislavski and Isadora Duncan made frequent reference to expression theory. Stanislavski's description of Duncan's dance shows how the Russian theater director apprehended expression theory as a spectator experience leading back to the visual origin of sensation: "I watched her during her performances and her rehearsals, when her developing emotion would first change the expression of her face, and with shining eyes she would pass to the display of what was born in her soul." Stanislavski quoted in Isadora Duncan, *My Life*, p. 168.

7. *Trattato dell'Arte del Ballo di Guglielmo Ebreo da Pesaro* (Bologna: Presso Gaetano Romagnoli, 1873), p. 31.

8. Guillaume Colletet, preface to "Le Ballet de l'Harmonie," in Paul Lacroix, *Ballets et Mascarades de Cour de Henri III à Louis XIV* (Geneva: J. Gay et fils, 1868), vol. IV, p. 209 (my translation).

9. Ibid., pp. 208–209.

10. See Engel, *Idées sur le Geste et l'Action Théâtrale* (1795; rpt. Geneva: Slatkine Reprints, 1979), p. 68 (my translation and emphasis).

11. See Merce Cunningham, "The Functions of a Technique for Dance," in *The Dance Has Many Faces*, ed. Walter Sorell (New York: World Publishing, 1951), pp. 250–55.

12. Merce Cunningham, "Choreography and the Dance," in *The Creative Experience*, ed. Stanley Rosner and Lawrence E. Abt (New York: Grossman, 1970), p. 176.

13. Merce Cunningham, "The Impermanent Art," in *Esthetics Contemporary*, ed. Richard Kostelanetz (Buffalo: Prometheus, 1978), p. 311. This essay was originally written in 1955. According to James Klosty, the very first use of chance operations in Cunningham's work occurred in the 1951 *Sixteen Dances for Soloist and Company of Three*. See Klosty, *Merce Cunningham* (New York: Limelight, 1986), p. 13. In this work, choreographic sequence was determined by artificially imposed options while dance and sound were linked only by their matching length. When explaining what chance operations such as tossing coins or dealing cards can bring to the process of composition, Cunningham repeatedly uses terms such as "field of juxtaposition," "multi-vision," "events," "unlinear thinking." Some of these phrases have lent themselves as names to dances. For Cunningham, the removal of intention clearly corresponds in a significant manner to the suppression of the spatial frame. Or, we might say that the suppression of the spatial frame serves to index the implicit theory according to which chance procedure has been used to remove personal intention.

14. It is difficult to pinpoint when his work began to be interpreted with increased personal neutrality by his own company, though this probably happened by the late seventies.

15. Merce Cunningham and Jacqueline Lesschaeve, *The Dancer and the Dance* (New York: Marion Boyars, 1985), p. 106. Cunningham continues, "That's not something I thought of when I made the dance, but it's in my experience."

16. "Music and Dance and Chance Operations: A Forum Discussion," recorded and broadcast February 16, 1970, by radio station WFCR in Amherst, Massachussets. Also present were composer Robert Stearn, dancer Marianne Simon and interviewer Anita Page.

17. As Sontag points out in that same interview, Cunningham has two ways of explaining his aesthetic concerns: He speaks in a very workman-like fashion of pedestrian human movement as a given which can be constantly manipulated out of a sort of inspired and tireless curiosity on the part of the choreographer; on the other hand, he is given to saying that dancing provides a unique amplification of energy, making reference thereby to its transformative capacity. The first discourse purveys an egalitarian ideology whose rhetoric all but submerges the second discourse. I am arguing that the second, rarer discourse, one of detached expressivism, is secretly more central to Cunningham. The first discourse in its very pragmatism has become an overlay (much as the dreaded additions of expressive attitude) which, after its initially liberating effect, may have paradoxically contributed to an anti-intellectual climate in American dance criticism.

18. Cunningham and Lesschaeve, *The Dancer*, p. 68.

19. Cunningham, "The Impermanent Art," p. 311.

20. Gotthold Ephram Lessing, *Laocoön*, trans. Edward Allen McCormick (Baltimore: Johns Hopkins University Press, 1984), chap. 16, p. 78. See also Roland Barthes, "Diderot, Brecht, Eisenstein," in *Image-Music-Text*, trans. Stephen Heath (New York: Noonday, 1977), pp. 69–78.

21. Cunningham, "The Impermanent Art," p. 311.

22. Ibid., p. 313.

23. These are the terms with which Althusser and Balibar explain the Leibnizian concept of expression: "It presupposes in principle that the whole in question be reducible to an *inner essence*, of which the elements of the whole are then no more than the phenomenal forms of expression, the inner principle of the essence being present at each point in the whole, such that at each moment it is possible to write the immediately adequate equation: *such and such an element . . . = the inner essence of the whole*." See Louis Althusser and Etienne Balibar, *Reading Capital* (London: Verso, 1979), pp. 186–87. Thus, Cunningham's dance is not authentically "un théâtre énergétique," that is, one that replaces a political economy with a libidinal economy, as Jean-François Lyotard prematurely claimed in *Des Dispositifs pulsionnels* (Paris: Christian Bourgois, 1980), p. 96.

24. Whether the current performance style had always been the desired end for which the true means have only recently been found or whether it betokens a regrettable loss of personality will continue to be argued. Deborah Jowitt's recent comments on this subject confirm my point of view in this article. "Not all of Cunningham's dancers," she writes, "especially in recent years have been/are able to 'allow' the power of the instant to speak through them, and may instead express their nervousness, their preoccupation with being correct, or even their desire to remain neutral." *Time and the Dancing Image* (New York: William Morrow, 1988), p. 285.

25. I am referring to the New York premiere of that work at the Hunter College Playhouse in December, 1966. At those performances, *How to Pass, Kick, Fall and Run* was danced by Merce Cunningham, Carolyn Brown, Barbara Lloyd, Sandra Neels, Valda Setterfield, Albert Reid and Gus Solomons, Jr. John Cage sat at a table stage right, talking and appearing to drink champagne.

26. *Suite by Chance* worked with the random structuring of a dance as early as 1953. See Merce Cunningham, *Changes: Notes on Choreography* (New York: Something Else, 1968).

27. See Calvin Tomkins, *The Bride and the Bachelors: Five Masters of the Avant-Garde* (New York: Penguin, 1968), pp. 239–46.

28. Together with Martha Graham, Paul Taylor, Alvin Ailey and Alwin Nikolais.

The hierarchizing of a dance world previously distinguished by rugged individualism was facilitated by the creation of an Association of American Dance Companies, a "coordinating" organization "designed to act as the official voice for dance, especially in the area of application for federal funds for cultural projects." See "New Dance Body Formed in June," in *Dance News* (September 1966): 4.

29. Irving Sandler, *The New York School* (New York: Harper and Row, 1978), p. 166.

30. By this I do not refer to indeterminacy, the extension of chance procedure to the dancer by allowing him or her to determine when certain movements will occur.

31. Jowitt, *Time*, p. 297.

32. See *Salmagundi* 33-34 (spring, summer 1976): 162.

33. Klosty, *Merce*, p. 79.

34. See Vernon Shetley, "Merce Cunningham," in *Raritan* 8, 3 (winter 1989): 73.

35. See chapter 1.

36. Ramsay Burt, "Dance, Masculinity and Postmodernism," in *Postmodernism and Dance: Discussion Papers*, p. 23. Burt associates the evasiveness with regard to content and gender to a gay male strategy of the repressive 1950s in America. See Burt, pp. 27–28.

37. See Vaughan, "Merce Cunningham," in *Performing Arts Journal* III, 3 (winter 1979): 4. This article appears to have been written in response to accusations of the new "anonymity" of Cunningham's dancers and in defense of the Cunningham company as it was then constituted.

38. Ibid., p. 5.

39. Marcia B. Siegel, *Shapes of Change: Images of American Modern Dance* (Boston: Houghton Mifflin, 1971), p. 323. I do not mean to imply that Cunningham choreographed faces although photographs from the early fifties suggest that he may have been experimenting with facial plasticity even as he initiated the first chance procedure operations. His own face appears choreographed in *Sixteen Dances for Soloist and Company of Three* (1951). In the solo for himself in *Septet* (1951), certain set expressions flickered across his face framed by a presenting action of his hands. I thank Michael Bloom of the Cunningham Foundation for enabling me to see the 1964 video of this solo.

40. Carolyn Brown, untitled essay in *Dance Perspectives* 34 (summer 1969): 29. She continues, "an earlier solo, *Root of an Unfocus*, seemed to tell a story, to be *about* something (Merce denies this . . .). But, at this time both Cage and Cunningham were dealing in more dramatic terms with regard to content . . . the movement [of *Untitled Solo*] itself is vibrantly dramatic." Paul Taylor, another member of Cunningham's original company, writes, "Presumably, the dances were not about anything, and as performers, we were to execute rather than interpret. This puzzled me, because the dances seemed to have subjects, or at least emotional climates, and because Merce danced his own roles dramatically. Each of his movements, be they sharp or soft, shouted or whispered, startled or stealthy, clearly meant something to him." See Paul Taylor, *Private Domain* (New York: Knopf, 1987), pp. 48-49.

41. In a broader sense, the sum of their actions are symptomatic of a theory whereby they deliberately bracket intentionality. Thus, each movement points outside of the dance to the egalitarian ideals of freedom that chance procedure has been chosen to foster. In this view, emotional intensity would just be a residual aura clinging to our perception of movement as human action, or a trace of the move from self to chance.

42. In Peter Bürger's terms, it becomes neo-avant-gardist because it negates the avant-gardiste intentions once inscribed in the work. "Neo-avant-gardiste art is autonomous art in the full sense of the term, which means that it negates the avant-gardiste intention of returning art to the praxis of life." Most interestingly, Bürger holds that this change can occur in the status of the work as product while the consciousness the artist has of his activity may remain unaltered. In the case of Cunningham,

the "status of the product" has much to do with the dancers' minds and bodies, and, ultimately, with their performance. See Peter Bürger, *Theory of the Avant-Garde* (Minneapolis: University of Minnesota Press, 1984), p. 58.

43. "Each story in its telling would take a minute. He [Cage] tells on an average of fifteen stories in the course of the twenty-four minutes, so there are lengths of silence as the dance continues. Using a stopwatch, he governs the speed of each telling, a story with a few words being spaced out over the minute, a story with many having a faster rhythm. Since from one playing to another playing of the dance he never tells the same story at the same point in time, we cannot count on it to relate to us." Merce Cunningham, "Choreography and the Dance," p. 184.

44. Richard Kostelanetz, "Metamorphoses in Modern Dance," in *Dance Scope 5*, 1 (fall 1970): 12.

45. This is particularly evident in the 1968 film of the work. The audience laughs only at the text, which, despite its disconnected fabric, it is willing to take on as an intentionally funny text. Roger Copeland criticizes similar critiques of *How to* by claiming that they betray an ignorance of Cunningham's interest in an anti-Wagnerian *Gesamtkunstwerk*, one that would display dis-unity among, rather than a harmonious fusion of, the arts. Yet, I continue to wonder whether dis-unity is automatically accomplished when conventional unity has been thwarted. By conserving the nonrelatedness of dancing and talking, Cunningham and Cage symbolically rejected Wagnerian conceptions of theatrical wholeness. Yet, by doing it the way they did in *How to*, they also unwittingly suggested a pre-Wagnerian model of the theatrical whole—composite spectacle of the late Renaissance—in which the text effectively dominated. The very domination of the text suggests a desire for unity and wholeness. See Franko, *Dance as Text*, and Roger Copeland, "Merce Cunningham and the Politics of Perception," in *What Is Dance?*, pp. 307–24.

46. I am not referring to a "movement" in dance but rather to an interest in reprocessing the objectification of inner state in choreography. I contend that such attempts must have a profoundly theoretical basis and are thus unlike the opportunistic "cluster of anti-minimalist tendencies" of the late seventies as described by Noël Carroll in "The Return of the Repressed: The Re-Emergence of Expression in Contemporary American Dance," in *Dance Theatre Journal* vol. 2, no. 1 (1984): 17.

47. Klosty, *Merce*, p. 39.

48. There are, of course, broader issues addressed by Dunn in these works. The group works clearly examine the dynamics of male-female relationships, as suggested by the text of Milton's *Paradise Lost* behind the title *Light, O Tease*: "Communicating Male and Female Light, Which Two Great Sexes Animate the World."

49. This work specifically addresses a conventional set of relationships between dancing and music, though talking also played a key role in it. Here again, however, the issues are more complex than we have space to indicate. "Haole" means white person in Hawaiian, and Dunn concludes the work, which is essentially an extended self-portrait, with a hula dance. As with the sections of *Sky Eye* performed to African drummers, one could mistakenly take portions of Dunn's work for politically incorrect statements or super-cool correctives to political correctness. Rather, in both cases, a negative symbolism is employed by which whites are portrayed through their nonblackness.

50. *Light, O Tease* was first performed at Dunn's studio in New York City on April 14, 1987; *Matches* premiered March 17, 1988, at the Kitchen; *Haole* received its world premiere at the Whitney Museum of American Art on September 8, 1988; *Sky Eye* was first performed at St. Mark's Church on March 9, 1989.

51. Another, though different, post-Cunningham tendency is to experiment with emotion as if it were another physical material. This approach acknowledges expression theory while introducing a radical difference: the "hidden scene" is deprived of its originary and transcendental status. In some of the work of Pina Bausch, for example,

impression and expression seem reversed. Despite the recognizable expressionism of the dance, dancers' identities take shape in the wake of what they do or what is done to them. Thus, the hierarchy of impression and expression is reversed and subjectivity becomes a construct of action. This is the most interesting contribution of what the Germans now call the "neue Sachlickeit" in dance. In its direct use of materials, on the other hand, it seems derivative of American happenings of the sixties.

5. WHERE HE DANCED

1. My title alludes to Elizabeth Kendall's *Where She Danced*, a study of modern-dance innovators who were women. Kendall suggests that a feminist approach to the history of modern dance can be quite productive, but she staunchly refuses men a place in that history. My reference to Kendall's title signals an attention to male issues in the context of modern and postmodern performance. I wrote an earlier version of this essay for the forum on the artist's exploration of death, organized by Curtis Carter in April 1990 at the Haggerty Art Museum of Marquette University (Milwaukee). I wish to thank Kimberly Benston, Ann Daly, Susan Foster, and Eric Wirth for their helpful critical insights during subsequent revisions of this essay.

2. The current ethos of gay discourse underpins, for example, some recent work by Douglas Crimp. For an implicit critique, however, see Jonathan Dollimore's "Different Desires: Subjectivity and Transgression in Wilde and Gide," in *Genders* 2 (summer 1988): 24–41.

3. For a discussion of previous archeologies of homosexuality that, paradoxically, also treat gay identity as a historical by-product, see David M. Halperin's critique of Harald Patzer in "One Hundred Years of Homosexuality," in *Diacritics* 16:2 (summer 1986): 34–45.

4. The issue of essentialism in the writing of Luce Irigaray and Hélène Cixous is beyond the scope of this essay. Their essentialist gestures may be strategies of in-dressing, ways of mythologizing aspects of feminine identity to counteract influential cultural stereotypes. Cixous's early fiction in particular is driven by a third androgynous term relevant to my discussion of Ohno in what follows. See Hélène Cixous, *Le Troisième Corps* (Paris: Grasset, 1970).

5. Alice A. Jardine, *Gynesis: Configurations of Woman and Modernity* (Ithaca: Cornell University Press, 1985), p. 155.

6. Judith Butler has begun to confront gay, lesbian, and feminist theory, reading the feminist back through the gay and lesbian. Her purpose in *Gender Trouble* (New York: Routledge, 1990) is "to enlarge the scope of possible gender configurations" (p. 38), which is also my focus here. The new archeologies of sexuality spurred by Michel Foucault's *Uses of Pleasure* also imply a more speculative and creative perspective. Drawing on feminist anthropology, John J. Winkler points out the dissociation of a variety of sexual practices from any discourse of desire in the classical world. Rather, the discourse subsuming sexualities is one of kinship or sociopolitical ethos. David Halperin stresses, reciprocally, the absence of desire from the juridical and medical category of "homosexuality" in the last one hundred years. The imprimatur of desire is the mark of a historically unique discourse. Yet a discourse of desire risks a sort of constructedness as "natural." The objection is often raised that the AIDS crisis is not a time for theorizing, but the exciting cultural analysis the crisis has engendered does not *talk* theory, it *uses* theory. The concern for the duality of material and linguistic signifiers—the body as both "a text and an anti-text" (Erni)—is a theoretical problem that dance scholarship has been grappling with for some time. Cultural analysis about AIDS rejuvenates the Saussurian "referent," putting it into play with Foucauldian discursivity and the master narratives of Jean-François Lyotard. In short, the use of theory in the very midst of cultural mystification is encouraging, as are indications of a shift in attitude toward theory: "Perhaps what we need most urgently in gay and

lesbian theory right now," writes Diana Fuss, "is a theory *of* marginality." See her introduction to the collection *Inside/Out: Lesbian Theories, Gay Theories*, ed. Diana Fuss (New York: Routledge, 1991), p. 5.

7. "Militancy and Mourning," in *October* 51 (winter 1989): 11.

8. This tension between a classical humanism under political stress and a politically astute postmodernism without a theory of otherness speaks to some conflicts within gay activism. AIDS as a gay crisis has two political routes to travel. On the one hand, it can be conceived as a "progressive" issue: Human beings who are dying deserve to be cared for and healed because they have the *same* rights as other human beings. But the AIDS crisis also invokes a "separatist" issue. Gay men who are dying deserve to be cared for and healed inasmuch as they constitute a threatened community *distinct* from others. This splintered politics corresponds to the "universalizing" versus "minoritizing" definitions given the terms "homo-" and "hetero-" sexual in recent history, as described by Eve Kosofsky Sedgwick. See her "Across Gender, Across Sexuality: Willa Cather and Others," in *Displacing Homophobia: Gay Male Perspectives in Literature and Culture*, ed. Ronald R. Butters, John M. Clum, and Michael Moon (Durham: Duke University Press, 1989), p. 58.

9. See Judith Butler's discussion of Monique Wittig on the lesbian as third sex in *Gender Trouble*, p. 113. Butler classifies all gender identity as performance, because it is artificially constituted. Yet there is a discrepancy between those who were born wearing their costumes, as it were, and who perform for an appreciative audience and those who must conceive and create their own costumes and script their own genres.

10. Barbette was the stage name of the Texan Vander Clyde. For background on Barbette's act and Cocteau's essay, as well as on the motif of the androgynous acrobat in modern art, see Naomi Ritter, "Art and Androgyny: The Aerialist," in *Studies in Twentieth-Century Literature* 13/2 (summer 1989): 173-93. Cocteau's essay on Barbette was originally published in *La Nouvelle Revue Française* 13me année, 154 (Juillet 1926): 33-38, and reprinted shortly thereafter as an appendix to Cocteau's *Antigone: Les Mariés de la Tour Eiffel* (Paris: Gallimard, 1928). Page numbers from Cocteau's essay on Barbette refer to the 1928 edition, and translations of the essay are my own.

11. Cocteau, "Leçon," p. 160.

12. Ibid., p. 162.

13. Ibid., p. 158.

14. Ibid., pp. 158-59.

15. Ibid.

16. Ibid., p. 159.

17. Barbette's masculinity is defined throughout by his athletic performances and pranks. For example, on the way from the dressing room to the stage, he slides down a banister in his skirts. His contained feminine gestures, however, are equally stereotypic. In Cocteau's 1932 film *Le Sang d'un Poète*, Barbette appears briefly as an elegant society lady who, seated on a theater balcony overlooking a courtyard, blithely applauds the poet's suicide. Barbette's travesty gestures are microscopic, fluttery, and self-absorbed.

18. In further observations of Barbette, Cocteau reinforces his own "faux-naïf" response to the theatrical sleight-of-hand. For example, just before the show, he sees Barbette test the aerial apparatus with markedly masculine gestures—muscle flexing and grimaces—and then survey the divan like an anxious host before the arrival of guests. Once transformed, Barbette may flip back and forth from beneath the disguise, but his turns are always a full 180 degrees.

19. See Julia Epstein, "Either/Or—Neither/Both: Sexual Ambiguity and the Ideology of Gender," in *Genders* 7 (spring 1990): 99-142.

20. Cocteau, "Leçon," p. 169.

21. Ibid.

22. This transformation is perhaps another example of what Gaylyn Studlar, in her

discussion of the Josef von Sternberg/Marlene Dietrich films, has called the masochistic heterocosm whose requirements are "disavowal, fetishism, suspension." See Studlar, *In the Realm of Pleasure: Von Sternberg, Dietrich and the Masochistic Aesthetic* (Urbana: University of Illinois Press, 1988), p. 91.

23. Jean Cocteau, "The Fine Arts Considered as a Murder," in *The Essay of Indirect Criticism*, trans. Arno Karlen in *Quarterly Review of Literature* 12, no. 4 (1964): 381.

24. Andrew Ross, *No Respect: Intellectuals and Popular Culture* (New York: Routledge, 1989), p. 161.

25. *Essay*, p. 374.

26. One could undertake an entire analysis of Cocteau's visual-poetic work with this overarching polarity as an interpretive grid.

27. The inaccessibility of his image is particularly apparent in *Plain-Chant*. In a very Nietzschean sense, the dream for Cocteau is an Apollonian construct haunted by invisible action.

28. Cocteau, "Leçon," p. 164.

29. Cocteau, *Le Mystère Laïc: Essai d'Etude Indirecte (Giorgio de Chirico)* (Paris: Editions des Quatre Chemins, 1928). Translations are drawn from Karlen's translation of *The Essay of Indirect Criticism* (see note 23), p. 375. Karlen translates *Le Mystère* as revised in 1932 and published along with Cocteau's "The Fine Arts Considered as a Murder" in one volume titled *The Essay of Indirect Criticism*. It is referred to hereafter in notes as *Essay*.

30. See Janet Flanner's account of Barbette's act in *Paris Was Yesterday* (New York: Viking, 1972), p. 73. Beginning with *Opium* in 1930, Cocteau's graphic work evidences an obsession with falling figures. His ascending figures can be less convincing, especially in his cinematic work. See, for example, the ascending couple in the final moments of the 1946 film *La Belle et la Bête.*

31. "Leçon," p. 164.

32. *Essay*, p. 333. During the late 1920s, Cocteau was frequently fascinated with the incongruous dramatic scenography implicit in architectural arrangement: "a rubber glove hung near a plaster head, a deserted street, an egg placed in evil solitude, a lightning of plague and eclipse" (ibid., p. 334).

33. "We should have found his affectation insupportable. The basis of his number bothers us. So? There remains this unclassed thing moving beneath the lights." (Cocteau, *Essay*, pp. 374–75). René Galand has called sex equals death equals poetry Cocteau's sexual equation. See Galand, "Cocteau's Sexual Equation," in *Homosexualities and French Literature: Cultural Contexts/Critical Texts*, ed. George Stambolian and Elaine Marks (Ithaca: Cornell University Press, 1979), pp. 279–94.

34. For Cocteau, inanimate objects with an allegorical charge are poetic objects *par excellence*. Indeed, poetry itself is only one such object, a fact Cocteau was at pains to demonstrate by his incursions into "visual poetry," including "objets" and montages. The centrality of Cocteau's essay on Barbette to his aesthetic of the late 1920s and early 1930s begins to reveal itself, but, rather than develop that theme here, I mention only the 1926 exhibition of his "objets," including one called "le numéro Barbette." In *Le Mystère Laïc* (1928), he deals extensively with de Chirico's object-aesthetic. Moreover, Cocteau's most important collection of poetry in the 1920s, *Opéra*, construes poetic language as "objective" by rejuvenating the punning procedures familiar to "la grande rhétorique" of the early French Renaissance.

35. The figure is donned with a white, curly wig that did not make the final version of the film. The wig appears on the "Louis XV friend" in a later scene, and Cocteau also wears it in his role as the poet in his last film, *Le Testament d'Orphée* (1960).

36. See Jean Cocteau, *Le Sang d'un Poète* (Monaco: Editions du Rocher, 1957), pp. 46–48.

37. In the script of *Le Sang d'un Poète*, further details of this scene, evidently cut or

never filmed, emphasize the either-or dilemma of the Hermaphrodite becoming a nei-ther/both. Shirts, skirts, white ties, and socks are scattered about the Hermaphrodite to the sound of drum rolls. As night abruptly follows, a male and a female voice conflict over whether to turn off the light. We also hear sounds of water. See ibid., pp. 47–48.

38. The idea that Barbette's audience was unsympathetic is presented in "Une Leçon de Théâtre" by a Cocteau in heterocritical drag. That Barbette's act became a rallying point for the Parisian avant-garde of the 1920s—the very audience, as Flanner re-marks, that had attended Diaghilev's Ballets Russes—does not obscure Cocteau's aware-ness of the Cirque Médrano as a venue of popular culture. But unlike Andy Warhol, Cocteau did not massively appropriate popular culture; Rather, he maintained the irony of a double audience for Barbette. Cocteau targeted a double audience for his cinema as well, if one excepts the first experiments and the final testament, and he actually became a writer of "boulevard" theater late in his career.

39. My discussion of Ohno's *Suiren* refers to his performance of the work at the Lila Acheson Wallace Auditorium of the Asia Society, New York, June 28–30 and July 1, 1988. Butoh is a highly humanistic form of theater dance that developed in Japan after World War II. It draws on the expressionism of early-twentieth-century German modern dance but only fortuitously reinvents the stylistic similarities it has with No and Kabuki traditions. For more information on Butoh, see Mark Holborn, Yukio Mishima, Tatsumi Hijikata, Haven O'More, *Butoh: Dance of the Dark Soul* (New York: Aperture, 1987). For more information on Ohno, considered one of the founders of Butoh, see Ohno, "Selections from the Prose of Kazuo Ohno," in *Drama Review* 30:2 (summer 1986): 156–62; Lizzie Slater, "Kazuo Ohno and Butoh Dance," in *Dance Theatre Journal* 4/4 (winter 1986): 6–10; Kazuo Ohno, "Through Time in a Horse Drawn Carriage," in *Ballett International* 12/9 (September 1989): 10–13. Ohno's im-pressionist woman bears some comparison to Mme. Alec Weisweiller's role as "une dame distraite qui se trompe d'époque" (a distracted woman in the wrong epoch) in Cocteau's last film, *Le Testament d'Orphée*.

The process of representing unconventional sexualities is now being afforded par-ticular reexamination in the context of Shakespeare's theater. See, in particular, Lisa Jardine, *Still Harping on Daughters: Female Roles and Elizabethan Eroticism* (Sussex: Harvester, 1983), especially pp. 9–36. In many literary instances familiar to the Re-naissance, however, the androgyne is neither ambiguous nor uncanny. This is as true for Leone Ebreo's *Dialoghi d'Amore*, in which the androgyne is a figure of Adam, as it is for the sonnets of Maurice Scève and Louise Labé, in which the androgyne is a figure dependent on heterosexual reciprocity. Yet the heterosexual matrix of the Re-naissance seems founded on ambivalent ground. This state of affairs is brilliantly clari-fied by Stephen Greenblatt, who shows that cross-dressing in Shakespeare's comedies underwrites conventional gender identities ideologically even as it undercuts them vi-sually and narratively. See his "Fiction and Friction," in *Shakespearian Negotiations: The Circulation of Social Energy in Renaissance England* (Oxford: Clarendon, 1988), pp. 66–93.

40. See *Le Japonisme* (Paris: Editions de la Réunion des Musées Nationaux, 1988).

41. See Daniel Wildenstein, *Monet's Years at Giverny: Beyond Impressionism* (New York: Metropolitan Museum of Art, 1978).

42. Emile Benveniste explains the middle voice as a form of ancient Greek and historical Indo-European, whose opposition to the active voice predates the active-passive dichotomy. While the active voice indicates the subject as exterior to the verbal action, the middle voice conveys the subject within the action's process, affected by it. See his "Actif et Moyen dans le Verbe," in *Problèmes de Linguistique Générale* I (Paris: Gallimard, 1966), pp. 168–75.

43. Roland Barthes, "The Dolls of Bunraku," trans. David Savram in *Diacritics* (winter 1976): 46.

44. Johan Huizinga reminds us of the etymology of illusion: "By withdrawing from the game he [the spoil-sport] reveals the relativity and fragility of the play-world in which he had temporarily shut himself up with others. He robs play of its *illusion*—a pregnant word which means literally 'in-play' (from *inlusio, illudere* or *inludere*)." See Johan Huizinga, *Homo Ludens: A Study of the Play Element in Culture* (Boston: Beacon, 1955), p. 11.

45. Barthes, "Dolls," p. 45.

46. Kevin Kopelson, "Wilde, Barthes, and the Orgasmics of Truth," in *Genders* 7 (spring 1990): 25.

47. Roland Barthes, *Roland Barthes by Roland Barthes*, trans. Richard Howard (New York: Hill and Wang, 1977), p. 69.

48. This phrase is quoted from Verena Andermatt Conley's gloss of Hélène's Cixous's *Le Troisième Corps*. See *Hélène Cixous: Writing the Feminine* (Lincoln: University of Nebraska Press, 1991), p. 30.

49. Barthes, "The Dolls," p. 44.

50. Kazuo Ohno quoted in Mark Holborn et al., *Butoh: Dance of the Dark Soul*, p. 36.

51. Richard Dellamora draws this conclusion, for example, in a different context when he shows that, historically, the androgyne, whose ambivalence is gendered, has been able to express homosexual concerns—and even to theorize them preliminarily. This manner of androgyny still relies heavily on gender polarities even as it blurs them in an attempt to suggest an other sexual experience. Its ambivalence, that is, its connection to the unambivalent, keeps it safely in the ken of a marginal but recognizable sexual-aesthetic discourse. See *Masculine Desire: The Sexual Politics of Victorian Aestheticism* (Chapel Hill: University of North Carolina Press, 1990).

52. David Halperin writes, "I see nothing wrong with being truly singular in the annals of history." See *One Hundred Years of Homosexuality and Other Essays on Greek Love* (New York: Routledge, 1990), p. 49. It would seem that Halperin's deconstruction of the category "homosexual" could ultimately engage a thirdness whose fiction purveys historical facticity in and through the present.

53. "Choreographies," in *Diacritics*, trans. Christie McDonald, vol. 12 (1982), p. 76.

54. "Le Menteur," in *Nouveau Théâtre de Poche* (Monaco: Editions du Rocher, 1960), p. 115.

Bibliography

Abrahms, M. H. *The Mirror and the Lamp: Romantic Theory and the Critical Tradition.* New York: Oxford University Press, 1971.

Adams, Hazard. *Philosophy of the Literary Symbolic.* Tallahassee: University of Florida Press, 1983.

Adelman, Katherine M. "Statue-Posing in the Late Nineteenth Century Physical Culture Movement." *Proceedings of the Fifth Canadian Symposium on the History of Sport and Physical Education.* University of Toronto (August 26–29, 1982): 308-17.

Adler, Norma. "Reconstructing the Dances of Isadora Duncan." *Drama Review [Reconstruction]* 28, no. 3 (fall 1984): 59–66.

Aesthetics and Politics. Trans. Ronald Taylor. London: Verso, 1980.

Agee, James, and Walker Evans. *Let Us Now Praise Famous Men.* Boston: Houghton Mifflin, 1988.

Alcoff, Linda. "Cultural Feminism versus Post-Structuralism: The Identity Crisis in Feminist Theory." *Signs* 13 (spring 1988): 405–36.

Alderson, Evan. "Metaphor in Dance: The Example of Graham." *Dance History Scholars Proceedings.* Riverside: Dance History Scholars, 1983: 111–18.

———. "Utopies Actuelles." *La Danse au Défi.* Montreal: Parachute, 1987: 60–72.

Allerhand, Ruth. "The Lay Dance." *New Theatre* (April 1935): 26.

Althusser, Louis, and Etienne Balibar. *Reading Capital.* London: Verso, 1979.

Ardis, Anne L. *New Women, New Novels: Feminism and Early Modernism.* New Brunswick: Rutgers University Press, 1990.

Bachelard, Gaston. *The Poetics of Space.* Trans. Maria Jolas. Boston: Beacon, 1969.

Banes, Sally. *Terpsichore in Sneakers.* Middletown: Wesleyan University Press, 1987.

Banes, Sally, and Noël Carroll. "Cunningham and Duchamp." *Ballet Review* 11, no. 2 (summer 1983): 73–79.

Banes, Sally, and Susan Manning. "Letters from Sally Banes and Susan Manning." *Drama Review* 33/1 (spring 1989): 13–16.

Barba, Eugenio. *Beyond the Floating Islands.* New York: PAJ, 1986.

Barthes, Roland. "The Dolls of Bunraku." Trans. David Savran. *Diacritics* (winter 1976): 44–48.

———. "Diderot, Brecht, Eisenstein." *Image-Music-Text.* Trans. Stephen Heath. New York: Noonday, 1977: 69–78.

———. *Roland Barthes by Roland Barthes.* Trans. Richard Howard. New York: Hill and Wang, 1977.

Bathrick, David. "Affirmative and Negative Culture: Technology and the Left Avant-Garde." *The Technological Imagination: Theories and Fictions.* Ed. Teresa de Lauretis, Andreas Huyssen, and Kathleen Woodard. Madison, Wis.: Coda, 1980: 107–22.

Bentivoglio, Leonetta. "Danza e Futurismo in Italia: 1913–1933." *La Danza Italiana* 1 (autumn 1984): 61–82.

Bentley, Eric. "Martha Graham's Journey (1953)." *What Is Dance?* Ed. Roger Copeland and Marshall Cohen. Oxford: Oxford University Press, 1983: 197–202.

Benveniste, Emile. "Actif et Moyen dans le Verbe." *Problèmes de Linguistique Générale I.* Paris: Gallimard, 1966: 168–75.

Berger, Maurice. *Labyrinths: Robert Morris, Minimalism, and the 1960s.* New York: Harper and Row, 1989.

Bois, Yve-Alain. "Kahnweiler's Lesson." *Representations* 18 (spring 1987): 33–68.

Brogue, Ronald, ed. *Mimesis in Contemporary Theory: An Interdisciplinary Approach. Vol. 2: Mimesis, Semiosis and Power.* Philadelphia: John Benjamins, 1991.

Bryson, Norman. *Word and Image: French Painting of the Ancien Regime*. Cambridge: Cambridge University Press, 1981.

Buchwald, Nathaniel. "A Revolutionary Gentleman." *New Theatre* (March 1935): 24.

Bürger, Peter. *Theory of the Avant-Garde*. Minneapolis: University of Minnesota Press, 1984.

Burgin, Victor. "The Absence of Presence: Conceptualism and Postmodernisms." *The End of Art Theory: Criticism and Postmodernity*. Atlantic Highlands, N.J.: Humanities Press, 1986: 29–50.

Burke, Owen. "A Note on the Modern Dance." *New Masses* 22, no. 4 (January 11, 1937): 18.

———. "The Dance." *New Masses* 22, no. 3 (January 12, 1937): 28.

———. "Martha Graham: Revolutionary Dancer." *New Masses* 26, no. 9 (February 22, 1938): 26–27.

———. "Music Lovers and Martha Graham." *New Masses* 27, no. 10 (May 31, 1938): 30.

———. "Dance Holiday." *New Masses* 34, no. 4 (January 16, 1940): 30.

Burnshaw, Stanley. "The Dance." *New Masses* 22, no. 8 (November 30, 1934): 27.

———. "The Dance." *New Masses* 16, no. 9 (February 26, 1935): 27.

Burt, Ramsay. "Dance, Masculinity and Postmodernism." *Postmodernism and Dance: Discussion Papers*. West Sussex: Institute of Higher Education, 1991: 23–32.

Butler, Judith. *Gender Trouble: Feminism and the Subversion of Identity*. New York: Routledge, 1990.

Butoh: Dance of the Dark Soul. New York: Aperture, 1987.

Carroll, Noël. "Post-Modern Dance and Expression." *Philosophical Essays on Dance*. Ed. Gordon Fancher and Gerald Myers. New York: Dance Horizons, 1981.

———. "The Return of the Repressed: The Re-Emergence of Expression in Contemporary American Dance." *Dance Theatre Journal* 2, no. 1 (1984): 16–18.

Certeau, Michel de. *The Writing of History*. Trans. Tom Conley. New York: Columbia University Press, 1988.

Cheetham, Mark A. *The Rhetoric of Purity: Essentialist Theory and the Advent of Abstract Painting*. Cambridge: Cambridge University Press, 1991.

Chinoy, Helen Krich. "The Poetics of Politics: Some Notes on Style and Craft in the Theatre of the Thirties." *Theatre Journal* 35, no. 4 (December 1983): 476–98.

Church, Marjorie. "The Dance in the Social Scene." *Dance Observer* 4, no. 3 (March 1937): 27, 30.

Cixous, Hélène. *Le Troisième Corps*. Paris: Grasset, 1970.

Clark, Timothy J. "Jackson Pollack's Abstraction." *Reconstructing Modernism: Art in New York, Paris, and Montreal, 1945-1964*. Ed. Serge Guilbaut. Cambridge: MIT Press, 1990: 172–238.

Cocteau, Jean. *Poésie Plastique: Objets—Dessins*. Paris: Aux Quatre Chemins, 1926.

———. "Une Leçon de Théâtre: Le Numéro Barbette." *Antigone: Les Mariés de la Tour Eiffel*. Paris: Gallimard, 1928.

———. *Le Mystère Laïc: Essai d'Etude Indirecte*. Paris: Editions des Quatre Chemins, 1928.

———. *Opium: Journal d'une Désintoxication*. Paris: Stock, 1930.

———. *Opéra: Oeuvres Poétiques, 1925-1927*. Tours: Arcanes, 1952.

———. "Plain Chant." *Poèmes (1916-1955)*. Paris: Gallimard, 1956: 35–61.

———. *Le Sang d'un Poète*. Monaco: Editions du Rocher, 1957.

———. *Le Testament d'Orphée*. Monaco: Editions du Rocher, 1961.

———. "The Essay of Indirect Criticism." Trans. Arno Karlen. *Quarterly Review of Literature* 12:4 (1964): 310-90.

———. *La Belle et la Bête*. Paris: Pierre Belfond, 1990.

Cohen, Selma-Jeanne. "The Achievement of Martha Graham." *Chrysalis* 11, nos. 5–6 (1958): 3-11.

Cohn, Robert Greer. *Mallarmé's 'Coup de Dés': An Exegesis*. New York: AMS, 1949.

Colletet, Guillaume. "Le Ballet de l'Harmonie." In Paul Lacroix, *Ballets et Mascarades de Cour de Henri III à Louis XIV*. Geneva: J. Gay et fils, 1868.

Conley, Verena Andermatt. *Hélène Cixous: Writing the Feminine*. Lincoln: University of Nebraska Press, 1991.

Conner, Lynne. "'Bristling with Revolutionary Protest': Socialist Agendas in the Modern Dance, 1931–1938." *Crucibles of Crisis: Performing Social Change*. Ed. Janelle Reinelt. Ann Arbor: University of Michigan Press, forthcoming.

Copeland, Roger. "Merce Cunningham and the Politics of Perception." *What Is Dance? Readings in Theory and Criticism*. Ed. Roger Copeland and Marshall Cohen. Oxford: Oxford University Press, 1983: 307–24.

———. "Postmodern Dance and the Repudiation of Primitivism." *Partisan Review* 1 (1983): 101–21.

Cott, Nancy F. *The Grounding of Modern Feminism*. New Haven: Yale University Press, 1987.

Craig, Edward Gordon. "Memories of Isadora Duncan." *Gordon Craig on Movement and Dance*. Ed. Arnold Rood. London: Dance Books, 1978: 247–52.

Crimp, Douglas. "Militancy and Mourning." *October* 51 (winter 1989): 3–18.

Cunningham, Merce. "The Functions of a Technique for Dance." *The Dance Has Many Faces*. Ed. Walter Sorell. New York: World Publishing, 1951: 250–55.

———. *Changes: Notes on Choreography*. New York: Something Else, 1968.

———. "Choreography and the Dance." *The Creative Experience*. Ed. Stanley Rosner and Lawrence E. Abt. New York: Grossman, 1970: 175–86.

———. "The Impermanent Art." *Esthetics Contemporary*. Ed. Richard Kostelanetz. Buffalo: Prometheus, 1978: 310–14.

Daly, Ann. "Dance History and Feminist Theory: Reconsidering Isadora Duncan and the Male Gaze." *Gender in Performance: The Presentation of Difference in the Performing Arts*. Ed. Laurence Senelick. Hanover, N.H.: University Press of New England, 1992: 239–59.

Dana, Margery. "Dancing to the Tune of the Times: Young Anna Sokolow among the Leading Modern Dancers of America." *Daily Worker* (November 10, 1937).

———. "Anna Sokolow and Dance Unit in Prominent Debut." *Daily Worker* (November 30, 1937).

David-Ménard, Monique. *Hysteria from Freud to Lacan: Body and Language in Psychoanalysis*. Trans. Catherine Porter. Ithaca: Cornell University Press, 1989.

Davis, Bette. *The Lonely Life*. New York: Putnam's Sons, 1962.

Dell, Floyd. *Women as World Builders: Studies in Modern Feminism*. 1913; rpt. Westport, Conn.: Hyperion, 1976.

Dellamora, Richard. *Masculine Desire: The Sexual Politics of Victorian Aestheticism*. Chapel Hill: University of North Carolina Press, 1990.

De Mille, Agnes. *Martha: The Life and Work of Martha Graham*. New York: Random House, 1991.

Denby, Edward. *Dance Writings*. Ed. Robert Cornfield and William Mackay. New York: Knopf, 1986.

Derrida, Jacques. "Choreographies." Interview with Christie McDonald. Trans. Christie McDonald. *Diacritics* 12 (1982): 66–76.

Dijkstra, Bram. *Idols of Perversity: Fantasies of Feminine Evil in Fin-de-Siècle Culture*. New York: Oxford University Press, 1986.

Dollimore, Jonathan. "Different Desires: Subjectivity and Transgression in Wilde and Gide." *Genders* 2 (summer 1988): 24–41.

Douglas, Paul. "Modern Dance Forms." *New Theatre* (November 1935): 26–27.

———. "Modern Dance Forms." *New Theatre* (December 1935): 26–27.

Dudley, Jane. "The Mass Dance." *New Theatre* (December 1934): 17–18.

———. "Jane Dudley Talking to Tobi Tobias." Oral History Archive, Dance Collection of the New York Public Library (June 28, 1976).

Duncan, Isadora. "Emotional Expression." *The Director* 1, no. 4 (March 1898): 109–11.

———. *Der Tanz der Zukunft (The Dance of the Future): Eine Vorlesung.* Trans. Karl Federn. Leipzig: Eugen Diederichs, 1903.

———. "The Dance: By Isadora Duncan: With an Introduction by Mary Fanton Roberts." *Touchstone* 2, no. 1 (October 1917): 3–15.

———. "America Makes Me Sick: Nauseates Me." *San Francisco Examiner* (March 4, 1923).

———. "The Dance in Relation to Tragedy." *Theatre Arts Monthly* XI, no. 10 (October 1927): 755–61.

———. *Ecrits sur la Danse.* Paris: Editions du Grenier, 1927.

———. *The Art of the Dance.* Ed. Sheldon Cheney. New York: Theatre Arts, 1928.

———. *My Life.* New York: Boni and Liveright, 1927; rpt. New York: Liveright, 1955.

———. *Isadora Speaks.* Ed. Franklin Rosemont. San Francisco: City Lights, 1981.

Duve, Thierry de. *Pictorial Nominalism: On Marcel Duchamp's Passage from Painting to the Readymade.* Trans. Dana Polen. Minneapolis: University of Minnesota Press, 1991.

Eisenberg, Emanuel. "Diagnosis of the Dance." *New Theatre* (July/August 1934): 24–25.

———. "Ladies of the Revolutionary Dance Movement." *New Theatre* (February 1935): 10–11.

———. "A Reply by E. Eisenberg." *New Theatre* (March 1935): 24.

Eksteins, Modris. *Rites of Spring: The Great War and the Birth of the Modern Age.* New York: Anchor, 1990.

Elias, Norbert. *The Civilizing Process: The History of Manners.* Trans. Edmund Jephcott. New York: Urizen, 1978.

Elion, Harry. "Perspectives of the Dance." *New Theatre* (September 1934): 18–19.

Eliot, T. S. "Tradition and the Individual Talent." *Selected Essays.* London: Faber and Faber, 1934: 13–22.

Encyclopedia of the American Left. Ed. Mari Jo Buhle, Paul Buhle, Dan Georgakas. New York: Garland, 1990.

Engel, Johann Jacob. *Idées sur le Geste et l'Action Théâtrale* 1795; rpt. Geneva: Slatkine, 1979.

Epstein, Julia. "Either/Or—Neither/Both: Sexual Ambiguity and the Ideology of Gender." *Genders* 7 (spring 1990): 99–142.

Erick Hawkins: Theory and Training. New York: American Dance Guild, 1979.

Erni, John. "A.I.D.S. and the Cultural Politics of the Body." Unpublished paper presented at the conference "Bodies: Image, Writing, Technology." University of California at Irvine, April 1990.

Evan, Blanche. "The Star Spangled Dance." *New Theatre* (October 1934): 24.

———. "From a Dancer's Notebook." *New Theatre* (April 1936): 31, 44–45.

———. "Her Chosen Theme: A Modern Dancer's Credo." *New Masses* 26, no. 5 (July 26, 1938): 17–19.

Fishbein, Leslie. *Rebels in Bohemia: The Radicals of "The Masses," 1911–1917.* Chapel Hill: University of North Carolina Press, 1982.

Flanner, Janet. *Paris Was Yesterday.* New York: Viking, 1972.

Foster, Hal. "The 'Primitive' Unconscious of Modern Art." *October* 34 (fall 1985): 45–70.

Foster, Steve. "The Revolutionary Solo Dance." *New Theatre* (January 1935): 23.

Foster, Susan Leigh. *Reading Dancing: Bodies and Subjects in Contemporary American Dance.* Berkeley: University of California Press, 1986.

Foucault, Michel. *Uses of Pleasure*. Trans. Robert Hurley. New York: Vintage, 1985.

Franko, Mark. *The Dancing Body in Renaissance Choreography*. Birmingham: Summa, 1986.

———. "Emotivist Movement and Histories of Modernism: The Case of Martha Graham." *Discourse* 13, no. 1 (fall/winter 1990-91): 111–28.

———. "Expressivism and Chance Procedure: The Future of an Emotion." *Res* 21 (spring 1992): 144–60.

———. "Where He Danced: Cocteau's Barbette and Ohno's Water Lilies." *PMLA* (May 1992): 594–607.

———. *Dance as Text: Ideologies of the Baroque Body*. Cambridge: Cambridge University Press, 1993.

———. "History/Theory—Criticism/Practice." *Corporealities*. Ed. Susan Foster. London: Routledge, 1995.

———. "Some Notes on Yvonne Rainer, Modernism, Politics, Emotion, Performance, and Its Aftermath," *Meaning in Motion: New Cultural Studies of Dance*. Ed. Jane Desmond. Durham: Duke University Press, 1995.

Freedman, Ezra. "Dance: Which Technique?" *New Theatre* (May 1934): 17–18.

Freud, Sigmund. "The Uncanny." *On Creativity and the Unconscious*. New York: Harper and Row, 1958.

Friedman, Martin. *Noguchi's Imaginary Landscape*. Minneapolis: Walker Art Center, 1978. Especially "Designs for the Stage": 25–37.

Fuller, Loïe. *Fifteen Years of a Dancer's Life*. New York: Dance Horizons, 1978.

Fuss, Diana, ed. *Inside/Out: Lesbian Theories, Gay Theories*. New York: Routledge, 1991.

Galand, René. "Cocteau's Sexual Equation." *Homosexualities and French Literature: Cultural Contexts/Critical Texts*. Ed. George Stambolian and Elaine Marks. Ithaca: Cornell University Press, 1979: 279–94.

Garafola, Lynn, ed. *Studies in Dance History (Of, By, and For the People: Dancing on the Left in the 1930s)*, vol. 5, no. 1 (spring 1994).

Giedion, Siegfried. *Mechanization Takes Command: A Contribution to Anonymous History*. New York: Norton, 1948.

Gilbert, James Burkhart. *Writers and Partisans: A History of Radicalism in America*. New York: John Wiley, 1968.

Gold, Michael. "The Loves of Isadora." *New Masses* 4 (March 1929): 20–21.

———. "Change the World." *Daily Worker* (June 14, 1934): 5.

———. "Remembering Isadora Duncan." *New Masses* 25, no. 1 (September 28, 1937): 16–17.

———. *The Mike Gold Reader*. New York: International, 1954.

Goldberg, Marianne. "She Who Is Possessed No Longer Exists Outside." *Women and Performance* 3, no. 1, issue 5 (1986): 17–27.

Goldstein, Malcolm. *The Political Stage: American Drama and Theater of the Great Depression*. New York: Oxford University Press, 1974.

Goodman, Paul. *The Empire City*. Indianapolis: Bobbs-Merrill, 1942.

Graff, Ellen. "Stepping Left: Radical Dance in New York City, 1928–1942." Dissertation: New York University, 1993.

Graham, Martha. "Seeking an American Art of Dance." *Revolt in the Arts: A Survey of the Creation, Distribution and Appreciation of Art in America*. Ed. Oliver M. Sayler. New York: Brentano, 1930: 249–55.

———. "Affirmations, 1926–37," and "Graham 1937." Merle Armitage, *Martha Graham*. New York: Dance Horizons, 1966: 96-110, 83–88.

———. "How I Became a Dancer." 1965; rpt. *The Dance Experience*. Ed. Nadel and Nadel. New York: Praeger, 1970: 237–39.

———. *The Notebooks of Martha Graham*. New York: Harcourt Brace Jovanovich, 1973.

———. "A Modern Dancer's Primer for Action." 1941; rpt. *Dance as a Theater Art.* Ed. Selma-Jeanne Cohen. New York: Dodd, Mead, 1975: 135–43.

———. "Dancer's Focus." Barbara Morgan, *Martha Graham: Sixteen Dances in Photographs.* Dobbs Ferry, N.Y.: Morgan and Morgan, 1941; rpt. 1980: 10–11.

———. *Blood Memory.* New York: Doubleday, 1991.

Greenberg, Clement. "The New Sculpture." *The Collected Essays and Criticism: Arrogant Purpose.* Ed. John O'Brian. Chicago: University of Chicago Press, 1988: 313–19.

Greenblatt, Stephen. "Fiction and Friction." *Shakespearian Negotiations: The Circulation of Social Energy in Renaissance England.* Oxford: Clarendon, 1988: 66–93.

Guidieri, Remo, and Francesco Pellizzi. "Editorial." Trans. John Johnston. *Res* 1 (spring 1981): 3–7.

———. "Shadows: Nineteen Tableaux on the Cult of the Dead in Malekula, Eastern Melanesia." *Res* 2 (autumn 1981): 5–69.

Guilbaut, Serge. *How New York Stole the Idea of Modern Art: Abstract Expressionism, Freedom, and the Cold War.* Trans. Arthur Goldhammer. Chicago: University of Chicago Press, 1983.

Halperin, David. "One Hundred Years of Homosexuality." *Diacritics* 16:2 (summer 1986): 34–45.

———. *One Hundred Years of Homosexuality and Other Essays on Greek Love.* New York: Routledge, 1990.

Heller, Agnes. *A Theory of Feelings.* Assen, The Netherlands: Van Gorcum, 1979.

Heppenstall, Rayner. "The Sexual Idiom." *Apology for Dancing* (1936); rpt. *What Is Dance?* Ed. Roger Copeland and Marshall Cohen. Oxford: Oxford University Press, 1983: 267–88.

Heymann, Jeanne Lunin. "Dance in the Depression: The WPA Project." *Dance Scope* 9, no. 2 (1975): 28–40.

Hicks, Anny Mali. "Vital Art." *Mother Earth* 1, no. 3 (May 1906); rpt. *Radical Periodicals in the United States, 1890-1960: Mother Earth Bulletin.* Series 1, Vol. 1 (1906-1907). New York: Greenwood, 1968: 48–52.

Holborn, Mark, et al. *Butoh: Dance of the Dark Soul.* New York: Aperture, 1987.

Horst, Louis. *Manuscripts.* Dance Collection, New York Public Library for the Performing Arts at Lincoln Center.

Horst, Louis, and Carroll Russell. *Modern Dance Forms in Relation to Other Modern Arts.* San Francisco: Impulse, 1961; rpt. New York: Dance Horizons, 1975.

Huizinga, Johan. *Homo Ludens: A Study of the Play Element in Culture.* Boston: Beacon, 1955.

Ignatin, Irving. "'Revolutionary' Dance Forms." *New Theatre* (December 1935): 28–29.

Irigaray, Luce. *Ce Sexe qui n'en est pas un.* Paris: Editions de Minuit, 1977.

I-Wan, Chen. "The Soviet Dance: The Basis for a Mass Dance Culture." *New Theatre* (January 1935): 17–19.

Le Japonisme. Paris: Editions de la Réunion des Musées Nationaux, 1988.

Jardine, Alice A. *Gynesis: Configurations of Woman and Modernity.* Ithaca: Cornell University Press, 1985.

Jardine, Lisa. *Still Harping on Daughters: Female Roles and Elizabethan Eroticism.* Sussex: Harvester, 1983.

Johnson, Barbara. *A World of Difference.* Baltimore: Johns Hopkins University Press, 1987.

Johnson, Oakley. "The Dance." *New Theatre* (February 1934): 16–18, 27.

Johnston, Jill. "The New American Dance." *Salmagundi* 33-34 (spring-summer 1976): 149–74.

Jowitt, Deborah. "Images of Isadora: The Search for Motion." *Dance Research Journal* 17/2, 18/1 (1985-86): 21–29.

———. *Time and the Dancing Image.* New York: William Morrow, 1988.

Kendall, Elizabeth. *Where She Danced: The Birth of American Art-Dance.* Berkeley: University of California Press, 1979.

Kermode, Frank. "Poet and Dancer before Diaghilev." *Puzzles and Epiphanies: Essays and Reviews, 1958–1961.* London: Routledge and Kegan Paul, 1962: 1–28.

Kirstein, Lincoln. "Revolutionary Ballet Forms." *New Theatre* (October 1934): 12–14.

———. "The Dance as Theater." *New Theatre* (May 1935): 21–22.

———. *Ballet: Bias and Belief: Three Pamphlets Collected and Other Dance Writings of Lincoln Kirstein.* New York: Dance Horizons, 1983.

Klosty, James. *Merce Cunningham.* New York: Limelight, 1986.

Kopelson, Kevin. "Wilde, Barthes, and the Orgasmics of Truth." *Genders* 7 (spring 1990): 22–31.

Koritz, Amy. *Gendering Bodies/Performing Art: Dance and Literature in Early Twentieth-Century British Culture.* Ann Arbor: University of Michigan Press, 1995.

Kostelanetz, Richard. "Metamorphoses of Modern Dance." *Dance Scope* 5, no. 1 (fall 1970): 6–21.

———. "Profile of Merce Cunningham." *Michigan Quarterly Review* 14 (fall 1975): 363–82.

Kracauer, Siegfried. "The Mass Ornament (1927)." *New German Critique* 5. Trans. Barbara Correll and Jack Zipes (spring 1975): 72–73.

Krauss, Rosalind E. *The Originality of the Avant-Garde and Other Modernist Myths.* Cambridge: MIT Press, 1985.

Kuspit, Donald B. *Clement Greenberg: Art Critic.* Madison: University of Wisconsin Press, 1979.

Lauretis, Teresa de. *Technologies of Gender: Essays on Theory, Film, and Fiction.* Bloomington: Indiana University Press, 1987.

Lawler, Lilian. *The Dance in Ancient Greece.* Middletown: Wesleyan University Press, 1964.

Lepczyk, Billie. "Martha Graham's Movement Invention Viewed through Laban Analysis." *Dance: Current Selected Research* 1. Ed. Lynnette Y. Overby and James H. Humphrey. New York: AMS, 1989: 45–64.

Lesschaeve, Jacqueline, and Merce Cunningham. *The Dancer and the Dance.* New York: Marion Boyars, 1985.

Lessing, Gotthold Ephram. *Laocoön.* Trans. Edward Allen McCormick. Baltimore: Johns Hopkins University Press, 1984.

Levin, David Michael. "Balanchine's Formalism." *What Is Dance?* Ed. Roger Copeland and Marshall Cohen. Oxford: Oxford University Press, 1983: 123–45.

———. "Postmodernism in Dance: Dance, Discourse, Democracy." *Postmodernism—Philosophy and the Arts.* Ed. Hugh J. Silverman. New York: Routledge, 1990: 207–33.

Leys, Ruth. "Mead's Voices: Imitation as Foundation, or, the Struggle against Mimesis." *Critical Inquiry* 19 (winter 1993): 277–307.

Liebertson, Joseph. *Proximity: Levinas, Blanchot, Bataille and Communication.* The Hague: Martinus Nijhoff, 1982.

Lloyd, Margaret. *The Borzoi Book of Modern Dance.* New York: Dance Horizons, 1974.

Lorca, Federico García. *Poet in New York.* Trans. Ben Belitt. New York: Grove Press, 1955.

Love, Paul. "Martha Graham." *Dance Observer* 1, no. 2 (March 1934): 17.

Lynes, Barbara Buhler. *O'Keeffe, Stieglitz and the Critics, 1916-1929.* Chicago: University of Chicago Press, 1991.

Lyotard, Jean-François. *Des Dispositifs pulsionnels.* Paris: Christian Bourgois, 1980.

MacDougall, Allan Ross. *Isadora: A Revolutionary in Art and Love.* New York: Thomas Nelson, 1960.

Magriel, Paul D., ed. *Isadora Duncan*. New York: Holt, 1947; rpt. *Nijinsky, Pavlova, Duncan: Three Lives in Dance*. Ed. Paul Magriel. New York: Da Capo, 1977.

Mallarmé, Stéphane. *Oeuvres Complètes de Stéphane Mallarmé*. Ed. Henri Mondor and G. Jean-Aubry. Paris: Gallimard, 1945.

Man, Paul de. *Allegories of Reading*. New Haven: Yale University Press, 1971.

Manning, Susan. "Modernist Dogma and Post-Modern Rhetoric." *Drama Review* 32, no. 2 (winter 1988): 32–39.

———. "The Mythologization of the Female: Mary Wigman and Martha Graham—A Comparison." *Ballett International* 14, no. 1 (November 1991): 10–15.

———. *Ecstasy and the Demon: Feminism and Nationalism in the Dances of Mary Wigman*. Berkeley: University of California Press, 1993.

Mansback, Steven A. *Visions of Totality: Laszlo Moholy-Nagy, Theo Van Doesburg, and El Lissitzky*. Ann Arbor: UMI Research Press, 1980.

Marin, Louis. *La critique du discours: sur la "logique de port-royal" et les "pensées" de Pascal*. Paris: Minuit, 1975.

Marinetti, Filippo T. "Manifesto of the Futurist Dance." 1917. *Marinetti: Selected Writings*. Trans. R. W. Flint and Arthur A. Coppotelli. New York: Farrar, Straus and Giroux, 1972: 137–41.

———. "Manifesto della Danza Futurista (1917)." *Teoria e Invenzione Futurista*. Ed. Luciano De Maria. Verona: Arnoldo Mondadori, 1968: 123–30.

"Martha Graham and Her Dance Group." *Dance Observer* 2, no. 9 (March 1934): 100–101.

Martin, Carol. *Dance Marathons: Performing American Culture in the 1920s and 1930s*. Jackson: University of Mississippi Press, 1994.

Martin, John. *The Modern Dance*. 1933; rpt. New York: Dance Horizons, 1965.

———. "Martha Graham." *Introduction to the Dance*. New York: Dance Horizons, 1939: 251–56.

———. *America Dancing: The Background and Personalities of the Modern Dance*. 1936; rpt. New York: Dance Horizons, 1968.

Martin, Randy. *Performance as Political Act: The Embodied Self*. New York: Bergin and Garvey, 1990.

———. "Dance Ethnography and the Limits of Representation." *Social Text* 33 (winter 1992): 102–22.

"Mass Dance in Soviet Union." *New Theatre* (February 1934): 4–5.

Mazo, Joseph H. "Martha Remembered: Interviews by Joseph H. Mazo." *Dance Magazine* (special issue: Martha Graham). (July 1991): 34–45.

McDonagh, Don. *Martha Graham*. New York: Praeger, 1973.

Millett, Kate. *Sexual Politics*. New York: Doubleday, 1970.

Murphy, James F. *The Proletarian Moment: The Controversy over Leftism in Literature*. Urbana: University of Illinois Press, 1991.

"New Dance Body Formed in June." *Dance News* (September 1966): 4.

Nietzsche, Friedrich. *The Basic Writings of Nietzsche*. Trans. and ed. Walter Kaufmann. New York: Modern Library, 1968.

Noguchi, Isamu. *A Sculptor's World*. New York: Harper and Row, 1968.

Ocko, Edna. "Whither Martha Graham." *New Theatre* (April 1934): 5–6.

———. "The Revolutionary Dance Movement." *New Masses* 11, no. 11 (June 12, 1934): 27–28.

———. "Reply to Michael Gold." *New Theatre* (July-August 1934): 28.

———. "The Dance." *New Masses* 13, no. 10 (December 4, 1934): 30.

———. "Martha Graham Dances in Two Worlds." *New Theatre* (July 1935): 26–27.

———. "Artist and Audience." *New Theatre* (March 1937): 18, 49, 64.

Ohno, Kazuo. "Selections from the Prose of Kazuo Ohno." *Drama Review* 30, no. 2 (summer 1986): 156–62.

———. "Through Time in a Horse Drawn Carriage." *Ballett International* 12, no. 9 (September 1989): 10–13.

"Olympic Protest." *Dance Observer* 3, no. 4 (April 1936): 38.

Ortega y Gasset, José. *The Dehumanization of Art and Other Essays on Art, Culture, and Literature*. Princeton: Princeton University Press, 1968.

Ortner, Sherry B. "Is Female to Male as Nature Is to Culture?" *Woman, Culture, and Society*. Ed. Michelle Zimbalist Rosaldo and Louise Lamphere. Stanford: Stanford University Press, 1974: 67–87.

Parker, H. T. *Movement Arrested: Dance Reviews of H. T. Parker*. Ed. Olive Holmes. Middletown: Wesleyan University Press, 1982.

Pellizzi, Francesco. "Adventures of the Symbol: Magic for the Sake of Art." *Lectures on Constructed Thought*. New York: School of Architecture of Cooper Union, 1988.

Pesaro, Ebreo da. *Trattato dell'Arte del Ballo di Guglielmo Ebreo da Pesaro*. Bologna: Presso Gaetano Romagnoli, 1873.

Phelan, Peggy. "Feminist Theory, Poststructuralism, and Performance." *Drama Review* 32, no. 1 (spring 1988): 107–27.

Pietz, William. "The Problem of the Fetish, 1." *Res 9* (spring 1985): 5–17.

Pinchot, Amos. "The Failure of the Progressive Party." *The Masses* 6, no. 3 (December 1914), issue 43: 9–10.

Polcari, Stephen. "Martha Graham and Abstract Expressionism." *Smithsonian Studies in American Art* (winter 1990): 2–27. See also Polcari, *Abstract Expressionism*.

Prickett, Stacey. "From Workers' Dance to New Dance." *Dance Research* 7, no. 1 (spring 1989): 47–64.

———. "Dance and the Workers' Struggle." *Dance Research* 7, no. 1 (spring 1990): 47–61.

Pridden, Dierdre. "L'Acte Pur des Métamorphoses." *The Art of the Dance in French Literature*. London: Adam and Charles Black, 1952: 126–62.

Rainer, Yvonne. *Work, 1961–73*. New York: New York University Press, 1974.

Re, Lucia. "Futurism and Feminism." *Annali d'Italianistica* 7 (1989): 253–72.

Ringbom, Sixten. "Art in 'the Epoch of the Great Spiritual': Occult Elements in the Early Theory of Abstract Painting." *Journal of the Warburg and Courtauld Institutes* 29 (1966): 386–418.

Ritter, Naomi. "Art and Androgyny: The Aerialist." *Studies in Twentieth-Century Literature* 13:2 (summer 1989): 173–93.

Rivière, Jacques. "Le Sacre du Printemps." *What Is Dance?* Ed. Roger Copeland and Marshall Cohen. New York: Oxford University Press, 1983.

Roach, Joseph R. "Darwin's Passion: The Language of Expression on Nature's Stage." *Discourse* 13, 1 (fall/winter 1990-91): 40–58.

Ross, Andrew. *The Failure of Modernism: Symptoms of American Poetry*. New York: Columbia University Press, 1986.

———. *No Respect: Intellectuals and Popular Culture*. New York: Routledge, 1989.

Roth, Moira. "The Aesthetic of Indifference." *Artforum* (November 1977): 46–53.

Rubenstein, Annette T. "The Cultural World of the Communist Party: An Historical Overview." *New Studies in the Politics and Culture of U.S. Communism*. Ed. Michael E. Brown, Randy Martin, Frank Rosengarten, and George Snedeker. New York: Monthly Review Press, 1993: 239–60.

Rudhyar, Dane. "Modern Dance Group at the Cross-Road." *Dance Observer* 2, no. 8 (November 1935): 85, 92–93.

Ruyter, Nancy Lee Chalfa. *Reformers and Visionaries: The Americanization of the Art of Dance*. New York: Dance Horizons, 1979.

———. "The Intellectual World of Genevieve Stebbins." *Dance Chronicle* 11, no. 3 (1988): 381–97.

Saint-Point, Valentine de. "Manifesto della Donna Futurista" (1912) and "Manifesto Futurista della Lussuria" (1913); rpt. in Claudia Salaris, *Le Futuriste: Donne e*

Letteratura d'Avanguardia in Italia (1909/1944). Milan: Edizioni delle donne, 1982: 31–36 and 36–40.

———. "La Métachorie." *Montjoie! Organe de l'Impérialisme Artistique Français* 2 (1914).

———. "Festival de la Métachorie." New York, April 3, 1917. Program file: Glans de Cessiat-Vercell, Valentine de. Dance Collection, New York Public Library at Lincoln Center.

———. "Le Théâtre de la Femme" (1915) and "La Métachorie" (1914). Giovanni Lista, *Futurisme: Manifestes-Proclamations-Documents*. Lausanne: l'Age d'Homme, 1973: 263–66, 255–56.

Sandler, Irving. *The New York School*. New York: Harper and Row, 1978.

Satin, Leslie. "Valentine de Saint-Point." *Dance Research Journal* 22/1 (spring 1990): 1–12.

Scarry, Elaine. "Three Paths from Bodies to Artifacts." *Choreographing History*. Bloomington: Indiana University Press, 1994.

Schwartz, Hillel. "Torque: The New Kinaesthetic of the Twentieth Century." *Zone* 6 (*Incorporations*). Ed. Johnathan Crary and Sanford Kwinter. Cambridge: MIT Press, 1992: 71–127.

Sedgewick, Eve Kosofsky. "Across Gender, Across Sexuality: Willa Cather and Others." *Displacing Homophobia: Gay Male Perspectives in Literature and Culture*. Durham: Duke University Press, 1989.

Segal, Edith. "Directing the New Dance." *New Theatre* (May 1935): 23.

Sennett, Richard. *The Fall of Public Man*. New York: Knopf, 1974.

Shaw, Mary Lewis. "Ephemeral Signs: Apprehending the Idea through Poetry and Dance." *Dance Research Journal* 20, no. 1 (summer 1988): 3–9.

Shelton, Suzanne. "Jungian Roots of Martha Graham's Dance Imagery." *Dance History Scholars Proceedings*. Riverside: Dance History Scholars, 1983: 119–32.

Shetley, Vernon. "Merce Cunningham." *Raritan* 8, no. 3 (winter 1989): 72–90.

Siegel, Marcia. *The Shapes of Change: Images of American Modern Dance*. Boston: Houghton Mifflin, 1971.

———. "The Truth about Apples and Oranges." *Drama Review* 32, no. 4 (winter 1988): 24–31.

Slater, Lizzie. "Kazuo Ohno and Butoh Dance." *Dance Theatre Journal* 4:4 (winter 1986): 6–10.

Snyder, Diane. "The Most Important Lesson for Our Theater." *Ballet Review* 10, no. 4 (winter 1983): 6–20.

Sontag, Susan. "For 'Available Light': A Brief Lexicon." *Art in America* 71 (December 1983).

Sparshott, Francis. *Off the Ground: First Steps toward a Philosophical Consideration of Dance*. Princeton: Princeton University Press, 1988.

Spector, Jack J. "The Avant-Garde Object: Form and Fetish between World War I and World War II." *Res* 12 (autumn 1986): 125–43.

Stanislavski, Constantin. *An Actor Prepares*. Trans. Elizabeth Reynolds Hapgood. New York: Theater Arts, 1948.

Stebbins, Genevieve. "Artistic Statue Posing." *Delsarte System of Expression*. 1902; rpt. New York: Dance Horizons, 1977: 444–56.

Stieglitz, Alfred. *Alfred Stieglitz, Georgia O'Keeffe: A Portrait*. New York: Metropolitan Museum of Art, 1978.

Studlar, Gaylyn. *In the Realm of Pleasure: Von Sternberg, Dietrich, and the Masochistic Aesthetic*. Urbana: University of Illinois Press, 1988.

Swanson, Amy. "Isadora Duncan: à propos de son enseignement et de sa filiation." *La Recherche en Danse* 2 (1983): 63–74.

Taylor, Charles. *Human Agency and Language: Philosophical Papers*. Cambridge: Cambridge University Press, 1985.

Taylor, Paul. *Private Domain*. New York: Knopf, 1987.

Taylor, Ralph. "Isadora and the Dance of the Future." *Dance Observer* 1, no. 2 (March 1934): 16, 20.

Taylor, Ronald, trans. and ed. *Aesthetics and Politics*. London: Verso, 1977.

Tisdal, Caroline, and Angelo Bozzolli. *Futurism*. London: Thames and Hudson, 1977: 154–55.

Tomkins, Calvin. *The Bride and the Bachelors: Five Masters of the Avant-Garde*. New York: Penguin, 1968.

Torgovnik, Marianna. *Gone Primitive: Savage Intellects, Modern Lives*. Chicago: University of Chicago Press, 1990.

Tormey, Alan. *The Concept of Expression: A Study of Philosophical Psychology and Aesthetics*. Princeton: Princeton University Press, 1971.

Untermeyer, Louis. "The Dance." *The Seven Arts* (November 1916): 79–81.

Valéry, Paul. "Philosophy of the Dance." *Aesthetics*. Trans. Ralph Mannheim. New York: Pantheon, 1964: 197–211.

Vaughan, David. "Merce Cunningham." *Performing Arts Journal* 3, no. 3 (winter 1979): 3–14.

Wald, Alan M. *The Revolutionary Imagination: The Poetry and Politics of John Wheelwright and Sherry Mangan*. Chapel Hill: University of North Carolina Press, 1983.

Walkowitz, Abraham. *Isadora Duncan in Her Dances*. Girard, Kan.: Haldeman-Julius, 1950.

Welsh, Deborah J. "Martha Graham: The Other Side of Depression." *American Journal of Dance Therapy* 13, no. 2 (fall/winter 1991): 117–29.

Wheeler, Mark. "New Dance in a New Deal Era." *Dance: Current Selected Research* 2. Ed. Lynnette Y. Overby and James H. Humphrey. New York: AMS, 1990: 33–45.

Wigman, Mary. *The Mary Wigman Book: Her Writings*. Ed. and trans. Walter Sorell. Middletown: Wesleyan University Press, 1973.

Wildenstein, Daniel. *Monet's Years at Giverny: Beyond Impressionism*. New York: Metropolitan Museum of Art, 1978.

Williams, Raymond. *Keywords: A Vocabulary of Culture and Society*. Guildford, Surrey: Fontana, 1976.

———. *Culture and Society: 1780–1950*. 1958; rpt. New York: Columbia University Press, 1983.

Winkler, John J. *The Constraints of Desire: The Anthropology of Sex and Gender in Ancient Greece*. New York: Routledge, 1990.

Winnicott, D. W. *Playing and Reality*. New York: Basic, 1971.

Young, Stark. *Immortal Shadows: A Book of Dramatic Criticism*. New York: Hill and Wang, 1948.

Index

Abrahms, M. H., x
aesthetic modernism, ix–x; modernist object in, xi
agit-prop dance, 27, 36–37
Alderson, Evan, 10, 62
Allerhand, Ruth, 29–30
avant-gardes, 28, 50

Bachelard, Gaston, 14
Banes, Sally, 39, 44
Barba, Eugenio, 151n.54
Barbette (Vander Clyde), 95–100
Barthes, Roland, 104–105
Bois, Yve-Alain, 44–45
Brown, Carolyn, 89, 171n.40
Bryson, Norman, xiii
Bürger, Peter, 171n.42
Burke, Owen, 67
Burnshaw, Stanley, 59–60
Butler, Judith, 173n.6

Cage, John, 77, 81–82, 85
Certeau, Michel de, xiii
Chinoy, Helen Krich, 145n.14
Clark, Timothy J., 157n.8
classical ballet, 5, 27
Cocteau, Jean, 93–100
    —works by: *The Blood of a Poet,* 100;
    "Une leçon de théâtre," 95–100
Colletet, Guillaume, 76
Copelande, Roger, 160n.60
Cornell, Katharine, 70
Crimp, Douglas, 94
Cunningham, Merce, xii, 56, 72, 77–87; and
    chance procedure, 77; and expression,
    78–80, 85
    —works by: *Winterbranch,* 77–79; *How to
    Pass, Kick, Fall and Run,* 81–82, 85; the
    dancer of *How to Pass, Kick, Fall and
    Run,* 81–85

Daly, Ann, 149n.31, 152n.69
Davis, Bette, 38
Dellamora, Richard, 177n.51
de Man, Paul, 148n.21
Denby, Edwin, 44
Derrida, Jacques, 106
Douglas, Paul, 28
Dudley, Jane, 29–30, 156n.43
Duncan, Isadora, x, 1–20, 24, 26, 109–13,
139–40, 142–44; and the solar plexus,
1–2, 12; and "natural movement," 1;
and classical ballet, 5; and choreographic syntax, 5–6; and color essentialism, 9; and light vibration, 16, 150n.40;
sexual politics of, 9, 14, 16; and subject
position, 11, 16; and pre-expressive
level, 11–12; and post-expressive level,
18; and class politics, 7–8, 148n.30; and
the Greek chorus, 17–19; and the wave
figure, 20
    —works by: *Mother,* 10
Dunn, Douglas, 87–92; relation to chance
    procedure, 87–88
    —works by: *Light, O Tease,* 90; *Matches,* 90

Eisenberg, Emanuel, 26, 28–30
Elias, Norbert, 146n.21
emotion, x–xi, 32–33, 37, 48, 50, 56, 62, 70–
72, 145n.10
emotionalism, 29–30, 40–41, 44, 51, 53
Engel, Johann Jacob, 76
Evan, Blanche, 32, 60–62, 66
expression theory, x, xiii, 8–9, 12, 14, 75–77,
79–80, 91–92, 170n.23; internal
critiques of, xi–xii, 145n.21; as a
politics, xiii

fetish, 1
Fuller, Loie, 14–15, 75

Giedion, Siegfried, xi
Gilfond, Henry, 68
Gold, Michael, 59, 63–64, 66
Graham, Martha, xii, 28, 36, 124, 140–41;
and abstraction, 44; and modernism,
39–40, 49–50, 60; and formalism, 44,
52, 57, 59; and emotion, 48, 50, 52,
62–63, 70–72; and primitivism, 48, 51–
53; critical reception of, 49–50, 56–57;
and Americanism, 51–55, 66, 68–69;
sexual politics of, 44, 54, 57, 68; and
political radicalism, 57–72; and flow,
59; and training, 59–62; and race, 67
    —works by: *American Document,* 68–69;
    Appalachian Spring, 43; *Chronicle,* 67;
    Course, 66; *Deep Song,* 67–68; *Every
    Soul Is a Circus,* 72; *Frontier,* 54;
    Lamentation, 45–46, 64
Greenberg, Clement, 39, 157n.7

Horst, Louis, 42–43, 47

Jardine, Alice, 94
Jowitt, Deborah, 153n.98, 170n.24

Kendall, Elizabeth, 47, 56, 173n.1
Kermode, Frank, 15
Kirstein, Lincoln, 27, 155n.11, 167n.80
Kostelanetz, Richard, 50

Lauretis, Teresa de, 16–17
Levien, Julia, 4
Levin, David Michael, 158n.10
Love, Paul, 60

machine dance, 153n.101
Manning, Susan, 39, 49, 151n.64
Marin, Louis, 146n.21
Marinetti, Filippo, 21
Martin, John, 41, 43–44
Martin, Randy, 147n.13, 151n.63
mass dance, 29, 64–66, 119–22, 135–37
McDonagh, Don, 57
metaphor, 14–15
modern dance, xiii; as modernism, ix;
    primitivism in, x–xi; impersonality in,
    xi, 15–16; as a feminist practice, xii, 9–
    10, 146n.16; as a discursive field, 7; and
    public space, 12, 15–16; and gender, ix,
    xiii, 21–24; revolutionary style in, 26–
    33; and technique, 28, 122–24; left-wing
    theory of, xi, 75, 146n.11; and class
    politics, xii

New Theatre, 35, 63, 154n.5
Nijinsky, Vaslav, x

Ocko, Edna, 27–28, 34–37, 62, 164n.129,
    165nn.143,145

Ohno, Kazuo, 100–107
O'Keeffe, Georgia, 41–43
organic society, 147n.9

Pellizzi, Francesco, xi, 161n.62
Pesaro, Guglielmo Ebreo da, 76
Pietz, William, 1
Pollack, Jackson, 56

Rainer, Yvonne, 40
reconstruction, 4
religious allegory, 1
revolutionary dance, 25–37, 59, 124–27
Rivière, Jacques, x–xi
Ruyter, Nancy, 40, 150n.50

St. Denis, Ruth, 38, 40, 47, 139
Saint-Point, Valentine de, 21–24; and
    futurism, 21
Schwartz, Hillel, 6
self-expression, 1, 7, 16
Sennett, Richard, 58, 149n.38
Siegel, Marcia, 75
Sokolow, Anna, 61, 167n.177
Sontag, Susan, 50
Sparshott, Francis, 75, 168n.3
Stanislavski, Constantin, 5–6
Stebbins, Genevieve, 11, 150n.50

Tamiris, Helen, 32, 141
Taylor, Charles, 12

Valéry, Paul, 1, 15
Vaughan, David, 85

Williams, Raymond, 147n.9
Winnicott, D. W., 12
Workers Dance League, 26, 30, 154n.4
Worker's Theatre, 154n.5

Mark Franko teaches in the Theater Arts Board of Studies, University of California, Santa Cruz. He is the author of *The Dancing Body in Renaissance Choreography* and *Dance as Text: Ideologies of the Baroque Body*.